BEAT RECESSION: PROVEN MARKETING TACTICS

139 Proven Sales Letter Writing, Direct Marketing & Business Development Tactics Make Short Work of Recession Fears

Volume 1

Carol A E Bentley

Beat The Recession: Proven Marketing Tactics

139 Proven Sales Letter Writing, Direct Marketing & Business Development Tactics Make Short Work of Recession Fears
Volume 1

ISBN: 978-0-9549206-2-3
Published by Sarceaux Publications, Dorset, England.

Cover Design by Susan Glasgow, Glasgow Graphics
www.glasgowgraphics.com

Catalogue Data:

Bentley, Carol A. E.
1. Copywriting 2. Marketing 3. Direct Response Marketing
4. Business Development

More advice on copywriting and direct response marketing is available at www.copywriting4b2b.com

Carol A E Bentley is the author of the popular business book 'I Want to Buy Your Product... Have You Sent Me a Letter Yet?' rated 5* on Amazon.

If you would like to talk to Carol's office about having her consider working on your current or next direct sales campaign call UK freephone 0800 015 5515 (outside UK call +44 1929 423411) or send an email to info@CarolBentley.com

In Memory of my Father,
Robert Francis Charles Cliff
(1928 – 2008)

How Effective Are These Tactics? Read What My Blog Readers Say..

In a survey I asked the people who read the postings on my **www.copywriting4b2b.com** blog what they thought of the material I deliver (in my book 'I Want to Buy Your Product... Have You Sent Me a Letter Yet?' and on the blog); if they'd used any of my advice and if/how it had helped them.

Here are just a few of the comments I received:

> "I've studied your book and used the knowledge gained to write many letters to my existing customers and as a result, I am **getting more repeat work** from my existing carpet & upholstery cleaning customers. I am achieving about **30% more results** from using these techniques."
>
> *Gerwyn Jones*

> "I bought several copies of your book for my franchisees and as a result sales letters have been more impactful."
>
> *John Davidson,*
> *West Drayton, Middlesex.*
> www.gas-elec.co.uk

> "Carol, Your book was a real eye opener and although pointing out the obvious, it is ideas I would never have thought of. Your blogg's are also a wealth of knowledge and something

I look at every day."

I look at every day."

I look at every day."

John Walmsley
Scot Lift Systems Ltd.
Edinburgh

"Yes it did. I was aiming at retailers and I got the attention of some big restoration mail order companies. Good quality, considered information. I've read your book a couple of times and read most posts on your blog."

Nigel West,
Operations Support (Software) Limited
Cranleigh, Surrey
www.operations-support.co.uk

"Very useful step by step instructions with real life examples helps to cement the lesson. Great...very personable and helpful. Supportive and creative."

Gail Doby
Design Success University
Denver, CO USA
www.renaissancedesign.com

"I read all your techniques you give. I learn a lot from you about everything. Excellent I don't miss any of it."

Brenda Jarrold
Innovative Information
West Dereham, Norfolk
www.ebaycashpump.com

"Very helpful if I am ever writing any letters,

brochures or web pages I always pick up your book first for some inspiration and know that I am on the right track if I follow your easily understandable tips."

Rob Chisholm
Ebay Profit System
Eltham, London
www.ebay-niche.com

"The well tempered hand holding I know will pay off. [The blogs are] Balanced, broad, innovative, clear and extremely informative."

Tim Bell
Aerodomes Ltd
Natchet, Somerset

"YES, although I have been doing this for quite a number of years with great success, I took on board your advice about putting my Order Form on a separate sheet."

Paul Petulengro
Gypsy Paul Petulengro
Granada, Espña
www.petulengro.com

"I have found the articles and your advice in writing sales letters invaluable. I am just starting to see results greater than before. Thank you."

Brian Kennard
Chipping Sodbury, South Glos
www.briankennard.co.uk

"Your book covers so much, plus the blog adds to this - the general Sales Letter / layout / what order to put things in / what to include in the mailing is all excellent, plus the added extras from the blog! Your thorough approach is really excellent Carol."

Alan Jones
Chester, Cheshire

"The material I have seen has been comparable with the best of them out there."

Keith Watson
Creative Eye
Poole, Dorset
www.wats-on.net

"Improved my copywriting skills and understanding of the processes involved. One word – excellent!"

Laurie Housley
Casvor Publishing
Redbourn, Hertfordshire
www.casvor.com

"Very specific in each post. so I know what to read and what not to read. sometimes I read anyway."

Stevie Wilson
Los Angeles, CA USA
www.LA-Story.com

"Good practical and usable stuff with a down to earth no BS approach. [*Did blog help*?] Yes, by making me think more about the copy I write. But let's not underestimate the enormity of going from ground zero to a truly effective copywriter. There are probably a handful of great copywriters in this country.

My strategy is to be a bit better than most out there who don't use or can't afford these few stars!"

Graham Rowan
National Nutrition Clinic
Richmond, Surrey
www.nationalnutritionclinic.com

Table of Contents

AUTHOR'S INTRODUCTION

Why This Book?

Many businesses grow and prosper, even in a global economic downturn. The reason they grow is because they focus on marketing that continues to work; continues to find sales, both from existing customers and new prospects.

Following these tips, taken from my online blog at **www.copywriting4b2b.com**, gives you the insights you need to come through a recession stronger than when you entered it. I'm not just talking about surviving... I'm talking about *real* business growth.

I first started my online blog to connect with business people and share these valuables tips, which include advice on copywriting, marketing and other business issues and resources.

But I realised that anyone finding the blog was likely to miss all the gems and valuable snippets in the earlier posts (that's not bragging – it's what my regular readers have told me in surveys I've held). After all, how often do you trawl back through the archives of new websites you've found – especially if just one blog post caught your attention? For me, it is certainly not going to happen!

Plus – you need this crucial advice fast!

And a book is easy to flick through. You can

highlight content that is particularly relevant to what you need. In fact I've already marked specific Recession Busting Marketing Tips with an *.

And check out the other tips I've included to inspire you or make you smile.

These People Are To Blame! ☺

Before I explain how the book is organised let me tell you about some of the people to 'blame' for the existence of the blog itself and the brilliant content you will find in the Bloggers' Insights section of this book.

Starting with the instigator; Ed Rivis. My first post on the blog (and in this book) describes how Ed encouraged me to start the blog and even gave me the technical know-how I needed.

Making an on-line blog vibrant and relevant is not only down to the content and me, the blog writer. It is enhanced when my posts point to other blogger's posts and articles. Their contribution gives a different perspective or additional information or even, in some cases, valuable free reports.

I'd like to thank the following (in no particular order) for agreeing to have their material included in this book so you can enjoy their recession-beating wisdom too.

- **Ed Rivis** (of course) for his insight to web marketing;

- **Jill Konrath** for her great advice on dealing with large companies;

- **Marc Kline** of AWeber explains how to use Email marketing to coincide with holiday dates;

- **Tui Bijoux** giving us life-value perspective;

- **Martin Russell** for telling the story of the dentist who doesn't advertise, yet has a thriving practice and for providing a great marketing tool;

- **Mark Brownlow** for his amusing post on a marketing Santa;

- **Cindy Silbert** who reveals that positive thinking may not be all it's cracked up to be;

- **Rich Schefren**, my inspirational business mentor, who delivers great value;

- **Hill Robertson**, a self-confessed techi-geek who none-the-less manages to deliver great advice in plain English (plus one of his products cancels some of the frustration your visitors might experience when viewing your websites and remember a frustrated web-visitor could be a lost sale!);

- **Terry Dean** for his 21 great PR ideas that get your mind buzzing;

- **Lindsay Polson** whose spinning girl certainly created a lot of discussion in our office – to say nothing of the fascinating examples of advertising and promotional ideas he collects and shares on his blog.

And one person I must not forget, because she did a great deal of the manuscript preparation work for me, is my indispensable PA, **Kelly Twomey**.

How This Book Is Organised

Posts on my blog are shown in date order and allocated to categories. So you can look at a specific category or just follow the (almost) daily posts.

If I'd organised this book in the same double-entry structure it would have been twice the size it is! So I decided the most useful layout is to arrange it by categories – that way you can choose the area you want to check on, browse the posts and mark the ones you want to take ideas from.

Each post appears exactly as it was shown on the blog. And you can read later, up to date posts – free – at **www.copywriting4b2b.com**.

Where posts refer to another blogger's article, and I've been able to contact them and get their permission, you'll see their full post in the **Other Bloggers' Insights**.

Web Addresses Made Easy

Scattered throughout my posts are web links to other websites (including my fellow bloggers). Some of the original web URLs are extremely long – I'm talking anything up to 129 characters, or more in some instances.

When you decide to visit those websites there is a chance you may type the long URLs into your web browser incorrectly – which would be very frustrating for you.

To make some of the longer ones easier to type I've created redirect links, with shorter address codes, through my website to include in this book for you – this means there is a higher chance you'll reach the web page you're looking for first time.

Exclusive Blog Gifts

People who read my blog can choose to use an RSS feed to keep up to date with new posts or they can subscribe. Subscribers get an email notice each time a new article is posted.

They also get exclusive access to useful gifts from time to time. The gifts are shown in private posts, which are password protected. And the password is sent by email.

Of course that means anyone who was not subscribed when the original post was made doesn't get that particular gift.

In this book I have included the private gift posts, including the download links, so you too can claim those gifts. Some are reports; some are audio MP3s; all contain valuable information.

Will I Do This Again?

To be honest – I don't know for sure. Although the content was already written, creating the layout, editing, getting the link URLs and contacting other bloggers, to get permission to include their material in this book, took a considerable amount of time and effort – although I thought it was worthwhile because I'm sure many business owners can use these insights to great effect.

I suppose it depends upon you, the reader; *how useful is this book for you*? Are you glancing through, never to look at it again or are you using it as treasure trove of ideas to dip into on a regular basis? Using it to keep your business soaring above the turbulent waters of recession?

Write and let me know how you are using this material. If I get an avalanche of *'Yes – it's useful!'* then I may produce further volumes.

You can send a message through the contact link on my blog at www.copywriting4b2b.com or send an email to **carol@carolbentley.com**

You can even send a (*gasp!*) letter by snail-mail to

Carol Bentley
Promote Your Business Ltd
Freepost NATW661, Swanage, BH19 1BR UK

Or phone and leave a message with Kelly, my PA on +44 (0) 1929 423411

This book contains a wealth of recession-proof business knowledge, but it won't do you any good if you don't take any action. The challenge is not to let the talk of a global recession paralyse you.

Check the table of contents, particularly those entries marked with the *, then decide which tip you are going to use first. Monitor the result and then choose your next action. You'll find that employing a combination of these insights gives you the greatest results.

I hope you benefit from these advisory tips and enjoy reading them as much as I have writing them. And I wish you all the best in your business-growth journey.

Kind regards

Carol Bentley
Author

INTRODUCTION...

And About Time Too...

I've been threatening to set up a copywriting blog for what seems like for ever and a day but never quite got around to it.

I think one of the things that discouraged me was not knowing how to get a good, professional looking blogging layout set up. But now, thanks to my good friend Ed Rivis who created an easy to follow DVD on the simplest way to set up your own blog, I've done it. And here's the proof!

(You can check Ed's **Ultimate Business Blogging** at www.carolbentley.org/rubb.html).

So what can you expect to see here? Well, in spite of the website address being www.copywriting4b2b.com, the insights I plan to share apply as equally to 'business to consumer' markets.

Bookmark this page, or sign up for blog announcements, if you want to know about writing sales letters and other marketing materials; marketing strategies and ideas; business promotion tools; business networking - in fact anything I come across that I find helps me in my business - because then there's a fair chance it could help you too.

And if there are any specific copywriting or marketing questions you'd like to ask, that you think would be interesting for my other blog visitors, visit www.copywriting4b2b.com and use the 'ask a question' link to send it in. Your question and my answer might appear on the blog at a later date.

~ Carol Bentley

Date: Tuesday, October 23rd, 2007 at 5:31 pm

COPYWRITING

It Must Be True.. The Scientists Have Told Us

Yes - it's true... we buy emotionally.

Mind you that's something we copywriting and marketing experts have always known; emotions probably play the greatest part in our decision making. And the scientists have proven what we've known all along.

That's why in any sales situation; whether face-to-face, on the web, in an advertisement or through direct response letters painting the picture of the pleasure or satisfaction a purchaser gains or the problem or pain they avoid or cure they find is the most powerful way of persuading people to buy and is frequently used in marketing material, especially direct response material.

Scientific Proof...

Unsurprisingly, that's what scientific research says too according to the studies carried out by Dr Joe Arvai, who is a professor of judgement and decision making and heads up the Skunkworks Lab at Michigan University.

He and Dr Robyn Wilson ran a study on decision

making; they asked 210 participants to judge how much of a budget should be allocated to risk prevention in two areas in a National Park; Mugging and Bag Snatching or Accidents Caused by Wandering Deer within the park.

They published their results in March 2006. And even though statistics indicated the deer problem was actually a slightly higher risk the volunteers judged it as lower and therefore a higher budget allocation was given to the emotive problem of mugging.

So how does this impact on our marketing material? It demonstrates that emotion, experience and perception all affect our decisions. Which is why it is crucially important to really understand your target prospect.

What are their experiences; what appeals to them; what excites them; what angers them; what worries them; what do they REALLY WANT - rather than need? What **colours** their world and **influences** their thoughts?

Remember people take more notice of their emotions than any logical argument.

And of course we see this all the time - why do people buy high-status cars or houses or designer clothing when a cheaper unbranded item does the job just as well? They want to enjoy the status, and maybe even envy, in the eyes of their friends and colleagues.

Before starting to write any sales letter, advert, brochure, email, web page or even a blog post like this, define your ideal customer. Then when you craft your message keep this picture in mind and describe the results they can expect to enjoy.

Once your prospect has made a decision to buy they need to justify the purchase to themselves - and perhaps other people - especially if your product or service has a high-ticket price. You can help them do this by describing the features and reasons why their decision to buy from you is a wise choice to make.

Having trouble describing or picturing your target prospect? Look at your existing customers; why did they buy from you? What influenced their decision? Is it something you can use to encourage other prospects to make a good buying choice in your favour?

~ Carol Bentley

Date: Sunday, October 28th, 2007 at 8:50 am

*A Tense Situation...

The tense you use in your writing makes a surprising difference.

Present tense is so much more **active** - it *breathes* life into your sales letter.

Describe something as if your reader is experiencing it right now and it is easier for them to visualise owning whatever it is you are selling; whether a solution to a problem, a service or a product.

So should you always use present tense?

Absolutely not!

Let me explain...

Anything written in future tense is not so vivid; it's something that *may* happen - but could just as easily not. And your reader may not see himself in that particular scenario. And there are times when you don't want him to.

Here's an example...

You write your letter or advert or web page describing the pain or problem he **is** experiencing; or the pleasure he **is** missing. You paint the glowing picture of the relief or joy or satisfaction or status he **does** have because he took up your offer. That's how you want him to see himself.

Offer a guarantee and your prospect is ethically persuaded to take your offer; especially if you include a risk-free money-back guarantee. But *you do not want your new customer to visualise himself asking for a refund.* So you use future tense:

"If you are unhappy, for any reason, all you **have to do** is ask for a refund and we **will** give you your money back, no questions asked".

In this way you are showing that asking for a refund is a *possibility* - but **not a definite**.

~ Carol Bentley

Date: Monday, October 29th, 2007 at 11:43 am

Don't Make The Same Mistake I Did...

Do you use clichés when you're talking to people? You know, things like 'he's as good as gold'?

And do you use them when writing your sales letters? After all, the best sales letter is written in the same way that you'd talk to someone, so you might include a common phrase. If you do, learn from my mistake and think carefully about what you use.

This is what happened. Earlier in the week I sent an email to my subscribers to tell them about Ed's blogging programme. I started off with...

> "How do you find time to keep in constant communication with customers and prospects - without tearing your hair out?"

So, what's wrong with that you might ask. Or, if you're like one of my subscribers who replied to my email, you may have spotted my faux pas!

His reply was simply: "I'm bald"

Was my face red!

So, whilst popular phrases can help to bring your letter alive and make it more vibrant, be careful that what you use isn't alienating part of your audience.

~ Carol Bentley

Date: Friday, November 2nd, 2007 at 10:00 am

If An Opera Singer Can Do It... So Can You

One of the interesting people I met at the weekend seminar I attended was Kirsty who is an Opera Singer and Manager. Her experienced confirmed what I've always believed and told people...

You see Kirsty needed to supplement her income - her passion is Opera - but as she said, it doesn't pay a huge amount of money. She tried various ways of getting an additional income, including temping which she did not take to.

Then, because she likes writing, someone asked her to

help with writing the copy for their web page.

She said "I was a bit nervous about it, but they gave me a guide to follow which took me step-by-step through what I needed to do and it was OK!" Since then she has helped other people with their copywriting tasks and now has a successful second business.

Which just goes to prove, **with expert guidance**, anyone can write effective copy for a business and you can write the material for yours.

If you don't already have a copy of my book, which gives you all the insider secrets and techniques for creating your business boosting marketing material, in simple to understand and easy to follow steps, download **Chapters 1 & 3** completely **FREE** and without obligation at **www.carolbentley.com/offer**.

~ Carol Bentley

Date: Monday, November 5th, 2007 at 4:28 pm

*Here's 8 Elements For A Powerful Sales Letter. . .

Your sales letter is extremely powerful when you use the proven science behind good copywriting . Simply adopt this 8-element structure to give you a head-start:

When selling (and remember you *are* selling in your letter or advert) most professional sales people tell you to follow AIDA; no I'm not talking about a person called AIDA, I'm talking about the acronym **AIDA** which stands for:

Attention, Interest, Desire, Action. Add an extra sprinkling of **A** for **Attention** and your sales letter sparkles.

Let's go through the copywriting techniques that match these elements:

1) Grab **ATTENTION** with your headline – spend the majority of your time on this. Use eye-catching words such as You/Your; Who Else; Which; Now; New; Bargain; Free; How/How to; Hurry or Breakthrough.

2) Whatever your headline promised **your first paragraph must reinforce**. Keep it short and to the point. Resist the temptation to ramble. Keeping it focused keeps your reader's **INTEREST**.

3) Draw your reader on - **describe exactly what you are offering**, what it does for him, how he benefits. If there are a number of steps to a process describe exactly what they are so you start to create his **DESIRE**.

4) Remember human nature. Something's good? We want it too! Give your reader feedback from your delighted customers. Make sure the testimonials are descriptive and identify the problem your customer had

or the result he wanted and the solution or outcome you delivered. You keep your reader's **DESIRE** high.

5) Lose – It is <u>your job</u> to make sure your prospect understands why he cannot possibly ignore your offer. Make absolutely sure he understands exactly how much less his life is if he does not respond to your valuable proposition. You are harming him by not doing everything possible to clearly show the loss he would experience.

So tell him what he loses if he doesn't taken up your valuable offer. How he's missed out on key benefits or results, how his life will never be the same again...

OK, so I'm exaggerating, but I'm sure you get the picture. As I've said before, people make buying decisions based on their emotions and then use logic to justify the decision. If we weren't influenced by our emotion, people would never buy expensive cars, designer clothes or larger houses. After all a small, cheap car gets you from A to B, just as a more expensive car does.

Appeal to your prospect's emotional wants and desires – the detail of features you provide helps him justify the logic of buying from you.

This is still part of his **DESIRE** – his desire not to lose what you have already created an interest in.

So, having '*depressed*' your reader with what he might

lose if he doesn't take your offer, now you must...

6) Repeat the benefits – raise the desire again to own or experience your service or product. Get your reader excited about what he can expect to enjoy.

And then...

7) Action – tell him EXACTLY what to do now. This is where many sales letters fall down. There is no specific 'call to action' describing, in simple to follow steps, how to get what you've been promising throughout your letter.

So go on, tell him to send the completed request form in the envelope provided. Tell him to call the Freephone number and place his request NOW. Tell him to send the email confirming his interest. Don't let him 'cool off' by not leading him through the steps he needs to take immediately.

And finally add the P.S. – your second headline (and the final sprinkling 'A' of the AIDA-A acronym). Having spent so much time preparing your main headline you have already discovered your second strongest – and that is probably a natural P.S.

Make your P.S. as compelling as your headline. Its job is to get your prospect to read your letter and remind him of the most important reason why he should respond.

These - and other - insights are described in my book, 'I Want to Buy Your Product... Have You Sent Me a Letter Yet?'

If you haven't already got a copy why not invest in yourself and go to **www.carolbentley.com/offer** or give it as a business gift to a colleague or friend.

You might not want to give it to a competitor though; after all you do want some advantage, don't you?

~ Carol Bentley

Date: Wednesday, November 7th, 2007 at 11:06 am

What If?

I'm a newsletter junkie - especially anything to do with marketing and copywriting. And one of the newsletters I always take time to read is the Copywriter's Roundtable (which you can read at www.jackforde.com) by John Forde. I love his quirky humour and his way of reminding me of copywriting techniques I know work.

And this week was no different. In his newsletter John talked about 'What if. . .' here's what he shared:

Who is Ravi Vora? He's a young guy who runs a motivational blog "for People with Big Dreams."

(www.ravivora.com). One recent post claims you only need two words, in the form of a question, to always inspire creativity. *What are the two words*?

Very simply; "**What if?**"

Ravi calls this single question the "root of imagination." It's here, and I think he's right, that every creative moment begins.

"The possibilities are endless with this question," says Ravi. "You open up new realms of discovery; new worlds; whole new universes of opportunities. There is no end with this question. There is no way to say 'No, we can't' or 'That isn't possible.' The only thing you can do with a 'what if' question is dream."

Well said.

This is a powerful phrase you can use in your copy-writing. . .

- *what if* you could double or triple response to your marketing activity?
- *what if* you could improve efficiency by 42%?
- *what if* you could reduce costs without reducing quality or service?
- *what if* you could show your customers how you can help them achieve their dreams?

Include a few *what if* statements in your sales letter and see what happens. And don't forget... *what if* can also be used to describe the less than ideal situation your customer experiences by **not** taking your offer.

Next week we'll take a look at some print newsletter tips.

~ Carol Bentley

Date: Thursday, November 8th, 2007 at 10:30 am

The Long and Short of It

I've just read a post by James Brausch in which he says 'long copy sucks and other heresies' and quotes tests and experiments he's carried out. All of which are web-based.

He points out that he fully expects copywriters to jump on him and say long letters do work.

And he's right. Including me - but let me qualify that a bit further...

Do you remember the Opera Singer turned copywriter I mentioned in a post last week? (read *If an Opera Singer can do it... so can you* (page 16) or on *my blog at www.copywriting4b2b.com/archives/14*)

One of the first questions Kirsty asked me was:

"What's your view of long versus short letters? Do

you get people arguing about it when they ask you to do the copywriting?"

When I said **"I've proven long letters work and yes, I do get sceptics!"** her face was wreathed in a smile.

"What do you say to them?" she asked.

So I told her... Want to know what I said?

"When you're writing a letter you have to bear in mind that there are two types of people who are likely to read it; the detail people - like engineers. They want to be absolutely sure they understand *every detail* there is to know about whatever is on offer. Then you have the skimmers; the people who are too busy to read everything in your letter.

Now - think about it; **what's the real purpose of your letter?**

It *isn't* to be read. Its **sole purpose is to get the recipient to take the action you want!**

So you've got to satisfy both types of audience with one letter. And that's where the formatting of your letter - as well as the wording - comes into play. (I'm going to assume you are writing an <u>interesting</u>, benefits-crammed, focused-on-your-reader type of letter).

For the detail people you must give the answers to all the questions they are asking themselves;

- 'How will it help me?'
- 'Why should I buy this?'
- 'Will I regret spending the money afterwards?' (*known as buyer's remorse*)
- 'Who else has got results from this?' (*genuine testimonials are needed here*)
- 'Will I get the same or similar result?'
- 'What's the risk I take by buying?' (*your guarantee gets around this concern*)

You have to provide all the detail to back up their emotional decision to purchase. You can only do this in a long letter. For the skimmers, your sub-headlines give an overview of what your offer is.

If you get it right, as they scan your letter they pounce on the sub-headline that is answering their burning question or catches their attention with a promise they like.

This is why it is imperative to make sure at least one of your subheads also clearly identifies how they can take up your offer; your call-to-action. Your skim-reader does not want to waste time searching for how to get whatever you are selling.

Something along the lines of '**3 Easy Steps to Get Your...**' or '**How To Get Your...**' or '**What To Do Now...**' is OK.

I have had people contact me saying "I got your letter. I didn't read it, it was too long..."

Do you think I care? Not a jot - they got in touch didn't they?

So my letter has done **exactly** what I wanted, it's compelled them to take action.

Read your letter. Does it answer all the questions your prospect is asking? (Some people call it sales objections, but that seems a bit harsh to me. After all he just wants to know enough to be sure he's making the right decision for him). Check your sub-headlines; do they give the gist of what the letter is about? Do they draw the reader in to your letter? Are they succinct and supportive or just cute and clever without any substance?

Try this: Give your letter to other people to read. Then ask them did they read the whole thing or just skim? If they skimmed, did they get a feel of what it was about? If they read the whole thing, did they find it interesting or boring? Use their feedback to fine-tune your content, but don't let the skimmers persuade you to shorten your letter just for the sake of doing so.

How Long is Long?

Again there are different views; some people say anything longer than 1 page is a long letter; others say 17, 20 or more pages have proven to be their best sellers. It's a matter of testing.

For one client I upped their standard sales letter length from 1 uninteresting page to 4 reader-focused pages and it almost doubled the response for them.

For another client, who always sent out very long letters, we tested a 1-page 'announcement type' letter that got a great result. It may be because it was a contrast to what his prospects normally got from him.

There is no definitive answer.

Web Copy Length

So does the same apply to web based copy - should they be long letters?

Perhaps not according to James' tests. But at the seminar where I met Kirsty, which was hosted by a multi-million $ turnover internet marketing company, they said their best selling letter was 55 'printed pages' long!

As with any advice given by experts the only answer is to **check what works for you...** test both short and long copy in any marketing campaign regardless of whether it is online or offline.

~ Carol Bentley

Date: Wednesday, November 14th, 2007 at 10:00 am

A Great Resource For Copywriting

After yesterday's blog I was mulling over what I could do to help you keep your letters interesting and compelling.

You see there are techniques to making your letter flow so your reader is swept through, like a white-water raft on an exciting, fast flowing river. And - not surprisingly - the words you choose to draw your reader from paragraph to paragraph makes their reading an enjoyable experience. At least - they can do.

So a resource that lists words and phrases you can use to bring your letter to life, phrases that have been proven over many years to work; in both on and off-line material has got to be a great tool to have, don't you think?

Well we're not the only people who do... because fortuitously Rich Schefren, a well-respected internet expert, thought so too and is offering a free download of **Phrases That Keep Attention** on his blog. The content is aimed at the American market, so you'll have to be selective about which ones you use. But, if nothing else, they should help your creative juices flow.

Why not pop over and have a look?

Visit Phrases That Keep Attention

(via www.carolbentley.org/phrases.html)

By the way, look out for tomorrow's post; **Choose Your Words Carefully** (page 287) - it might make you cringe or blush!

~ Carol Bentley

Date: Thursday, November 15th, 2007 at 10:00 am

Do Your Headlines Grab Your Reader's Undivided Attention?

Having a good headline is not enough. It has to be a compelling 'grab-them-by-the-throat' attention hold-ing headline if you are going to get the *undivided* at-tention of your prospect.

Let's face it - whether we are talking letter, advert or presentation headlines - your reader is unlikely to be concentrating absolutely 100% on what he (or she) is reading - unless it strikes a resounding chord with him. Unless you get him to say "How the heck did you know that?" when you ask the question that's been bugging him for ages. Or "This solution is *so* what I want - it's almost uncanny!" then your chances of keeping his interest may slip away.

It's a challenge we all have no matter what our line of business or how we go about our marketing.

Is there an easy way to come up with the most effective headline? Not really - there are techniques; there are attention words that help to make your headline stand out; but it still takes practice, experience and skill to find the one that pulls no punches, hits the mark dead on and delivers the best measurable results.

Having said that let me give you a few pointers to get you started...

Get Your Creative Juices Flowing

One of the biggest mistakes I see people making is writing one or two headlines and thinking "That's it!"

It rarely is.

When you start crafting your headlines you are only just getting warmed up - your creative performance is still in first gear. As you write more - allowing each headline to act as a catalyst for the next - they begin to flow, like sliding into the higher gears in a high performance car.

That's why I encourage people to write as many headlines as possible before deciding which ones to test. Personally I aim to write at least 100, if not more.

Study Successful Headlines

Find successful headlines. How can you recognise a

successful headline? Look for these attributes:

1. It's a headline for a direct response advert or sales letter. You can tell if it's a direct response marketing campaign because there is a reference code. You are asked to quote it or it is printed on the response form or in the advert.

2. You see the same headline frequently. If it is used in a direct response campaign, which means it is measurable and is being monitored, it is unlikely to be continually used if it isn't proving to be successful.

Study the headline.

Is it specific? (Being specific makes your headline more believable)

Does it contain the promise of a result or benefit that appeals? (People are only interested in results; 'What's In It For Me?')

Does it intrigue without being obscure? (Curiosity can hold your reader's attention provided your first paragraph is strong).

What is it appealing to; envy; greed; pride or status; generosity; well-being or health; peace of mind or something else? (You need to know what appeals to your target market - and you may have to test different appeals to see which is the strongest motivator).

Is it short or long? (Your headline should be long enough to put your message across).

Is it using any of the attention words that magnetically draw your eye and catch your attention? (See the list of words following the headline examples below).

Example Headlines

How many of **these** common gardening mistakes are causing **you** to work harder than you really have to?

Introducing the plain paper copier that's so low in price you can't afford not to own it

Here are **9 reasons** why you should claim your 'The Dangers of Handling Asbestos' report today

Now You Can Get a Business Loan - Even if **Your** Bank Has Turned You Down

Who Else Wants To Lose 10lbs In 28 Days?

Your Investment in Pinesuites Development Could Be Worth Up To £12,960 per Year in Income

Five Familiar Skin Troubles - **Which** Do You Want to Overcome?

Vinegar... Nature's **Secret** Weapon

I've shown the attention words used in these headlines

in bold.

Attention Words

Using specifics, identifying a benefit or result your reader can expect or a problem they have that you can solve makes your headline more attractive. Including one or more attention words increases the attraction because certain words are proven to draw the eye - just like a magnet.

Here's 15 you can use:

You / Your	Breakthrough
Amazing	Free
These	Who Else?
Proof	Last Chance
How / How to	Advice
Here's	Easy
Find Out	Secret
Announcing	

The Secret of How To Make Writing 30 Headlines Easy

When I said to aim at writing 100 headlines to give you the best chance of finding the winner, did you think "No Way!" or something similar? It seems like an insurmountable task - doesn't it?

Try this:

Grab a pen and paper

Look at the first word/phrase in the list above

Write a descriptive headline about your product or service; the result you can deliver or the problem you can solve, using that word. Follow the headline advice I've given you earlier in this post.

Now write a second one, using the same attention word.

Move onto the second word and do the same again; two headlines using the attention word.

Continue down the list - by the time you've used each word **you have 30 headlines**. They won't all be fantastic - some may even be ridiculous, but the point is your creative juices are starting to flow and...

You've written almost 1 third of 100 headlines.

Think you could repeat the exercise another 2 times? Do it and you've written 90 headlines! Not bad going eh?

Now you've got your headlines start working on your letter or advert. And remember the advice I gave you on 7 November in the post *Here's 8 elements for a powerful sales letter* (page 17) or read it on the blog at www.copywriting4b2b.com/archives/11 (did you notice the attention words and specifics in that post headline?)

~Carol Bentley

Date: Thursday, December 13th, 2007 at 10:00 am

1 Response to "Do Your Headlines Grab Your Reader's Undivided Attention"
1. January 13th, 2008 at 7:01 pm *CG Walters* Says:
    Excellent suggestions, Carol.
    Thank you,
    CG

How Annoying Is Your Voicemail?

It is inevitable that sometimes you have to leave a message when you're trying to contact someone and your call goes through to voice mail. How effective, or annoying, is the message you leave?

SpinVox revealed the top 10 most annoying voicemails through their survey. Have you experienced any of these – or perhaps you're guilty too? Check them out on www.modernselling.com

The one that really gels with me is number 2, **The Death March**.

At the moment everyone in my office knows to repeat that all important information - the number to call back on - at least twice. But I think I'm going to ask them to give the number earlier in the message as well as at the end. After all, we don't want to annoy or frustrate the people we are trying to reach, do we?

So, the message *you* leave - is it helpful, informative and designed to elicit the response you want? Or is it one of those most hated message types?

Constructing a well thought out message before you call - just in case the person you want to speak to isn't available - is also a good use of your copywriting skills, don't you think?

~ Carol Bentley

Date: Tuesday, January 15th, 2008 at 10:00 am

Death of The Long Letter

This is the last of the questions that were submitted for 'public consumption' and it is an interesting one because, in some respects, the answer may seem to contradict the advice I give many business owners. It was sent in by Ian Brodie from Lighthouse Business Consulting:

> "One area I'm really interested in is whether you think that in sales, "what works" changes over time.

I'm certainly finding that in my field (person to person selling for large, complex sales) what worked yesterday isn't working so well today. People have got so used to approaches that used to be novel (e.g. talking about the financial benefits of a product rather than its features) that they tend to blank them out (rather like the "banner blindness" Jakob Nielsen talks about in the web world).

When everyone from photocopier salesmen to high end strategy consultants is using the "would you like to hear about an approach that could save you 10% of your costs" technique it becomes devalued.

Similarly, both Michael Fortin and James Brausch have written about the 'death of the long sales letter'. My belief is that this definitely happens. Even the best techniques - once used by everyone - lose their power. Not that they become bad - just that they become the baseline that you must do even to play the game - but you need to do more to win the business. Your thoughts?"

My first thought was "Yes" if you do the same thing constantly or do exactly the same as everybody else then your prospect does become immune and getting a response becomes that much harder. Having said that, I still believe, and experience hasn't changed that belief, it is important to make sure your target market is fully aware of every nuance of what you can do for them; whether that is in the form of a service or supplying a product. And sometimes you have to ask them what they want to know.

For example, if you are in constant contact with your prospects and customers; informing and advising; interacting with comments and discussions - perhaps via a newsletter or web-based blog like this - then you may find that you don't need to use extremely long letters or jaded selling techniques every time you make a new offer.

This is because you have already educated your prospect who has come to know you and what you supply; he has a relationship with you and, possibly, already trusts your judgement and advice. So when you put a new offer into the market place all you have to do is clearly explain what it is and how it impacts on your prospect's life or business. You don't have to do quite so much 'selling'.

So I think the 'death of the long letter' is subjective; if it is an approach to a cold audience; to people who don't already know you or have any knowledge of what you can do for them then the long, explanatory, information-rich and value delivering (i.e. giving valuable free advice that is useful to the reader even if they don't do any business with you) letter still has its place.

If your target prospect is much warmer and already has a relationship with you then just making the new product or service available with a brief explanation of what it does for him may be enough. It is - like any other marketing approach - one that should be tested as my good friend, Grant Marsh (Managing Director of IC Office Solutions Group), realised when I posed the question to him.

He is a great believer in the effect of the long letter; purely because he has experienced the remarkable results this marketing has generated for him over the last 3 to 4 years. However, he has also found he needs to take a different direction occasionally as his reply indicates...

> "I've found a mixed approach does best. Whatever anyone says, there are people out there that will never sit down and read a 16 page letter and there are people who want to know every last detail before they make a decision. [**Carol**: *Often you can't be sure which type of person your reader is, which is why the structure of your letter is so vital, as I explained in my post* **The long and short of it** – page 23] Plus, of course, they get used to a big bulging letter coming to them every month and know it's from us - think "well I don't need a..." - so

they probably don't even open it.

The smallest full offer letter I've ever done was 4 pages, the longest 16 pages. I even rotate who the letters are from now to try and keep it fresh.

What I haven't tried (which I will now be-cause you've just given me the idea - so thanks!) is the same offer going out twice (maybe one week after another) one really shortened down in a short letter and one in a more explanatory long letter."

As I've said previously there is no definitive answer to what works or doesn't work in marketing.

There are theories; there are proven activities gener-ating results in certain industries or professions but when it comes to the crunch the only action that works for you is the one that gets the sales. And you'll only discover that by listening to what your customers and prospects have to say and testing different ap-proaches on your own target market.

~ Carol Bentley

P.S. Incidentally, it is interesting that you men-tioned James Brausch. He frequently uses his blog to explain how his programs work and the benefits both he and others have reaped from using them, before sending you to his 'short sales page'.

I'd be intrigued to know how many of his sales are purely from people who have found his sales letter page without any of the preamble on his blog - I'd be surprised if the proportion was significant.

Date: Monday, February 4th, 2008 at 2:45 pm

*Getting The Appeal Right!

Have you ever started a conversation or starting writing something intending to talk about one thing and then ended up with a completely different subject?

That's what happened when I was writing yesterday's blog post (**How Appealing Are You** on page 191) . I intended to share with you 36 different appeals you could consider when writing your sales letter. Instead I went off at a completely different tangent because, as I was thinking about how we identify our ideal target prospect, I remembered how sometimes recommending an apparent competitor instead of trying to 'close the sale' sometimes turns out to be the best action to take.

So I thought today I would get back on track and share my original thought with you...

Getting The Right Appeal

When you are deciding upon your offer and crafting your sales letter you need to know your target prospect in as much depth as possible, as I mentioned yesterday. Once you have that intimate knowledge of them you can position your offer to match what appeals best.

Here are some popular appeals that might resonate with your target audience:

He (or she) wants to:

1. Satisfy their curiosity
2. Be successful - in life or in business
3. Be comfortable
4. Make their work easier
5. Gain recognition or praise from their peers or superiors
6. Save money
7. Make money
8. Satisfy their ego
9. Gain self-respect
10. Be fashionable
11. Be a recognised expert
12. Protect themselves, their family & their possessions
13. Protect their reputation
14. Avoid embarrassment
15. Save time
16. Gain status through possessions
17. Get a bargain
18. Get something for free

19. Protect the environment
20. Prevent or relieve boredom
21. Get ahead - in their career or social status
22. Enjoy beautiful items
23. Be popular
24. Be their own boss
25. Enjoy leisure pursuits
26. Gain better health
27. Become fit
28. Get rid of aches and pains
29. Be sexually attractive
30. Satisfy their own sexual desires
31. Gain knowledge
32. Be good parents
33. Relax - with friends or alone
34. Be safe and secure
35. Live longer
36. Enjoy their life more

Which of these do your products or services satisfy? Could you make an offer that would match other desires?

The more of these appeals you can meet the better chance you have of increasing the response to your sales letters, adverts and web pages.

~ Carol Bentley

Date: Tuesday, February 12th, 2008 at 10:45 am

How To Structure Your Sales Letter . . .

I'm getting withdrawal symptoms - not having written my daily blog post for a few weeks. I'm getting back into it gradually (time still being taken up sorting my Father's estate) and I'm starting with an extract from my book that may be a reminder (if you have a copy) or a useful insight if you haven't.

It's taken from chapter 10 and is my unique way of looking at how to structure your sales letter.

But... I'm starting to get to grips with hubpages so I've put the whole article; **Outline of a Winning Sales Letter** online at www.carolbentley.org/hub2.html – or read it on page 377).

Take a look and, would you do me a favour; give me a thumbs up rating? Cheers!

~ Carol Bentley

Date: Thursday, February 28th, 2008 at 10:41 am

I Response to "How To Structure Your Sales Letter..."

1. February 28th, 2008 at 3:48 pm *Jeannie Monaghan* Says:

    It's a great book Carol - as ever you make it seem so simple!

Sometimes it's good when "life" takes us away from the computer for a while - be grateful for everything.
Regards, Jeannie

Reply from Carol

I am Jeannie, especially for the fact he didn't suffer in the long term as he could have.

And thank you for your comments about the book.

~ Regards Carol

Apparently I Am Nuts. . .

"I thought you were nuts about..." was the start of a comment on a hubpage I published on 9th February. But I had to smile as I continued to read because it went on to validate the advice I had given.

The subject of the hub is one I've mentioned in a previous post on this website... how taking time to write as many headlines as possible, before choosing the few you want to test, is time well spent.

On the hub I included a useful mind map, which gives an 'at-a-glance' reminder of my headline creating tips. You can download it from the hub page Crafting Headlines or from the link on page 370, where you can also read the full comment left by the reader I mentioned above, as well as those left by other readers.

Please give the hubpage a 'thumbs-up' rating when you visit it. Thanks.

~ Carol Bentley

Date: Monday, March 3rd, 2008 at 2:00 pm

Research and Write

I wonder if, like me, you turn to the internet as your first port of call when you want to find something; whether for business or personal use.

I'm always amazed at the stuff that is out there - literally at the end of your fingertips. And when I was looking for inspiration for verses for my Father's memorial service that's where I started to look.

Why am I sharing this with you? Because I found something unexpected - although I suppose I shouldn't have been surprised. It was an online website at which you can set up a memorial page. I thought it was a great way of sharing with family that is spread far and wide and is especially nice for those who can't attend a funeral. www.imorial.com/bobcliff

So what does this have to do with copywriting?

Everything!

Because there are times when your writing skills are needed for occasions outside your business; writing speeches for christenings, weddings, special birthdays and anniversaries and, of course, memorial services.

Writing for an emotional occasion is probably harder than when you are writing for your business. For me, I found that following the same principle of 'writing to a friend' helped me write Dad's eulogy and the natural flow of the words made it easier for my brother to read out at the service.

And writing can be therapeutic as well; it certainly helps with the healing process.

Isn't it nice to know that as you're developing your writing ability you are creating a skill that is useful in all aspects of your life, not just business?

~ Carol Bentley

Date: Tuesday, March 4th, 2008 at 11:36 am

4 Responses to "Research and Write"

1.   March 4th, 2008 at 1:39 pm *Nigel West* Says:

Dear Carol

I'm so sorry to hear about the loss of your father. I lost mine to prostate cancer last September and you are right, writing is therapeutic as well as moving.

My sister & I are committed to raising money for the hospice Dad spent his last days and for some reason we've decided to take a trip on the River Thames in a kayak.

Recently finishing the website for the sponsorship (www.thameschallenge.org.uk)
has brought up all sorts of emotions, but I'm glad I can do this, to hopefully make a difference to families needing the hospice in the future.

We did meet a while back at one of Paul Gorman's events.

Take care

Nigel

Reply from Carol

Hi Nigel,

thank you for your post. I think it's great that you and your sister are taking such positive action.

Good luck with your kayak trip - that's certainly something different. Is it a sponsored trip? If so reply to this post with a weblink where people can sponsor you if they wish - you never know it may help other people who have lost someone to cancer. I've activated the URL you included in case it is the one to follow.

See Nigel's reply below - this is a sponsored event, which you can support at www.thameschallenge.org.uk

~ Carol

2. March 4th, 2008 at 11:01 pm *Jeannie Monaghan* Says:

    Ah Carol, that was lovely - I didn't know your Dad and I was crying. What a nice thing to do.

    Hi Jeannie,
    You would have liked him - especially knowing how sensitive you are and I think your sense of humour would have found a match with him.

    Carol

3. March 5th, 2008 at 3:13 am *mishra* Says:

    Dear Carol,

    I was reading your blog daily for about 2 months I guess, but this post touched me, I also lost my father a few years ago.
    It's amazing, through internet how you can still feel people so close no matter how far. I'm from a tiny island in the Caribbean, Aruba. And I also started to leave my impressions through a blog I started recently. As you say we may never know how our writing skills can be useful.

Thanks for inspiring.

4. March 5th, 2008 at 10:29 am *Nigel West* Says:

Hi Carol

It is indeed a sponsored trip - we're aiming to raise £10,000. Thank you for activating the website link, sponsorship details are all on the website.

Nigel

---

*Bullets Hit The Mark. . .

Want to get your message across to your target audience? Want to get them excited and eager about your product or service? Want to draw them inexorably towards the sale without a moment's hesitation?

Master the art of writing powerful 'hit the mark' bullets and you increase your chances of success ten, even one hundred-fold.

Look at the winning sales websites; those used to launch highly successful products, programmes, self-study courses and marketing programmes and you'll see they all have one thing in common - bullet paragraphs drawing a clear picture of what you can expect when you take up the offer; or bullet descriptions of the problems you face to which they have the perfect solution.

Ever found yourself so caught up reading a website or letter you can't draw away? It's acted like a magnet to your eyes and senses? Why? What has fired your imagination?

Short, to the point, focused - *a rapid-fire* - of bullets.

Bullets are ideal for catching the skimmers - they are short and succinct. Great for highlighting the key benefits and results the offer is making.

Writing Bullets

You can learn how to write bullets. The easiest way? *Write them!*

- Find the web or sales letter that grabbed your attention, one that you found hard to resist (or maybe you didn't; maybe you succumbed!)

- Grab a pen and paper and find somewhere quiet, where you won't be disturbed.

- Copy the bullets in your own handwriting; absorb the phrasing, the rhythm. Notice the words.

- Repeat the exercise with other letters; just make sure the bullets you copy are vibrant, alive and speak to you.

Mark Hendricks, whose newsletter I receive on a regular basis, recommends taking the next step.

- Re-write every bullet point again for your own product or service.

Did You Know...

If you've followed some of my previous tips then you are already writing bullets - or at least the start of a bullet. Write 100 headlines, as I advised in my post **Do your headlines grab your reader's undivided attention?** (see the post on my blog at www.copywriting4b2b.com/archives/47) and on page 29. Some of those that are not powerful enough for your main headline are a good foundation for your bullets.

Examples of Stunning Bullet Writing. . .

Here's a few websites I've linked to where bullets are used to great effect...

Rich Schefren's Strategic Profits at www.carolbentley.org/ssp.html

Shrink Wrap Your Brain at www.carolbentley.org/rswyb.html

Ultimate Success Program at www.ultimate-success-program.com

Write Letters - Win Sales at www.carolbentley.org/wlws.html

I urge you to take the time to write these bullets out - it's the only way to really get the skill under your skin!

~Carol Bentley

Date: Monday, March 17th, 2008 at 12:00 pm

Copywriting: Blind Faith. . .

I read a great tip in a report for copywriters this week. Although it did seem a bit wacky, I thought it might just work. It is a tip that allows your creative juices to flow uninterrupted. Crucial for getting that great bit of copy written.

You see, one of the biggest problems I have when writing is stopping myself from editing as I go. I see a spelling mistake; I go back and change it. I check a phrase - doesn't read quite right - I'll stop to restructure it. And it breaks the creative flow - sometimes it even wipes out the great prose sparkling in my mind!

But this tip works! I tried it.

When you're typing your letter, or copy for your web page, switch your computer screen off!

Yep, that's what I said - *turn it off!*

With the screen off you can't see your mistyping and you aren't tempted to go back to correct or change things around.

When you've finished being creative *then* you switch the screen on and start editing, correcting any spelling mistakes as you go.

If you have a laptop set the text colour to white so it doesn't show on screen. Then select it all (Ctrl + A) and set it back to the default colour ready for editing.

The tip originally came from Dr Joe Vitale but Karen Martiny from www.copyprotege.com shared it in a report I got.

Give it a try - if nothing else you may give yourself something to smile at when you switch back on and read what you typed!

Have a good Easter break - catch up next week.

~ Carol Bentley

Date: Friday, March 21st, 2008 at 10:00 am

I Response to "Copywriting: Blind Faith. . ."
1.   March 21st, 2008 at 8:33 pm *Jeannie Monaghan* Says:

Cool idea Carol, thanks, Jeannie

Writing To Your Audience

A letter I received in the post this morning broke the two golden rules when writing to prospects, which are:

1. Target your audience
2. Write to your audience

The sender did successfully use some of the copy-writing techniques I share with you - but the funda-mental research hadn't been done. Either that or they purchased an inaccurate mailing list!

After the headlines, here's the start of the letter...

> "Dear Carol:
>
> As an active investor, you've experi-enced more than your share of losses.
>
> But did you know that professional traders also have losses? Yet they have skills and understanding of the market that makes them successful while others lose a fortune!"

A little later in the letter it said...

> "This FREE workshop is perfect for **anyone with an interest in invest-ing.**"

So what's wrong with that?

- I do not trade on the stock market so this is not relevant to me. I am *not* their target audience.

- If I did trade, the writer is making a huge assumption that I've made losses. You could say in view of recent events in the financial world this is probably a fairly safe guess. However it could alienate someone whose trading has been a bit more successful than he is implying, but who would otherwise be interested in what he has to offer.

This was a well written letter and if I had been correctly targeted I would probably have responded.

Learning From Others Mistakes

Why am I sharing this with you?

Because we can learn from the mistakes other people make in their copywriting. And it's often easier to see these mistakes in letters we receive, whereas sometimes we can be too close to our own material and not realise the trap we're falling into.

Tell me, how well targeted is your audience? How well do you know them? Are you writing your letters with their circumstances in mind and in such a way that you are not eliminating a good portion of your recipients?

And - just for a bit of fun and practice - how would you have started the letter (assuming it is going to a targeted audience of trade investors). Share your suggestions – send an email to carol@carolbentley.com

~ Carol Bentley

Date: Friday, March 28th, 2008 at 10:00 am

I Had A Doh! Moment...

I read other blogs - but you already knew that. And some of them give me food for thought. But the posting I've just read made me go "doh!" slap my head and go a little pink with embarrassment.

Why? Because it reminded me of a fundamental method of encouraging people to take note of what you are doing.

You can read the post here (and my comment in reply): **5 Powerful Ways to Increase Blog Readership.** . . (page 440 - or visit the post at www.edrivis.com/?p=253) It was the blue boxed paragraph in **tip number 1** that made me exclaim.

As a result I'll be changing my blog subscriber sequence to offer a gift, which hopefully, will encourage new visitors to subscribe.

A Gift for You...

If you're already subscribed then I'll make sure you get the gift as well.

I'll send a link for it by email and put an announcement in a post on here so you can keep a look out for it. I'm not sure when I'll do this because I want to check through all my material to find something useful for you. And this week is manic (it doesn't help that my PA is on holiday too) so I may not get time to do it before next week. [See **How To Get Your Two Report Gifts** on page 60]

But I won't forget! Promise!

~ Carol Bentley

P.S.   And NO! This is *not* an April's Fool prank! (I've just noticed the date).

Date: Tuesday, April 1st, 2008 at 10:00 am

Getting Your Creative Juices Flowing. . .

How do you get your creative juices to flow when you need to get that sales letter written?

When you are immersed in the day-to-day flow of your business it can be difficult to pull yourself away enough to allow those innovative, compelling words to materialise.

And sometimes we need to get back the imagination and free thinking of our childhood - see things through fresh eyes, with a new, vibrant perspective.

But how?

In my sales letter writing workshops I aim to get that free feeling in the delegates, before they even put pen to paper. Sure, I go through the 'science' behind writing an effective sales letter (or advert)...

- craft eye-catching headlines
- structure the letter to follow the skeleton outline described on page 377 and in the hubpage at www.carolbentley.org/hub2.html
- write a *personal* letter to your prospect
- paint the picture of what the reader gets - benefits - in a language that resonates with him

All of this is important. But facing a blank page or empty computer screen is a real dampener for many.

So I start off by giving everyone a **small bottle of champagne**.

What?!

Encourage people to drink - like a writing equivalent of *dutch courage*?

Absolutely Not!!

The bottle is champagne bubbles - the type you see at weddings.

Having fun - for some going back to the childhood pleasure of blowing bubbles - lightens your mood.

It generates laughter; lessens the sometimes sombre and serious mood of business. And thoughts and ideas start to percolate through.

And, happily, for many it does make writing easier, because writing about *your* passion; *your* business *is* fun! Isn't it?

Give it a go - what have you got to lose? You might surprise yourself with a flow of creative writing that 'hits the mark'.

~ Carol Bentley

Date: Tuesday, April 8th, 2008 at 10:49 am

How To Get Your Two Report Gifts...

If you are already subscribed to this blog you got an extra email today with information on how to get your subscriber gifts - check your Inbox or filtered email folder if you haven't seen it.

And if you are not a subscriber *yet* you can get these gifts too, as I'll explain in a moment.

Why am I giving these gifts?

Well, all is revealed in my original post on 1st April - '**I Had A Doh! Moment**' (read it for yourself on page 57 or at www.copywriting4b2b.com/archives/111).

You see, I decided to add to the value of this blog by giving these gifts to anyone who decided to keep up to date with my posts by subscribing for the email notices.

And I do try to be fair-minded, so I didn't want people who are already subscribed to miss out. Hence the email that was sent separately.

Subscriber Gifts

So what do you get as a subscriber?

Two Great Reports

Report 1:

Profit Mastery Series - Marketing: Paul Stewart Interviews Carol Bentley

In this 16-page transcript of the interview I had with

Paul I shared my thoughts about:

- Why targeting your market is crucial
- How marketing can give a return on investment
- Making your customer your best friend
- Breaking the £1m turnover barrier (or whatever level you are currently facing)
- Three copywriting mistakes you should avoid like the plague
- Using AIDA-A in your sales letter

And

Report 2:

How to Banish, Forever, The Hair-Tearing Frustrations of Microsoft® Word® When Writing Your Sales Letters!

31 tips make your writing a lot less stressful!

These quick tips get rid of the irritation you feel when Word suddenly 'does its own thing' - you can make it behave as **you** want. And they save you a great deal of time. Tips apply to all versions of MS Word since version 2002.

Claim Your Gifts Now

If you are a subscriber - check your email notices.

If you are not yet a subscriber simply visit my blog at www.copywriting4b2b.com pop your name and email address in the boxes in the panel on the right and click the **Tell Me!** button or you can use the pop-up invitation if you prefer.

By the way - once you are subscribed **you won't get the pop-up box appearing *ever* again.** *That's* good news isn't it?

~ Carol Bentley

Date: Wednesday, April 9th, 2008 at 11:34 am

I Response to "How To Get Your Two Report Gifts..."

1. April 11th, 2008 at 9:42 pm *Alan* Says:

   Hi Carol,
   many thanks for the 2 reports!
   have bought your book in the past as well!
   thanks again!
   Alan!

   Reply from Carol

   You are very welcome Alan. I hope you're getting some good results from the book and get some more with the gems in these reports.

   Carol

Conversation or Lecture?

Are you having a conversation with your customers and prospects? Or are you lecturing them?

We are the experts in our field. And we want to be sure our prospects - and customers - fully understand the results our offer gives them.

So, just like the experts tell us, we 'paint the picture' in our letters or on our web pages; clearly describing all the benefits our features deliver. And it reads well, because *we* know what we meant to say. And we know the tone we are using to express our thoughts.

The problem we all have - yes, me included - is making sure what we've written is read correctly.

There are two challenges we face:

1. The words we use. Are we friendly, persuasive and supportive without being condescending, dismissive or just downright 'in-your-face' annoying?

2. The emphasis that someone reading might put on the words you've given them.

I'm sure you know (or have read somewhere) that only 7% of our communication is in the words we use - the rest is made up of body language (55%) and voice tonality (38%)

So how do we get over these challenges in our writing where we don't have the benefit of body language or voice tone? Here's a couple of techniques I've developed that you might like to use:

1. After writing your letter, sales page, email or message, read it out loud. If you can record your reading, so you can listen back, that is even better. When you listen to your reading does it sound right? Do the words flow? Does it sound like you are having a conversation or does it come across as a speech or lecture?

   Writing in a conversational tone is not easy, which is why I so often recommend recording what you want to say and then transcribing it into your document. The words you use when you speak come across more naturally and, after using this technique a few times, you'll find it easier to write in that style as well.

   Now, ask someone else to read the same message aloud. Does it still sound as you expected? Or has the message changed? If so, why?

   Words in the wrong order can change the meaning.

   Let me give you an example. On my blog website, www.copywriting4b2b.com, a pop-over appears if you visit the blog and are not subscribed. I recently changed the pop-over to offer a couple of reports as an incentive to subscribe.

The wording I used for one of the reports was:

31 Word Time Saving Tips for Sales Letter Writers

I wanted the reader to know the report contains 31 tips on how to save time when you use Microsoft Word for creating sales letters. And that read OK, *didn't it?*

But when I looked at it again a bit later I realised it could be read as **31-Word** Time Saving Tips for Sales Letters. Do you see the difference? The way someone reads it could be entirely different to what I meant! So I changed it to say:

31 Time-Savers in Word for Sales Letter Writers

It's another good reason for putting what you've written to one side and coming back to review/revise it later!

2. Punctuation can sometimes create a problem as well. Pauses in the flow - created with commas, semi-colons, colons, dashes and other

punctuation marks - may not be in the right place. Missing punctuation can completely change your message!

3. Formatting can change the emphasis of words. Here's another example; read these sentences putting emphasis on the word in bold/italics in each one:

    o   *I* never said he stole the money
    o   I *never* said he stole the money
    o   I never *said* he stole the money
    o   I never said *he* stole the money
    o   I never said he *stole* the money
    o   I never said he stole the *money*

Do you see how changing the emphasis on a different word in each sentence changes the whole meaning?

So how do you handle this challenge - the challenge of emphasis? It is more difficult when you are writing, compared to speaking. Using different formatting (as I did in the sentences above) can help. Use italics, bold, underline and capitals as well as careful punctuation.

But again, I would strongly suggest going through the same 'reading aloud and checking' process as I recommended above just to be doubly sure it sounds OK.

The *good news* is once you've written a few letters or emails following these suggestions you'll develop your own natural, conversation style. And I'm confident your prospects and customers will respond more warmly to you as result.

~ Carol Bentley

Date: Tuesday, April 29th, 2008 at 9:30 am

I Response to "Conversation or Lecture. . ."

1. April 29th, 2008 at 10:41 am *Nigel West* Says:

> That's really good advice, thanks Carol. I'm helping a software development company improve their technical documentation and interestingly most of the advice you give here (and some in your book) can also be applied to improve technical documentation, whether business requirements or technical design.

How Informative Are Your Sales Letters?

I'm forever going on about making your letters to clients and prospects interesting and information-packed. (Are you sick of hearing it yet?)

Well sorry, I'm not going to apologise for emphasising it (oh - I just did, *sort of...* didn't I?)

No, seriously! Including useful tips, insider knowledge or understanding puts you at a higher level than your competitors, who do not do this, because you are giving value.

What's better - is you are giving value without obligation because you are making it freely available without your prospect having to pay a single penny. And they come to regard you as the 'go-to-expert' when they eventually decide to buy your type of product or services.

Adding Value

So what sort of thing is useful to your prospect; what gives your letter 'added value'?

The actual content you can offer is different in your industry or profession compared to another. Let's see if we can discover what would be useful for your target audience by going through a few questions:

1. When you have a face-to-face meeting with a prospect do they ask you questions? (*What?* Did I hear you say "Doh!" 'course they do!) Alright, what questions do they ask?

    Are any of the questions generic to your industry or profession rather than specific to your product or service?

    Those are the ones you should be answering in

your letter. And by doing so you are giving valuable information to your reader. (An added bonus for you is you might also be overcoming a possible objection to buying the reader might have had).

2. Along a similar vein - what tips do you share with your staff and customers? Again look for the more generic gems. Include these in your letters.

   Remember, something very simple and obvious to you can be a real eye-opener to a person who does not have your experience or knowledge. Sometimes it's easy to forget the wealth of expertise we accumulate over the years.

Offering free advice, from a position of knowledge, goes a long way towards encouraging people to decide in *your* favour when they make the decision to buy!

~ Carol Bentley

Date: Thursday, May 1st, 2008 at 10:00 am

How Do You Brainstorm Headlines?

A colleague has just finished recording an interview with me. He wanted to get some 'behind the scenes tips' on copywriting - specifically for sales letters. He asked a good many questions - but one came up that I'd never been asked before, or at least not in quite the way he put it.

And I thought it's a good one to share with you.

Q:
HOW DO YOU BRAINSTORM HEADLINES FOR A GIVEN PROJECT?

A:
For many people, getting started on headlines can be an insurmountable problem. And sometimes I think it is because enough research and thinking about it has not yet happened.

You see, first off I do research on the project so I know everything there is to know about the company I'm writing for, their business; their products (or services) and the specific offer they are making.

I find out who their ideal customers are and what result the customer is looking for. I pore over letters the company has received from customers, including letters of complaints and how they were dealt with. Reading about an unhappy customer who has been turned into a satisfied, sometimes delighted, customer can be a great catalyst for innovative ideas.

I research their competitors to see what else is on the market - not just direct competitors. We are often competing against something completely different when it comes to persuading people to part with their money. For example if you were selling a portable CD player, your competition is not just other makes of CD players it could be MP3 players, iPods - in fact any other technology that can deliver the result the customer wants; to be able to listen to their music on the move.

Then, having decided I want to write some good headlines, I let it brew. The important step here is to state your intention; "I need some cracking headlines" so your sub-conscious knows what it is supposed to be working on.

I move away from the project and go do something else. And the good ideas; the approach to take; the results purchasers gain when they take up the offer start to percolate through my sub-conscious.

This process helps with the letter itself, as well as the headlines.

When things are starting to 'bubble through' I create a mindmap of the proven response - or 'Power' words as some people call them, starting with the 79 in my book. These words also act as a catalyst as I start to formulate the headlines.

(I've shared the next section of this process with you before on this blog) For each response word I write 2 or 3 headlines. Some are absolute rubbish - especially in the early stages - but as I warm up the better ideas

start to flow.

By using a mindmap I can go back and forth between the different response words adding more headlines as they occur to me.

Using this method makes it really easy to create the 100 headlines I advocate in my book. And, more importantly, I find the stronger headlines to test as well as good ones that are natural sub-heads to use in the letter itself. And often a good P.S. can come out of this exercise.

So there you have it - my approach to crafting headlines.

If you are stuck on 'what to write' for your headlines - review all your material. Even if you are writing for your own product or service, take the time to refresh your mind. Then let your sub-conscious do the work for you. The combination of research and your sub-conscious is a powerful one, if you let it work for you.

~ Carol Bentley

Date: Thursday, June 12th, 2008 at 11:00 am

*Why Some Yellow Page Adverts Do Not Work

Some of the adverts in your local Yellow Pages haven't

got a cat-in-hell's chance of bringing enough business to cover the cost. Asking these three questions could prevent you making the same mistakes.

The adverts I'm talking about are frequently those 'designed' by the Yellow Ad's 'graphics team'.

You know the type I mean... the

'Name... Rank... Serial Number' style

Name: Business name; unless you have a highly descriptive business name this is not going to make you stand out from the crowd.

Rank: What the business does; standard wording that rarely describes any benefit to make the advert more appealing than the other entries.

Serial Number: Contact details; with a phone number as a minimum.

Here's Three Questions To Ask Yourself Before Deciding To Advertise in any Long Term Publication...

Q1. "Is this directory the *first* place my target audience is likely to look for someone who can provide my services/products?"

Q2. "How can I make my advertisement stand out from my direct competitors?" (I'll give you a hint -

think about the **results** your prospects are looking for).

Q3. "Is the advert I plan to use tested and proven elsewhere before committing to a 12 month publication?" Find a local business directory or publication that is issued more frequently - say monthly - that your prospects are probably looking at.

Test your advert:

Test

- the headline;
- the offer;
- the content;
- the layout

and remember to use a reference code so you can measure which version is the most successful. Then - and *only* then - should you agree to place that tested and proven advert in a long term directory like Yellow Pages.

Never, *ever* leave the design of something as vital as your advertisement to the directory publisher - you can't afford to waste money like that - *can you?*

Carol Bentley

Date: Wednesday, July 9th, 2008 at 4:56 pm

Does Any Advertising Work?

Anyone involved in marketing will have come across the quote from John Wanamaker, founder of the Philadelphia store of the same name:

"Half the money I spend on advertising is wasted, and the trouble is I don't know which half."

If you sometimes feel like this, then what I'm about to share will be an inspiration to you.

My good friend, Ed Rivis, knows the true power of advertising - *when* it is done properly. What do I mean by *done properly*? I mean it is...

- **Targeted** at the right audience like a master archer focusing his arrow on the bulls eye

- Written in the most effective style* - as an **advertorial** (an advert that looks like an article) so your reader is engaged in your message

- Contains an **offer that hits the reader's hot-spot** so they can't help but respond

- Thoroughly **tested** as a smaller advert before investing in larger, more expensive advertising space

- **Measurable** - either through coding or by using a unique response mechanism. You cannot test if anything is working if you have no way of measuring it.

* Incidentally, David Ogilvy said...

"There is no need for advertisements to *look like* advertisements. If you make them *look like editorial pages*, you will attract about **50% more readers**."

Would You Like 1,035 Responses To An Advert?

Pop over to <u>Ed's blog</u> where he shares, in a video clip, the details of what he did to get <u>**1,035 responses**</u> to his advert (www.edrivis.com/?p=359).

As I said it may inspire you to reconsider advertising if you've dismissed it as a "waste of money" in the past.

~ Carol Bentley

Date: Friday, July 11th, 2008 at 9:00 am

Do You Make These Writing Mistakes?

I know - it is a classic style headline, but if it has intrigued you then I guess it is still working.

There are some blatant writing mistakes that it is easy

to make when you are dashing off a quick email or two. And, as the article I've linked to below explains, that can be forgiven when it is between friends. Make those same mistakes in a business email and your credibility could be wiped out.

I'm talking about classic mix ups, like your and you're; its and it's and other faux pas.

Check out the 10 mistakes described in this article (www.carolbentley.org/mistakes.htm).

It makes interesting reading - and if you do spot something you have problems with it may help you avoid making that mistake again. Of course, if you are fully aware of all the examples and how they should be used... then you can congratulate yourself, can't you?

~ Carol Bentley

Date: Wednesday, July 23rd, 2008 at 10:55 am

MARKETING

*Marketing - Hot Topics

How can you grab your prospect's attention? If you've read any of my material you'll know I advocate talking about your prospect; *their* desires; *their* worries; *their* problems and describing solutions for *them*.

There's another way of catching their attention. Tie your offer in with a breaking news story; a seasonal event or a current trend like fashion or health. 'Piggy-backing' on events that are in the news places the focus more keenly on what you are promoting because the topic is already in your target's mind.

For example - at the moment a vast majority of people are concerned about their health. There is a huge industry based on the consumption of anything that promises to deliver health benefits.

- 5-a-day for fruit & veg;
- drink plenty of water;
- take vitamin supplements;
- eat so-called superfoods because of the antioxidant benefits they deliver.

But people still want to enjoy treats like biscuits, cakes and chocolate. That's why it was such 'hot news' when researchers discovered **dark chocolate** was *good* for protecting against heart disease. So it made sense that a chocolate producer would create a healthier chocolate that delivers the naturally occurring health-enhancing antioxidants found in cocoa beans.

Tying the indulgence of a chocolate treat with a real, scientifically researched health benefit makes marketing sense – check out what I mean; visit www.copywriting4b2b.com/delvaux

So how can you tie your product or service in with a news event or current trend? Scan the newspaper headlines or listen to what's going on around you. Can you put out a timely offer that fits neatly with what people are talking about and looking for? Is there a PR story you can send out?

Keep your eyes open for every opportunity to grab attention for your business.

~ Carol Bentley

Date: Friday, October 26th, 2007 at 4:12 pm

Spreading The Word...

On the web spreading the word about something - good or bad - is known as viral marketing. Think about it... it isn't new, is it? We've had viral marketing since the year dot! It's just got a rather fancy 'technical' term nowadays.

Of course I'm talking about 'word of mouth' recommendations. You know, when a friend or relative recommends a restaurant or suggests a good film or talks about a theatrical play or musical concert they attended, it's all 'viral marketing' because people are getting to know about it from someone else.

So how often are your customers and business colleagues talking about you? Is what they are saying a compliment or is it damaging your business?

Keeping your communication channels open with your customers is one way of making sure they don't have disparaging comments to make. You can do that by keeping them informed through newsletters, telephone calls, emails, occasional visits, seminars and open days, customer events, letters describing new products, services or offers - and of course you can create a web blog where you offer advice and help as I'm doing here.

Now I'm going to ask you to help me with some viral marketing...

A Gift In Exchange For Your Help..

This blog is new and I have a wealth of tips I plan to share over the coming months; tips you can adopt successfully in your business. Will you share with your friends and colleagues so they too can benefit? If you do, I have created an MP3 audio of powerful copywriting insights for you to listen to / download to show my appreciation of your support.

You can recommend your friends by clicking here (you can reach the web address via www.copywriting4b2b.com/blogtaf2.html) or by clicking the '**Click here to recommend**' link, in the right hand panel, on my blog website at www.copywriting4b2b.com.

Thanks.

~ Carol Bentley

Date: Wednesday, October 31st, 2007 at 1:00 pm

Lets Be Frank About Stamps

When sending out a mailshot should you use franked postmarks or live stamps? I've always maintained real stamps get a better response in most situations because the letter looks more personal - and I have proved it on many occasions for clients.

So I was intrigued to get a letter from Royal Mail - with a live stamp. Although I have to say the 'first impression' of a personal letter was rather spoilt by it being addressed to **RM Direct Customer**!

In the letter they were promoting their Christmas Stamps. It said:

"Imagine you have two letters in front of you. Which would you open first? The one with the postage stamp or the one with the printed postmark?"

They quoted independent research, carried out in the UK on their behalf by Quadrangle in February 2007, which reported:

"Anecdotal evidence suggests letters with stamps are perceived as having a positive, personal touch and are far more likely to be opened. And direct mail makes the recipient feel more valued than email or e-news-letters."

I'd like to add my 2p worth to that, based on my own testing and experience...

Does It Work?

I carried out a test for a client, sending half a mailshot using a franked stamp and the other half with ordinary 'stick-on' stamps. Result? The **stamps brought in 18.5% more bookings** (it was for a training course) which paid for the extra labour involved **and** brought in additional profit.

First or Second Class

Most direct mail is sent second class to keep costs to a minimum.

But - tell me, if you see a letter with a 2nd class stamp

on it, how important or urgent do you think it is? If the letter inside is urging you to act before a deadline doesn't that come over as a bit inconsistent with the subliminal message from the 2nd class stamp?

So does that mean you should send your letters 1st class? Could be hellishly expensive - especially if you're sending out thousands of letters!

No - here's my suggestion:

Check the actual postage price for your letter or package; for e.g. an ordinary 2nd class letter, at the moment, is 24p. Use denominated stamps to that value. Unfortunately Royal Mail do not help us by offering a 24p stamp, so you have to use multiple stamps. E.g. 10p & 14p.

People rarely check the value of stamps and what class postage rate they represent. So although the actual rate is for 2nd class, it won't give that impression when it is received.

Getting Your Stamps

Did you know.. if you buy stamps to the value of £35 or more Royal Mail delivers them to you next day free of charge?

It's a great way of buying your stamps for smaller, in-house mailing campaigns without going to your local post office and depleting their stock. You can order online at www.royalmail.com

Outside the UK?

This post is about UK mailing campaigns; I wonder if people in other countries get the same results? If you are a reader from outside the UK I'd love to know what you've discovered if you've ever tested franked mail against stamped mail.

~ Carol Bentley

P.S.   Thanks to everyone who emailed to say these frequent blog posts are OK because the contents are useful. I'll just take weekends off and the occasional day of holiday

Date: Friday, November 9th, 2007 at 10:00 am

1 Response to "Lets be frank about stamps"

Copywriter July 3rd, 2008 at 3:47 pm
Says:

I am a copywriter in the US and real stamps, in my opinion, out pull anything else.

Everything you said in this post is spot on.

Thanks for sharing your information with the rest of us. Jay

Too Early For Christmas Promotions

It would appear that we are not the only country where shops seem to stock Christmas goods earlier and earlier each year.

The post on a blog I regularly visit asked **'How Soon Is Too Soon?'**
(www.carolbentley.org/awblog.html)

Now, as a copywriting and marketing expert, I totally understand businesses wanting to make the most of a major holiday period like Christmas. And conversely I also join in the consumer irritation about Christmas promotions starting before the summer season is hardly finished. I suppose you could say I'm a bit contrary.

But the aweber post made a valid point about seeking a connection between your marketing and any celebration or anniversary. And an astute marketer looks for any opportunity to tie an event in with something he is offering.

So what event could you tie your promotional activity with - apart from the obvious ones like Christmas, New Year, Valentine's Day etc?

What ideas can you come up with?

Here's a few to get you started...

Product Anniversary.. celebrate the 1st anniversary of your product or service launch

Web Page Anniversary.. a good way of promoting your website - especially if you've had a makeover

It's My Birthday - sharing useful information or giving a handy gift - I know that's an obvious one

Chinese New Year - particularly good if you can tie the year into your product or service

I found some really strange celebration days for January 2008 at www.carolbentley.org/celebrate.html, give you any ideas you can use?

~ Carol Bentley

Date: Wednesday, November 21st, 2007 at 10:30 am

Cialdini and The Art of Persuasion

Understanding the art of persuasion when you write your sales letter gives you an edge.

Understanding the art of reciprocity when interacting with people in your network of business contacts can bring great rewards - for both sides. (Check the content of the example letter I gifted you in yesterday's post **You Met New Business People – Now What?** on page 262).

But it's not just about understanding these principles, it's about being genuine when you use them in your dealings with people.

And that's a clear point Dr Robert Cialdini makes both in his book **Influence - The Psychology of Persuasion** and in his presentation on **Power of Persuasion**. If you haven't read his book I strongly recommend you get yourself a copy.

The ISBN numbers are:

- **ISBN-10:** 006124189X
- **ISBN-13:** 978-0061241895

It will help you write more powerful, compelling and persuasive letters.

And whilst you're waiting for your book to arrive, take look at the video clips on YouTube showing Dr Cialdini's presentation, during which he describes the 6 principles you should know about when marketing your business (As at 29 April 2008, the video clips have been taken down due to a copyright dispute).

~ Carol Bentley

Date: Wednesday, November 28th, 2007 at 10:00 am

Another View On Business Cards

Is your business card just for handing out at business meetings, because everyone else does so? Or is it a <u>real</u> **marketing** <u>tool</u> for you?

Provided you've got the design and content right (see what I say about 'Your Hidden Marketing Tool' in the post on page 275) it can be one of the hardest working marketing weapons in your arsenal.

But only if you use it properly to position yourself.

And that's where the quality of the card you use counts. It speaks volumes about you and your business.

Quality Speaks Volumes

Start-up business people know they need business cards. But often they go for false economy by using the cheapest methods possible to get their cards organised. Now, don't get me wrong, I'm not saying you have to spend a fortune on your business cards. What I *am* saying is the card should look like a *quality* card – no matter where you got it from.

Self-Print Cards

The entrepreneur, sole-trader and individual professional sometimes print their own business cards using the many 'business card' products available and an inkjet printer. Be careful...

These cards are often flimsy in order to feed through the printer and consequently give the impression of 'a business with no experience or history'.

Handing these out, at business meetings in particular, can send out the wrong, damaging message. On top of that, inkjet printing smudges and runs if it gets wet – giving a less than favourable impression to the people you want to engage with.

On-line Printed Cards

There are many websites offering free business cards. A selection of designs is available and you can add whatever details you want. The cards are often a good quality weight and feel good to hand out.

There's just one thing that spoils these for you...

If you are only paying postage the company supplying the cards has to have some means of recompense. And they have... **YOU** are doing *their marketing* for them.

They print their website URL on the back of your cards, so every time you hand one out you are advertising their website and, by default, you are also implying you don't consider your business cards important enough to pay for them.

If **you** don't take your business cards seriously – why should anyone else?

By all means use these sites; they can be very cost effective. But, as a minimum, pay the small amount they ask to remove THEIR website details off the back of YOUR cards.

Of course if you've read my previous post : 'Your Hidden Marketing Tool' you know what should really be on the back of your card, don't you?

Does Your Card Pass The Tactile Test?

Test it for yourself: Close your eyes, and feel your business card. Does it honestly give the impression of quality, professionalism, trustworthiness and integrity?

If it doesn't, you just might be throwing future sales away when new business contacts get the wrong impression about you.

~ Carol Bentley

Date: Monday, December 10th, 2007 at 2:00 pm

*Word-of-Mouth Power In A Bricks & Mortar Business

Do you know of any business that is built and run

purely on word-of-mouth marketing? Or any that regard 'referrals' as their prime business source?

There aren't many.

Yet with today's emphasis on taking more notice of what your friends and peers say, rather than the marketing message companies put out, it is something every business owner should seriously consider.

And that's what an Australian Dentist, described in Martin Russell's blog post on page 390, (or you can read it at www.carolbentley.org/womm.html) has done extremely successfully.

Now imagine the power of harnessing this outstanding and innovative service approach with the power of peer marketing on the internet - the possibilities are breath-taking!

How can you adopt these ideas in your business? Got thoughts you'd like to share? Pop them in a comment for others to see and, maybe, benefit from.

~ Carol Bentley

Date: Friday, December 14th, 2007 at 1:00 pm

How To Show Your Expertise

In 1994 I worked with a savvy sales & marketing expert, Peter Thomson, who is a self-made millionaire. He gave me some sage advice:

"If you want people to recognise you as an expert in your field, you must write and publish a book!"

In those days getting a book published was no easy task. Finding a publisher who would take your work was like finding a needle in a haystack.

Self-publishing, called Vanity Press, was very expensive with the likelihood that none of your books would sell and you'd end up with a garage full of the thousand or so books you had to order.

I wrote hundreds of how-to manuals and programmes and created a number of tips booklets, but I didn't go down the print publishing route.

Then in 2003 I got the exact same advice from another marketing expert, Paul Gorman.

But one thing Paul said - that turned out to be true - is that no matter how many business people learn about this powerful market positioning tool very few take action and actually do it.

And that included me for another 18 months or so.

Then in 2005 I decided to 'buckle down' and write my book and it was a lot easier than I had expected. Now you might be thinking, "Well it is going to be easier for *you*, after all you *are* a copywriter!"

True! But, amazingly it wasn't my copywriting skills that came to the fore - it was my knowledge and passion about my subject. I wanted to share with other business people; to let them discover how they too could write their own effective marketing material.

The actual writing, *not the editing or getting it published and out into the market place*, took me a little over a week to achieve. Once I started it just poured out. And, as it did, I discovered a few tricks to writing a book that helped me enormously.

The book was finally published in November 2005. I still remember the elation of holding the first copy in my hands; the excitement of sharing it with family and business friends. And, even more, the thrill of seeing it listed on Amazon and receiving my first order from them.

Both Peter and Paul said a book is an amazingly effective marketing tool - and it is.

I've met people and gained new clients I would never have come across in a month of Sundays if they hadn't bought my book. Some came through Amazon sales; others came through website sales, book store sales and joint venture sales.

Over the next month, amongst these daily blog posts, I'm going to share some of those writing, publishing and marketing insights with you.

So, sharpen your pencil, clear your mind and get ready to create your most powerful marketing tool. And I promise... I'll help you make it as painless as possible.

~ Carol Bentley

Date: Tuesday, December 18th, 2007 at 10:00 am

You Don't Have To Write The *Whole* Book

A few posts ago I told you how I'd been told that publishing a book is one of the most powerful marketing activities you can do. And I'd proved it to myself.

I also explained that the experience had given me some insights I would like to share with you over the next month or so.

Before I do that, let me explore some alternatives with you...

"What?! Are you going to say *I don't need* to write a book?"

No, what I'm saying is you don't have to write 'war & peace' or a Tolkein masterpiece.

What your book should have is valuable insights your

target prospects find interesting and useful. Because that is how you demonstrate your expertise.

And, in fact, *you don't even have to write the whole book* to achieve that.

An idea that Peter Thomson suggested to the consultant's membership group I belonged to, back in the early 1990's, was to form a collaboration where each person wrote just 1 chapter. Obviously there would have to be a connection between the authors' topics so that they complemented each other.

The book was published with different jacket covers; each cover depicted one of the consultant authors on the back - with their short bio, a description of the chapter they'd written and a resume of the book content. The other authors were listed as contributing writers.

There are many books published under a co-authorship, so the idea made perfect sense.

Quite a few of the group membership did this and gained the benefit of being recognised as an expert author by their clients and prospects as a result.

Think about the people in your industry or profession or in associated disciplines. Who could you join forces with to write an informative book?

Not sure this would work for you? Don't worry, I've

got another thought for you - but that's the subject of another post...

~ Carol Bentley

Date: Thursday, December 20th, 2007 at 10:00 am

I Promised To Tell...

In my post on 21st December I said I'd let you know what I'm currently developing - and why. . .

How do you actually do what many marketing experts tell us is the most powerful action you can take? It can seem like an insurmountable challenge. But having done it I can assure you it is not as daunting as it may seem. But of course, it is a lot easier when you know exactly *what* to do as well as the how.

What am I talking about? Writing and publishing a book. As I've said in a previous post being a published author positions you as an authority on the subject; an expert.

I am currently discussing a joint book venture with a close friend and colleague. We plan to start preparing the book content towards the end of January. The project will include writing, preparing the manuscript for publishing, getting it out to bookstores and on-line stores, like Amazon, and all the marketing that needs to go into getting the book known.

So why should you be interested? Because as we go through the project I will be creating a video record of exactly how it is all done. My intention is to have an extremely easy to follow step-by-step instructional video programme that anyone can use.

During the project development I'll be sharing gems on this blog which, if you've thought about writing a book, will guide you through the process.

And I may be asking for your help because I will be looking for beta-testers before launching the programme as a live product.

In fact, if you *have* thought about it but have not done anything to get your book written and published. Or you'd like to write a book but you are not sure how to go about it, you could get some starting tips straight away.

Simply tell me what's preventing you from doing it.

What questions would you like answered?

What advice can I give that will help you get started?

How can I help you show your target market that **you** are the go-to expert in your field?

~ Carol Bentley

Date: Friday, January 4th, 2008 at 12:53 pm

2 Responses to "I promised to tell. . ."

I. January 9th, 2008 at 7:57 pm *Chris Ingham* Says:

Hi Carol,

Do hope that your [birthday] celebrations lived up to expectations; certainly caught my attention!

Your blog got me to thinking...... I've just finished helping my partner to complete an authoritative manual on their area of expertise and it does seem a natural to expand and spin this manual into a book.

It could be a first of its type.

We'd like to join in with your new project if possible. What's involved please?

Chris

2. January 9th, 2008 at 11:13 pm *Carol Bentley* Says:

Hi Chris,

Celebrations were wonderful, thanks for asking.

It certainly sounds intriguing. Are there any others out there dealing with the same / similar subjects or is it really a first? If it is, who would be interested in buying it? How would it be used to promote a business?

As regards getting involved: at the moment the only involvement with my project is to keep up with the posts that are talking about book publishing - they'll be scattered throughout the next few months or so whilst I'm developing the video tutorial.

When the tutorial is ready I'll put a post on this blog asking for beta testers - that's when you can get more actively involved.

Good luck with the book.

~ Carol Bentley

4 Easy Steps To Authorship. . .

If the thought of writing a whole business book is something you just can't see yourself doing, but you want the kudos of being a published author then there is a way you can start on a smaller scale.

Your published book can contain as few as 20 pages; the important thing is to make the content useful to the reader. One way to do that is to produce a **tips booklet**.

What To Include In And How To Write Your Tips Booklet

The good news is you probably already have all the

material you need to create your tips booklet. Here's a few things to keep in mind...

Structure your tips booklet as a series of useful hints and advice in an easy to read format.

Keep your tips interesting; not a boring '*you should do this or you should do that*' type of monologue. Do this by writing in active language - discover exactly how in a moment.

4 Easy Steps...

1] Gather all the questions you've been asked about your products or services and the answers you've given. How many of them are generic? Which ones are questions that would be asked of anyone in your line of business?

2] Turn each answer into an action statement that introduces a topic you can give expert advice on. Do this by starting your sentence with a verb. Here are some examples:

> (i) **Realise** it's the process not the price (taken from **117 Handy Haggling Hints** published by Derek Arden at www.derekarden.co.uk)

> (ii) **Avoid** backache when driving - take a break every 20 minutes

> (iii) **Write** about benefits and results, not features,

in your sales letters

(iv) **Listen** carefully to what your prospect is saying when you meet

(v) **Consider** the cost savings when you use...

(vi) **Plan** your business strategy to gain the highest success

3] Follow each introductory sentence with a more detailed explanation; it could be just one paragraph or more if needed.

4] Choose a compelling title for your booklet that appeals to your prospect (it's the same process as creating a headline for your sales letter).

Once you've got the content organised you can get your manuscript ready for printing.

Tips Booklet Format

Ideally your tips booklet should be small enough for your reader to carry with him/her in a pocket or handbag. Most tips booklets are 21cm x 10 cm, which fits neatly into a DL envelope and makes it a perfect size for sending out in the post.

Alternatively you could create an A6 size booklet (half of A5). Talk to your printer to find out which size is the most economical for printing.

Start off with a brief introduction to what the booklet is about. If your tips fall into different categories you might want to include a table of contents listing the categories.

Number your tips.

Show the first few words; the action sentence, in bold so it stands out.

At the back of the booklet include information on how your reader can get more copies of the booklet.

If you publish a series of booklets list your other titles in the series.

Your New Marketing Tool

Your intention is to use this booklet as a marketing tool. You can sell it on your website for visitors who come across your site through search engines or other incoming links.

Or you can give it away to targeted prospects. Like a book, it is far more powerful than a business card and, because it contains valuable information, it won't be thrown away.

It achieves two benefits for you:

- It demonstrates your expertise.

- It keeps your name fresh in your prospect / customer's mind.

So, make sure you include a page at the back with details of what you offer, your contact information and an invitation to use it.

You can also show your contact details on the back cover.

OK - what's the name of *your* tips booklet? Do let me know... it's your first step towards publishing a book!

~ Carol Bentley

P.S. If you've already created an informative report or have a set of Q&A pages or handouts, you have the foundation of your tips booklet. All you need to do is rewrite it in the style I've described in this post.

Date: Tuesday, January 8th, 2008 at 10:00 am

2 Responses to "4 easy steps to authorship..."

1. January 8th, 2008 at 1:29 pm *Ian Brodie* Says:

   Excellent idea Carol - particularly the use of a "giveaway" booklet as a sort of uber-business-card. Ian

2. January 20th, 2008 at 2:26 am *Tip Diva* Says:

   What about doing a PDF version instead of

printing? How do those fare? (See *What Do You Think . . . Print or PDF?*; page 183)

*Do You Make This Mistake With Your Letters?

You wouldn't expect the layout of your letterhead to cost you extra every time you send a sales letter to your prospects or customers would you? But it can.

I was talking with Phil Hutchinson, Managing Director of Direct Mailing Services, whose services I frequently use for my clients' and my own mailshots. We were discussing some of the mistakes people make with their sales letters and specifically the problems they create for themselves when they don't think to ask his advice before preparing their direct mailing material.

Even something as simple as the layout design of a letterhead can have a significant impact on the costs of a mailshot.

A bad design loses money...

How so?

Because when bulk mail outs are sent (and when I say 'bulk' it can be any quantity between 500 and 500,000 or more with Phil's services) you can enjoy a welcome saving on postage costs. But only if your packages comply with certain standards.

And that's where a letterhead design can create problems - as happened for one company.

You see, a vast number of letters sent to businesses use window envelopes. And Phil explained that postal companies are able to offer discounts because they use OCR (optical character recognition) systems to automate and speed up the sorting process.

But in order to do this it is crucial that nothing appears through the envelope's window, other than the recipient address. Showing any additional, unrelated text or graphics can cause the letters to be rejected, which means you lose your postage discount. That could be an **expensive £300 or more loss** on a mailshot of 15,000 items. Imagine the cost for larger numbers!!

Even if you've not yet reached these larger mailshot numbers, there are other important marketing reasons for keeping that address area as clean as possible.

An 'Aha!' moment

As Phil and I chatted I realised this is just one of the crucial aspects that need considering when you are creating your mailing campaign. Phil has a deep well of knowledge when it comes to direct mailing. And it occurred to me drawing on that knowledge could have immeasurable benefits for you.

So I'm going to twist Phil's arm and get him to spill the beans. I intend to draw these professional secrets out of him and share them with you. Each gem I weasel out of him will give you extra, powerful knowledge you can use to make your mailings even more successful. (By the way, we will be discussing specifics for the UK postal services but the vast majority of the topics we touch on apply to mailings in other countries too).

The telephone interview will be recorded and posted on this blog. [See **Survey Results In Gift** on page 120].

~ Carol Bentley

Date: Wednesday, January 9th, 2008 at 10:00 am

Ask Your Most Burning Question. . .

Most of the posts I've done so far have been on copywriting, marketing or business insights I wanted to share with you or topics that people have asked me about before.

As a regular visitor to this blog you possibly sit there thinking "I could do with knowing about this..." or "I wonder how I should do such and such?" Some of my visitors have already sent in questions, and you may be one of them. If not, now is your chance to ask your most burning question.

It can be on copywriting, marketing, business strategies or tips, the meaning of life and the universe... well maybe not the last one, I'm not a philosopher!

So ask away, send your question to carol@carolbentley.com

Then visit www.copywriting4b2b.com to check if it has been used. And don't forget to include the URL for your web page so I can include a link for you. Thanks.

(You can send in a question at any time – don't wait to be invited).

~ Carol Bentley

Date: Monday, January 14th, 2008 at 12:00 pm

Haven't Yet Written A Book?

I mentioned at the beginning of January I would be creating a video programme to show the easiest way to get a book written and published. And, because of that, I decided to talk to other business authors to get their views on why they decided to write a book and how they went about it. I figured the more approaches I revealed the better chance there was that you'd find something that hit the mark for you.

Last week I spoke to Jill Konrath, who wrote 'Selling to Big Companies'. We were discussing the reasons for writing a business book; one I've already shared with you is to position yourself as the expert in your field.

Jill told me that after publishing her book she was curious why there were very few business women authors. And she talked to successful business women, trying to encourage them to join her as an author. Their response surprised her...

You might be relieved to find you have the same thoughts.

I recorded my telephone conversation with Jill and I'll be sharing the full content with you at a later date, but for the moment, I thought you might like to listen to this short clip - only a few minutes - in which she shares the revelation those astute business women gave her and explains why some of them changed their mind.

Listen to the MP3 audio, which you can download at www.carolbentley.org/jkaudio1.html.

So - has this short audio given you some food for thought?

~ Carol Bentley

Date: Tuesday, February 5th, 2008 at 10:45 am

1 Response to "Haven't Yet Written A Book. ."

1. February 16th, 2008 at 1:38 am *Carol* Says:

> Yes, food for thought. I agree that appealing to the sense of generosity (helping others) and not a sense of selfishness (promoting myself) will motivate people to write books and promote their services.
>
> I wrote my soon-to-be published book with both factors in mind. I really want to share what I know (help people), but it would be nice if some of the readers then used my services (accounting in my case).

Reply from Carol B

> I agree with the thought that after reading your book some of your readers will gain the confidence to enquire about your services.
>
> I think that is still part of the real sense of helping others because without your accounting services they could find themselves financially disadvantaged.
>
> Not letting people know how your expertise can help them is doing them no favours - they need to know so they can take advantage of what you offer.

Good luck with your book Carol, I hope it goes really well for you.

~Carol Bentley

The Heart Of The Matter

I constantly advise that when writing a sales letter one of the most effective ingredients is a good testimonial. Not just one that says "Great job, would recommend", but one that is more specific about what was happening before, what solution you provided and the result your customer enjoyed.

An even better structure for your testimonial is what Alex Mandossian refers to as a heart-centred testimonial using the Before/After/After template. This is particularly powerful when coming from your long term customers. Check if Alex's post is still available at his blog www.carolbentley.org/testimonial.html and, if it is, go down to the visitor's comments because the one from Gail Doby is rather useful.

And when you've done that consider your existing customers.

- Which of these gained a great result from you?
- Which of these makes you feel proud of what you've done for them?
- Have you asked for their testimonial? If not, perhaps now is a good time to ask.

Use this question structure, not only does it produce a good testimonial for you; it also makes it easier for your customer to think of what to write or say. And one final point, the testimonial is no good if you can't share it with your prospects. So make sure you get permission to use it - along with your contact's name, company name (if appropriate) and location - in your marketing material.

~ Carol Bentley

Date: Thursday, February 7th, 2008 at 10:45 am

*Are You Newsworthy?

Whilst doing my usual browsing of other people's blogs a post on Ed Rivis' called '**Write Press Releases That Sizzle**' (read his blog post on page 393 or online at www.edrivis.com/?p=199) caught my eye. He described how to boost your company's visibility, with both on and offline PR... so I followed the link he included and found an interesting article on Terry Dean's blog offering some inspiring tips at **21 ideas for hot press releases** (which you can read on page 396 or at www.carolbentley.org/deanPR.html)

PR is a great way to get some free publicity. But you have to stand out from all the other businesses trying to get noticed. And news editors are looking for something that is interesting for their readers; something a little different from the 'norm'.

Some of Terry's ideas may seem a bit wacky - but they've all got merit. I particularly like number 20 - it made me smile.

Help Your News Editor Make Your PR An Attention-Grabber

When I first released my book I sent a press release to my local paper's Business Editor describing some of the tips it contained and how they help business people get a good result. I wanted to make sure I had the highest chance of the news release being printed so I sent a bit of an odd picture to catch his attention:

The editor asked if the money I was holding was real - it was!

He published the picture, and a long article about the book, on the first page of the business news section. *Great result!* [See www.carolbentley.com/offer]

In fact he used the picture again when a local Ottakar's

bookstore hosted my book-signing event a few months later.

So what can you do to promote your business? Perhaps Terry's tips have given you an idea or two?

If you have never included PR in your marketing toolkit maybe now is the time to try. See which of his 21 ideas appeals to you and give it a go.

~ Carol Bentley

Date: Friday, February 8th, 2008 at 10:45 am

Results Are In... Lessons To Learn...

If you are one of the many people who managed to spare me 5 minutes for the survey last week - thank you - I really appreciate your feedback.

In fact I was really chuffed with the number of completed forms we got in - far more that I'd expected. I do hope the e-book you got in appreciation is proving handy.

A number of people asked some very interesting questions; many about topics I intend to explore with you in future postings on this blog.

The exercise of carrying out this survey gave me some

valuable insights, which you might find interesting as well.

It's no surprise (see chart following) the highest score for what you'd like to see in these posts is copywriting; after all, that's what this blog is mainly about. But asking the question meant I found out what else interests people who visit this website so I can add variety to the content.

What would you like to see in these blog posts?

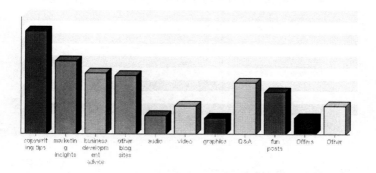

It is so easy when we are in the thick of our day-to-day business to lose sight of what is important to our customers and prospects. Holding a survey like this is a valuable way to discover what your customers think about you and your products or services.

Have you asked *your* customers recently?

You may be surprised at what they'll tell you and you may even discover something new they'd really value that you could provide, thus giving you a new reve-nue/profit stream. Worth asking, don't you think?

On a blog site like this it's a fine line between overbur-dening visitors and satisfying a thirst for knowledge. Of course that ties in strongly with the actual content too. As you can see in the following graph the over-whelming majority felt that 3 blogs per week is suffi-cient, with the remainder fairly evenly split between random and every weekday.

How frequently would you like to see new posts?

Why did I start by posting every weekday?

A few people asked why I posted so often... I promise it's not because I like the 'sound of my own voice' - there is a strategy behind this.

I've mentioned previously starting a blog is a great way of keeping in touch with existing customers and pros-pects. It's also a great way of finding new prospects... but only if they find your blog first.

To do that they need to become aware of it; search engines, other blogger's posts and 'word-of-mouth' recommendations are some of the ways to get a website known and encourage people to visit.

But...

- A stale website doesn't show up on search engines; they like dynamic sites with constantly changing content.
- Other bloggers only talk about someone's blog if there is something interesting to mention - that can't happen if the posts are infrequent.
- And why would anyone recommend a blog if very little useful content is delivered?

So it was a deliberate decision to make my posts as frequent as possible with the intention of delivering interesting content to everyone in my prospective and actual audience. If you've followed this blog for a while you'll know that I do try to cover a variety of topics to make sure there is something to suit every reader at some point and keep the blog as vibrant as possible.

I will continue to make regular posts - sometimes it will only be 3 during a week. But on other occasions, if there's something to tell you that I believe is important, I may slip a few extra posts in.

I hope that satisfies what you'd like to see.

Thank you once again for sharing your views and

helping me to make sure I deliver what you want to read.

~ Carol Bentley

P.S.   If you want to run a survey there are a lot of websites offering different solutions. The one I used for my survey, which automatically created the graphs above, is SurveyGizmo at www.carolbentley.org/gizmo.html where they offer a free account.

Date: Wednesday, March 19th, 2008 at 10:00 am

I Don't Know The Answer... But I Know Who Does

When I talk to business owners, clients or prospects the most frequently asked question is "What works best in a letter or web sales page?"

It is a question any marketing professional or experienced copywriter is asked time and time again.

And none of us know the definitive answer! In fact the only people who *do know* what's working are **your customers;** because they are the people who responded to your offer and bought.

That's all very well - but until you get the content of your message right; targeted specifically to the people you have identified as your ideal audience you're not going to get those customers, are you?

Test, Test and Test Again...

I've said it before - and any marketing expert worth their salt says the same thing - you **must test**. The 3 minimum things you should be testing are:

- **Your offer:**
  -what your prospect will receive
  -how it will be delivered (post; special delivery or, if online, digitally)
  -price
  -payment method (single charge or spread payments, or 'try before you buy')
- **Your headline**
- **Your guarantee**

Fred Black gives a good description of testing in his blog post **Test, Test, Test** (to read the blog post, go to www.pqinternet.com/127.htm)

Testing Takes Time...

Testing can be time-consuming - especially if you are testing and sending by post. And in this age of 'instant satisfaction' that delay may be too much.

If you are getting high traffic (large number of visitors) to your website you may decide to create an online sales page and use that for testing these different elements.

If you are not getting streams of traffic you can use Google Adwords - or a similar PPC (pay per click) advertising to drive traffic to your test sales page.

(If you want to know more about Google Adwords check Ed Rivis' Google Adwords Voyeur or visit this web page www.carolbentley.org/rgav.html).

One distinct advantage of using an online sales page is that you can test more than one element at a time. It is known as multivariate testing.

You can use testing software to control this more complicated testing.

Remember - *only your customers **truly** know what works*. I can only take an educated guess based on experience.

~ Carol Bentley

Date: Wednesday, March 26th, 2008 at 10:38 am

Survey Results in Gift

Wow! I was hoping I might get some useful feedback in the survey I invited you to visit, but I didn't expect such an overwhelming response. So I've just got to say 'Thanks' in my normal way...

I decided to talk to a very good friend of mine who is the Managing Director of a mailing house. We spent 40 minutes on the phone last night discussing some of the issues that impact on the success of a mailing campaign; how a badly structured mailing can dramatically suppress the open rate of letters and subsequently give a low response.

Actually - it was more of an interview than discussion - I wanted to be sure you got some extremely valuable insights so I asked rather a lot of questions for you. And I recorded our conversation so you could listen in like a 'fly-on-the-wall'. Because the conversation took place over the telephone the audio quality is not brilliant - but the content is.

My friend revealed some startling facts and, frankly, offered good advice - in fact this recording is the sort of thing some experts would make into an audio pro-gramme and sell. I'd say it's worth a good £100 or more, especially when you hear how one company cut their mailing costs in half, slashing it by over £400, in a way that you could too.

But I'm not 'selling it' - other than to persuade you to collect your free gift.

But this is yours only if you are subscribed to this blog. The download link is in a private, password protected post; another gift for my subscribers.

Download the MP3 at

www.carolbentley.org/mailing.html

The file is just over 11 Mbytes and is just under 40 minutes play time.

~ Carol Bentley

Date: Thursday, May 8th, 2008 at 10:00 am

Direct Mail Gems

I think this must be a 'business resource' week because this is the fifth business tool I've told you about since last Friday!

If you are subscribed to this blog then you got the private post in which I gifted the specially recorded audio of the conversation I had with Phil Hutchinson.

Since then Phil has generously said you are invited to request an audio-CD (complete with workbook) of a business presentation he gave. In the CD he shares 10 Direct Mail Secrets which, in his experience, make an impact on the success of a mailing campaign.

Listen whilst he tells us:

- How to determine who to write to
- How to trim your mailings costs whilst still generating the highest impact

- The single, most effective thing you can do to make sure your message is read
- Why the wrong presentation of your mailing can decimate response
- Why using the wrong addressing method can drastically cut your open rate

And, because the tips he gives are important, I've decided to make this a publicly available invitation so you can get your copy even if you are a casual visitor to this blog.

 Pop over to Phil's website at Direct Mail Services (www.directmailservice.co.uk) and click the **Free Direct Mail Secrets** graphic in the right panel.

Enjoy Phil's generosity and use the tips he reveals to boost your mailing responses.

Date: Thursday, May 15th, 2008 at 3:00 pm

*Ostrich or Hawk

In my 36+ years in business (oops! I think I've just given my age away!) I've gone through a fair few recessions. And time and time again I've seen businesses make a big mistake that, in some cases, has been the beginning of their demise.

You see, when the economy is good business people

actively engage in marketing; pro-actively look for new business. They are hawk-like, ready to use all their skills and resources to flush out prospects who want their products or services.

Then the economy dips, maybe a recession hits and suddenly some of these companies turn into an ostrich! They bury their head in the sand, stop marketing; stop spending on the one activity that could help beat recession and generate the sales they desperately need.

Why?

Whenever I've asked that question I'm invariably told "Because we aren't getting enough revenue and we haven't got the money to spend!"

It's a catch-22 situation, isn't it? If you stop or reduce your marketing you're less likely to find new or additional business, which in turn means your revenues slump and there's less money for your promotions.

But is this a wise decision? History might say otherwise. If you look at businesses that continued their marketing and advertising, in spite of a recession, they not only survived they often prospered. Prospered because their competitors, who **didn't** have the courage to invest in their business marketing had gone to the wall, leaving more of the market ripe for picking.

How To Give Yourself Confidence In Your Marketing

It's a scary time.

How can you be sure your marketing is a good investment?

Is it worthwhile?

How can you be confident about what you're doing?

There's only one way that makes any sense to me. . . and that's by knowing what your customer is truly worth to you in terms of the overall gross profit they generate for you. Not just on the first sale, but on all the purchases they are likely to place with you. And knowing your direct acquisition costs; how much you spent on your marketing to get that customer in the first place.

Then - *and only then* - can you calculate how good an investment your continued marketing is.

In fact I think if you carry out the exercise I've described above, you'll discover a stronger, more active marketing strategy could pay dividends.

So why not be a hawk, spread your marketing wings and flush out all that business that's waiting for you?

~ Carol Bentley

Date: Wednesday, May 28th, 2008 at 9:00 am

I Responses to "Ostrich or Hawk"

1.   May 28th, 2008 at 9:08 pm <u>Stevie</u> Says:

totally agree that if you want to make money in a *down* economy or a slow economy, you cannot sit on your hands and fret. You have to be more proactive.. get your name and face & work out there. People need more marketing to get the attention.. and it's pennies of cost compared to advertising.. or going down the tubes.

*Recession? Count Me Out. . .

When there's a cold going around I decide I'm not going to catch it. I know that sounds ridiculous, but it's worked for me for quite a few years now. And I regard talk of a recession as a bit like an unpleasant virus because it can be contagious.

Reports in the media about the credit crunch, escalating bills and reduced spending give a picture of general doom and despondency. Are you being infected?

Now, don't get me wrong I do appreciate many people, both consumers and businesses, are finding things more difficult. I also believe we, as business owners, have a decision to make; accept all the negative reports, take part in the recession and accept the dire consequences it can lead to.

Or, decide not to take part. Decide to take action that makes us - and our business - stronger.

Is it possible to come out of a recession stronger?

In my experience, yes. I was talking with a close friend (I'm godmother to his son) and business entrepreneur. And we realised that we had both come out of previous recessions stronger than we might have expected to. In fact, my original computer training business - back in 1990 - was born out of a recession when I was made redundant from my position of General Manager with a local computer supplier.

Why had we survived so well? Because we both avoided...

The Biggest Mistake Businesses Often Make in a Recession...

They stop actively looking for business from existing and new customers.

When I say actively I'm talking, as you've probably guessed, about marketing. Being seen as a vibrant, open-for-business company is vital to your survival, let alone your growth and success when there is an economic downturn.

Yet as soon as business is a bit slow and the order

books start to dwindle, for many the thought of investing in advertising and marketing is abhorrent to them. The mentality is "We can't afford to spend on advertising and marketing!"

Why is this when the reality is "Can they afford NOT to spend?"

Lack of Knowledge Can Lead to Your Downfall

I believe the reasons why some business people think this way is lack of knowledge in two specific areas...

- They don't know how effective their advertising and marketing is.
- They don't know the true value of each prospect they find who turns into a loyal customer.

Measuring your marketing spend against the value of the sales it attracts is the only way you can be sure of having control of your business at any time. When you've got this control you can choose not to take part in a recession, if it comes.

Back to Basics

Over the next few posts I'm going to suggest a few different marketing approaches for you to consider in your business.

Before I do that let me remind you of a few basics,

linked to the two points above. (Sometimes it's good to be reminded, don't you think?)

How to Measure The Effectiveness of Your Marketing

There's only one way to be sure **your** marketing spend - whether that's time or money - is a good investment... only use **direct response marketing** in your letters, adverts, web pages, newsletters and flyers. Gear them up to elicit a direct action from your target audience. And monitor the responses you get.

Here's an example of what I mean.

You decide to place an advertisement in a local publication targeted at your specific market.

You create a direct response advert and include a unique code so you can measure the response to that specific advert, in that specific publication in that specific issue.

The advert costs you £500.

The publisher tells you it has a readership of 25,000 - and says "It's only costing you 2p to reach each reader!" That would be a fantastic investment if all those readers are *real* prospects and there is a high chance they will respond. *You wish!* ☺

The only figure that is relevant to you is the **actual**

number of people who take action and respond to your advert.

Your advert goes out and you get 10 enquiries. You now know it cost you £50 to get each enquiry. Let's say you convert half into sales. You have 5 new customers, each cost you £100 to acquire. (The price of your advert divided by the total number of new customers).

The next point is the one that many businesses base their future marketing decisions on. And it's where they often go wrong.

Question: "Is running this advert worthwhile?"

On face value you could decide "No!" if the immediate sale - the first sale - does not deliver a high enough profit to cover the advertising cost. The real question should be "What is the profit value of all the subsequent sales I'll make to this new customer?"

If you are going to blossom in a recession you **must have a** strong, effective, follow-up system; sometimes called the back-end. Once your new customer buys, especially if you've delivered a good product or service, they are more open to considering other products or services you can deliver. Add these onto the initial sale and you could find that seemingly expensive advert is not such a drain on your resources after all!

Before you start any advertising or marketing campaign you need to know two things:

- The **average profit value** of each of your customer's transactions
- The number of purchases they are likely to make before they stop (*if they ever do*) buying from you.

Multiply these two figures and you have a fair idea of the **true worth** of your new customer (sometimes called lifetime value).

So, going on from my example...

let's be conservative here and say your first sale profit value is only £80. That means you are making a loss of £20 on each new sale. At first glance that looks as though this is not a worthwhile advert to run again. And, as I said, that's what many business owners base their decision on.

But if you've got your strong follow-up in place and you know that, on average, your customer's subsequent purchases deliver a £100 profit each and they normally buy another 6 times over a period of two years - then your total potential profit is £680. Take away the original cost to acquire the customer (£100) and that gives you an overall expected average profit of £580 per customer.

Now placing that advert makes more long-term economic sense, doesn't it?

Recession Proof Tip 1;

Have a Strong Back-End and make sure you know how to measure your *true* return on investment.

Look out for more Recession Proof Tips, including some direct response marketing ideas for you to consider.

~ Carol Bentley

Date: Thursday, July 24th, 2008 at 3:42 pm

*Make Profitable Connections..

In yesterday's post I mentioned it's easier to sell to a prospect who considers you favourably - a warm prospect - rather than a cold prospect who knows nothing about your company.

You get warm prospects when your customers recommend you to other people - but this is not always a reliable, constant source of prospective sales.

You can create a more structured and controlled way of getting those new, warm leads by connecting with other companies and arranging a joint venture. Businesses with an online presence often use affiliates to create the same result.

The idea behind this is to find a non-competing company who sells to the same market place you target. So, for example, a landscaping business could connect with a builder or a garden supplies centre or an estate agent. The company you are working with recommends your services or products in a letter sent to their customers. You write the letter and cover the mailing cost - if you ask the other company to do that they may think the reward doesn't justify the work or costs involved.

You pay a pre-arranged commission for any new business you get from this arrangement.

Organising Joint Ventures

How do you find companies:

a) you are happy to associate with

b) who feel confident about your ability to deliver what you promise

Selecting Companies to Approach

The first, most obvious criteria I've already mentioned, is finding companies whose customers are your targeted audience.

Second, check the company supplies a complementary rather than competing product /service (you can have arrangements with your direct competitors too, but I suggest you start with non-competing companies first).

Third, make sure the company you choose to approach has a professional reputation to match yours. If the company does not have a top-rate reputation then their recommendation does not do you any favours and could actually damage you.

Fourth, make sure your proposal benefits both sides; maybe even offer to recommend their services or products to your customers in return. Obviously make sure you are happy with the quality of what they supply before agreeing to do this.

Be prepared to do the work in progressing this - your prospective Joint Venture Partner may not see the real benefit to them when you first make the suggestion, especially if they've never taken part in this sort of arrangement before.

Making The Approach

If you've never considered this approach to finding new customers before it can be a little scary - especially if you're trying to convince companies who are sceptical about an arrangement like this. The way you make your proposal and follow through on your initial contact makes a huge difference.

You'll probably find the Strategic Profit's **Joint Venture Partnerships** course a useful resource. It looks at the whole area of creating joint ventures, including how to find companies to approach. The course is focused on creating *online* Joint Ventures but the process it describes is just as relevant to offline JVs.

Are Your Partner's Customers Interested?

Not all of your Joint Partner's customers are interested in what you offer and you do not want to upset your partner or his customers by constantly sending offer letters. Ideally you want the customers who are interested, either now or in the future, to show they want to know more so you only keep in touch with them.

The easiest way to do that - as I'm sure you already know - is to offer free information. You can send a tips guide/booklet, an audio or video or invite them to your website to download useful information (make sure you capture their name and email address). Once the customer accepts your offer of free information they have effectively demonstrated their interest and you can continue to keep in touch so that eventually - hopefully sooner rather than later - they become your customer. And, at that point any commission arrangement you have agreed can kick in.

Recession Proof Tip 3: Find Profitable Alliances

Use the joint venture principle to find warm prospects and generate more sales.

~ Carol Bentley

Date: Friday, August 1st, 2008 at 9:45 am

2 Responses to "Making profitable connections. . ."

1. September 10th, 2008 at 2:55 am *Elizabeth Potts Weinstein* Says:

    Joint ventures have been the #1 way I've built my business quickly. Not only do I access someone who has a list already of my target audience, but they are inherently giving me a testimonial by recommending me to their clients/customers/list. Once you find the right J/V partners, it's the fastest and easiest way to build a list, fast!

    ~ ElizabethPW

2. September 10th, 2008 at 12:02 pm *Carol Bentley* Says:

    Thanks for stopping by Elizabeth; it's great to hear from someone who is using connections so successfully.

    I agree that their recommendation is effectively a great testimonial for you too. Great point you made there.

    Carol

*Do You Have A (Marketing) Leg To Stand On...

In most areas the children go back to school this week, the start of a fresh new term and year for them. And for many people life is 'back to normal' and work.

So the children are starting a fresh year, taking a new look at their future. Is it time to do the same in your business - specifically take a fresh look at your marketing strategy? Because of the economic doom & gloom that seems to be forever in the news, perhaps it is time to do that.

How Solid is Your Marketing Strategy?

Marketing is like a well designed and made chair - but with more legs. Each leg is a particular marketing activity.

Your marketing activity supports the business [the more legs you have the better the support] and each activity should connect and complement the others.

But in many businesses marketing plans and campaigns seem to be carried out independently. For example the company may have a website - which runs as a separate marketing activity. There may be an advertising campaign that has no connection with the website - except perhaps the URL dropped in as a last minute thought.

They may run a PR campaign or direct mailing campaign with no thought of connecting with the advertising or website.

If all these different business-generating activities have no connection it's like having a DIY chair made with unmatched legs - it doesn't give a good pleasing result and could even topple over because there is no balance.

Connecting Marketing Legs

Let's have a look at an example of how different marketing activities could be linked together to give a strong, balanced business support (this is just a simple suggestion, yours could be far more extensive).

- An advertising campaign is devised to specifically draw visitors to a website page to request a free/low cost advisory guide.

- A PR campaign announces the guide is available from the website and people who've read the article visit.

- Online marketing through PPC (pay-per-click) advertising draws visitors to the website as well.

- A targeted mailing is sent to prospective customers offering them the guide, with the choice to send a request by post or visit the website.

- The website page is a focused landing page - not just a more general home page - telling the visitor about the benefits of the free/low cost guide. It does not have any distracting links to other pages or products. It could have audio and/or video links describing the information on offer.

- The visitor requests the guide, giving their contact information.

- The guide is delivered - either electronically in PDF format or as a printed report or CD/DVD - along with a direct response 'sales letter' giving more details of the main offer.

- If your offer is a high-value item you might have a tele-sales or field sales team who follow up on these warm leads; warm because they have expressed an interest by asking for the guide.

By the way, don't think that this 'giving a free guide' cycle is purely for 'information products'. Yes, it is used extensively in this way - I do it myself; giving free previews or samples of the products or service I'm offering. But even if you are selling a physical product you can give people useful tips such as...

- Questions to ask before deciding to buy - gives the reader guidance on avoiding any pitfalls when choosing a supplier or recognising less ethical companies in your industry or profession

- Tips on how to use the product you supply

- Tips on how to get the most out of the product you supply; perhaps care tips that make it last longer

- If you're selling to businesses, case studies of how other businesses have effectively used your product would be interesting

- FAQs - the classic Q&A information that prospective buyers look for. Just check what questions your current and previous customers have asked and you have your guide ready to go.

This whole strategy is geared towards attracting new prospects and, through careful nurturing, they become customers.

The Sales Are In The Back-End

But it doesn't stop there. Further direct response campaigns - whether through e-marketing or 'snail-mail' is used to keep contact with the new customer keeping them informed, including telling them about different offers as they come up. As a result they often become a long term buyer. This is known as a 'back-end' system.

And now a further strong marketing leg can be added with a formalised referral system; make a point of asking your satisfied customers for a referral (and testimonial you can use in your marketing). The best time to ask is when they've just taken delivery.

An example of this is the 'tell a friend' mechanism you see on many websites - by telling a friend about your experiences; what you've found on the website (a free guide) or your delight with the product or service supplied you are giving the company you've done business with a referral.

And, of course, it can continue with joint ventures - where another business recommends your guide and website to their customers giving you another marketing leg for your business.

Having many strong marketing activities that connect and complement each other gives stronger support for your business. If one marketing activity doesn't perform as well as normal, you have other activities which still deliver results for you.

So - is it time to think afresh on your marketing? Ask yourself these questions.

1. Does all my marketing bring in measurable results?

2. Are all my marketing activities connected and focused on the same end result?

3. What marketing activities are missing from my connect strategy?

4. Would adding additional activities weaken or strengthen my marketing strategy and deliver better results?

Before you make any changes, think of the adage 'if it ain't broke, don't try to fix it'. It is a good maxim to follow... but by the same context we know if we don't improve we stagnate and eventually fall behind. Continuous improvement, through testing, is vital to any business survival. And continuous improvement in our marketing means we have stronger, matched, legs supporting our business.

~ Carol Bentley

P.S. Before deciding your marketing strategy you might find it useful to review aspects of your business. Brian James' blog post "Become the business of choice for your customers" describes how to do that. (www.business-coachinguk.com/?p=35)

Date: Wednesday, September 3rd, 2008 at 11:55 am

How Do We Get Bums-On-Seats?

If, like me, you have ever held (or plan to hold) any public event... whether seminar, workshop or training course then one question uppermost in your mind is 'how do we get the room filled; how do we get bums-on-seats?'

Anything that makes achieving that a little easier has got to be worth looking at, would you agree?

My guest blogger, Andrew Ludlam, is a regular reader of this blog. When he sent an email to me last week commenting on a post, I took a look at his website (I can't help being nosy - I'm a woman!) and I was intrigued by what he had to say so I downloaded his book.

It contains such a down-to-earth, 'oh my god, that's so-oo obvious' type of marketing approach to getting people interested in seminars (one that very few people use) I wanted to share it with you. Which is why I invited Andrew to write a guest blog, provided he let you get your own copy of his book...

Discover The Secrets To Marketing And Selling Your Seminars SUCCESSFULLY!"

There is without doubt one thing... And *only* one thing, that can <u>truly</u> make a difference to the success, or otherwise, of your seminars or workshops. Essentially it all comes down to the **marketing**.

You see, I find that most consultants, trainers and coaches market their seminars in terms of what *they* would like to deliver. This strategy is essentially *always* flawed, because everything is focused on the *deliverer* and not the *attendees*. In fact many businesses follow this concept: falling into the trap of thinking, it's all about them... Let me tell you now, it's <u>never</u> about them, it's all about their **clients**.

Your client <u>does not care</u> about you, or your training. All they care about is acquiring some sort of result or solution to their 'problem'. Simply demonstrate how you — and your training — are the right choice, and further, *the only choice*, to solve your prospect's problem.

However to begin with, you must follow a correct and effective, plan of action. You see most business owners get it all **back to front**... For example, a date for the workshop is decided upon, then a very nice (and expensive) room at a local hotel is booked. Marketing materials are printed, adverts are placed... Time is getting on... And you still haven't had a booking! **Not a nice feeling**.

So what's the first thing you must do?

Your first and major priority — before you do anything else — is to build a <u>receptive</u>, and <u>passionate</u> audience: a large number of people who would *leap* at the chance to attend a seminar or workshop. *Then...* You market the event to 'your list'. A list that will be hungry <u>from the very start</u> to hear and learn more from you!

And one key strategy is all about positioning. Positioning yourself as the expert in your field; this simply means that clients come to trust, respect and acknowledge you. In fact, they place a high value on the information you give them, and most important of all, are willing to compensate you very highly for your products or service.

Okay, so how do you do this? Well you can discover this, as well as many more profitable strategies and techniques needed to successfully market and sell your seminars, absolutely FREE, simply click on the link below for more details on my latest book **"Discover The Secrets To Marketing And Selling Your Seminars SUCCESSFULLY!"** And – as I said - best of all, this A4 content-rich book, valued at £45, is 100% FREE... Plus, you will also receive a free 10-part 'mini seminar marketing email course' delivered to your inbox each week!

www.maverickmarketingconsultancy.co.uk/cboffer.htm [This is not an affiliate link].

There is no 'theory', theory has never paid the bills, or filled seats! Instead you have the opportunity (for a limited period) to gain practical — profitable — steps you can take to ensure that every seminar, workshop or training programme you run from now on, is marketed **purposefully** and **effectively**.

To your success... And do let me know how you get on!

Does this approach seem familiar? It should do because, as I've said many times before, it is the basic foundation of any successful business's marketing; building relationships that deliver value to your customers and prospects both before and after making a sale.

Thank you Andrew, for sharing this valuable guide - I'm sure the content will inspire many business owners who plan to run this type of event for their clients.

~ Carol Bentley

Date: Wednesday, September 10th, 2008 at 10:30 am

SELLING TECHNIQUES

Letter To The Seller

When I first started studying the techniques of the great copywriters I came across a poem written by Victor O. Schwab in 1942; '**Tell Me Quick and Tell Me True**'. It completely encapsulates the prospect's point of view about any marketing material we send out. Here are a few lines from this famous verse (which is pinned to the wall in my office):

So tell me quick and tell me true
(Or else my love to hell with you!)
Less - "how this product came to be";
More - "what the damn thing does for me!"

And then I found a modern take on this in Jill Konrath's letter to a seller (page 417) (or read it at www.carolbentley.org/konrath-letter.html).

It certainly struck a chord with me.

One of the tricks of copywriting is to imagine the person you are writing to. Understand what interests them; what sort of person they are; what problems they have; what dreams they have.

In fact some expert copywriters give their prospect a name and write specifically to that person; it makes the letter more personal and conversational.

And Jill's letter adds an extra dimension to this visualisation of your prospect. Because if you can tell what sort of day your prospect is probably experiencing, what pressures they're under then your letter, email or telephone call is more likely to stay focused and on track.

And that's good news for you, because you get a clear message across, and it's good news for your prospect because they get to understand more quickly how you can make life a little easier for them.

And if you don't know what the day-to-day pressures of your prospective customers are - why not ask some of your existing customers? If nothing else it will show you take an interest in their welfare and will help cement your business relationship with them even more. (If you'd like to tell me what your working day is like I'm a really good 'listener'.
Send your email to carol@carolbentley.com).

By the way if your target market is big companies I highly recommend Jill's book: **Selling To Big Companies** (at www.carolbentley.org/konrath-book.html). I have a copy in my reference library and give copies away to my clients who target the corporates.

~ Carol Bentley

Date: Tuesday, November 13th, 2007 at 11:00 am

Does The Thought Of Cold Calling Give You The Heebie-Jeebies?

It's not my favourite activity - in fact, I've always avoided it like the plague. Give me a nice pad and pen any day to write my first communication with someone and I'm as happy as a lark.

Give me a phone to call someone I don't know - and who doesn't know me - and you wouldn't see me for dust!

I know, it's the *way* I think about it. I suppose it's no different to people saying they are terrified of the thought of public speaking, which I have no problem with at all!

So why am I sharing this with you?

Because I discovered someone who is extremely comfortable with cold-calling and totally understands the fears many of us hold and is able to help allay those fears.

His name? Steve Brewer.

I saw his presentation at a business seminar and was totally impressed - he even motivated me to change my view about this marketing activity; well that's what it is isn't it? Because, as he said, you have to create a relationship before anyone is going to buy from you and that's what cold-calling is - the start of a relationship.

In the presentation he explored how our mindset is the key to being successful at cold-calling. Tell me, if I asked if you enjoyed cold-calling would you say "I love it!" as Steve does, or would you say "I'd do absolutely everything I can to put it off!" as I did?

Understanding this, knowing the best approach that empowers you and building on the successes you experience makes this not only a more pleasurable task but one you get more and more success from.

So what else did he share?

1. Use Customer Centered Selling. Focus on the real benefits for your prospect; think of the damage you'd be doing if you didn't make the effort to speak to him and explain how your company's offer delivers a solution for him.

2. Decide the 3 biggest things that would make an impact for him, write it on a post-it and place it on the screen in front of you - it helps keep you focused.

3. Don't regard the 'gatekeeper' as an obstacle. Make friends with her, ask for her help, use her name if she's given it.

4. Remember decision makers often work outside normal hours. Calling between 8am and 9am or between 5pm and 6pm may give you a better chance of getting through.

5. If you get through to voicemail leave a compelling message. Steve said to copy the style of a radio advert - you want your prospect to call you back or at least be happy to take your call when you get back to him. Review your Elevator Speech - can you turn that into a radio ad style message? [See **Your Wow! Introduction** on page 270].

6. When you call you have less than 30 seconds to intrigue your prospect enough for him to allow you to continue. You must be able to answer the 3 questions he is silently asking himself:
   1. Who are you?
   2. Where are you calling from?
   3. Why should I stop and talk to you? (What's in it for me?)

I know Steve only scratched the surface of the fund of valuable experience and knowledge he has. How do I know? Because I've got his new book and audio programme, in which he explains in plain English how to turn this spine-chilling activity into a more pleasurable experience.

Steve's not only good at what he does; selling, but he's also a great communicator presenting this difficult subject in a humorous and enjoyable style.

You can find out more about his programmes or visit his blog at www.stevebrewer.co.uk/blog

~ Carol Bentley

Date: Monday, December 17th, 2007 at 10:00 am

*It Is *So* Frustrating. . .

Breaking into larger organisations can be extremely frustrating as the question sent in by Tony Clarke of Fuel Dynamics Ltd indicated:

> "I want to do business with every Housing Association in the UK. I somehow or other have to 'get to' their chief purchasing officers.
>
> My experience is that because I'm only a small business they will not work with me. They will, it appears, only deal with 'big' companies who they know and have a strong market presence.
>
> Letters do not work even to the right man. Phone calls are never put through. Faxes, which I've found effective in some situations, don't get a response.

Maybe you have some tips for me and some of your other readers on how to deal with these very powerful people. They rule the roost and even their MD's give them a free hand in terms of control.

It's an interesting dilemma for me."

A: Changing the perception your target prospect has of you is key to getting that door open. And it takes more than letters, emails or faxes that introduce your company and the service or products you offer.

Sometimes you have to approach it from a completely different angle. So let me start by asking you some questions; see if they give you any ideas...

- Do you give the impression of being a small company? Check your image, both in terms of presentation - from your business card up - and what happens if anyone does attempt to contact you. Do you have an answer phone or are calls always answered personally?

  For example; many years ago when I was the sole representative of my company I made absolutely sure that anyone contacting me got a very favourable impression. I engaged a telephone answering service that offered a good personalised service; they didn't have a lot of other calls being answered in the background and knew that they must never, **under any**

circumstances, let on that they were a telephone answering service.

It worked, because one of my clients who I had worked with for some years, expressed surprise when he discovered that I didn't have an army of people behind me.

Now, the important thing is I did not deceive my client; he never asked about the size of my company - he just assumed that my company was large because the phone was always answered by a variety of different people whenever he rang; there was no voice mail or answerphone. And of course, he received superb service so had no reason to doubt my company's ability to look after him.

- Who, in the organisation, uses what you offer? Does the person (or people) who would benefit most from your product or service have any influence on the CPO? Could you recruit them as ambassadors for you and your company?

- What challenges is the CPO facing that your product or service could help with?

- Do you have expert knowledge that would help him in his job, without actually selling him anything? Advice freely given makes you more memorable than competitors who are only looking for the sale.

- Do you have a valuable, content-rich report, booklet (or book) you can send as a gift. It would have to deliver exceptional value; not just mundane 'facts & figures' he can get from anywhere.

- Have you thought about writing and publishing a book? Doing so positions you as the expert. It adds gravitas to your reputation and, when you send it as a gift, it raises the barrier for you; makes you stand out from the competition. And crafting a book is not as difficult as it may first seem.

- Do you have case-studies from other organisations that demonstrate innovative approaches to solving the problems the Housing Associations CPO faces? Collate them into a report; make sure you get permission to use the stories and check exactly how much detail your customers are happy for you to reveal.

- Do any of your present or past satisfied customers know the people you are trying to reach? Would they be prepared to recommend you, or write a letter of endorsement?

- Are you well known within your industry? If your prospect recognises your name as an industry expert he is more likely to give you time to talk. Apart from publishing a book you can achieve this by getting articles printed in the trade publications he is likely to read. Send letters to the editor with interesting 'industry specific' points. **Do not make even the *slightest* attempt to advertise or sell your product or company.** The editor is highly unlikely to print your letter if you do, which defeats the whole purpose of writing.

Enhancing your reputation within your industry works in your favour, even if you don't own the company you work for.

If any of the writing activities phases you then hire a ghost writer to create the material for you.

Like any large organisation, selling to a Housing Association needs a different approach. Don't *'sell'* - offer powerful advice that the CPO appreciates and looks forward to receiving. Demonstrate your expertise; demonstrate the higher level of personal contact and customer service he (or she) gets from you compared to a larger organisation where he may not always be able to deal with the same person continuously.

But most of all, remember you are still selling to a person who has his own problems; his own challenges, his own stressful situations. Eliminate some of that stress for him, make life easier and you have a better chance of getting his attention.

I have recommended it before... and it is worth mentioning again because I think it would help you in this situation - Jill Konrath's book **Selling To Big Companies** is worth getting. You can take a look at 2 chapters for free if you visit:

www.carolbentley.org/konrath-chapters.html

~ Carol Bentley

Date: Wednesday, January 16th, 2008 at 10:00 am

1 Response to "It is so frustrating. . ."

1. January 19th, 2008 at 9:15 am *Martin Russell* (website www.wordofmouthmagic.com) Says:

Well you got my attention Carol, by taking up an offer on my blog and then giving me an unsolicited testimonial for it. Then you left compliments on my blog at a later point too.

Those approaches are fairly irresistible.
People are much more likely to respond to someone who is giving first, rather than hard selling from the get-go.

As you said, there are certain times to "...not make even the slightest attempt to advertise or sell your product or company. "

Nice to see you being a true example of your words Carol.

*How Well Does Your Customer Know You?

It is far more difficult - and costly - to find new customers than it is to keep your existing customers happy by enhancing their experience with your business; making sure they do not miss out through your negligence.

And making your first sale is easier if you are introduced to your prospect by a trusted colleague. That's why business networking is so powerful - especially for smaller businesses.

These are two different aspects of the same approach - concentrating on people who are less sceptical about what you offer and may even be very inclined to do business with you.

I'm forever banging on about keeping in touch with your customers. Keeping them informed, giving great advice, perhaps even making recommendations. If you only supply a single type of service or product then making sure everyone you deal with knows what you can provide and the benefits they gain is very easy, isn't it?

Or is it? Because a wise business owner is always looking for innovations, for new ideas that complements what they offer. And sometimes - as the variety of products or services expands - we forget to tell existing clients about all the new solutions we've introduced.

In fact, if your company has a sales force and a wide array of products and services, are you confident that **everyone** knows the full product range and potential benefits - and actively promotes them? It's probably even more important now with talk of a recession.

Go through this exercise with your sales staff (or just do it for yourself)

Your Customer/Product Awareness Exercise

1) Take a piece of paper. Ask your sales team to list all the products and services your company provides - including any variations. Now compare the lists - do they all match? If they do then you have a great sales force because they are selling from a strong position, knowing what you can provide.

2) Now ask your sales people to think about their accounts and mark which products they have told their customers about. Are there any gaps? If so, they are selling opportunities for your sales team. And it is worth remembering that a selling opportunity isn't necessarily a direct sale to the customer, they may not need that particular product or service. But, if your customer knows you can supply it they can recommend you when someone mentions they are looking for that service or product.

This is a good exercise to repeat, just to keep it fresh in your mind. If you like visual reminders then an Opportunity Matrix could work for you and your team - perhaps on an office whiteboard or (as I've described later) in a spreadsheet.

Here's how to create a constant visual reminder...

1) Draw a grid shape. You need enough columns going across to list all your products and services in the top row; show one product/service at the top of each column, starting from the second column.

2) In the first column of the rows going down list your current customers.

	Book: IWTE	Audio Book	Bentley Makeover	Copywriting Services	Writing Blog	Self-Study Set	Book: Marketing Tips	New: Membership Site
ABC Ltd								
HelpMe Co								
WeTry It Ltd								
GoForIt plc								

3) Choose 2 strong colours. One to represent 'Told', the other for 'Sold' (you could add a third for 'Referred'; and use it when your customer has recommended your company to someone else). I've used Told=Grey; Sold=Black in my example chart).

4) When you tell your customer about another one of your products; you have supplied information so you

know he is fully aware of it and the benefits it offers, mark the colour for 'Told' against that company in the column for the specific product/service you've explained.

5) When your customer buys that product/service from you add the 'Sold' colour.

	Book: NOTE	Audio Book	Bentley Makeover	Copywriting Services	Writing Blog	Self-Study Set	Book: Marketing Tips	New: Membership Site
ABC Ltd								
HelpMe Co								
WeTryIt Ltd								
GoForIt plc								

6) If your customer recommends your product / service to someone else; 'refers you', you can fill in the 'Referred' colour.

If you include step 6 some of your boxes may have the Told and Referred, but not the Sold colour.

Now you can see, at a glance, which products your customers do not know about (in which case you can inform them) and, just as importantly, if they do know about the products whether they have bought from you or referred you to someone else.

A Free Gift For You...

As I said earlier, this works really well on a spreadsheet, such as Excel, using the conditional formatting feature. I have created a spreadsheet with the chart set up ready to use.

In fact the file, which I call the **Opportunity Matrices**, contains 3 **spreadsheets**: 1 to use for referrals within your business contacts circle, another to use for checking that your current customers know about everything you offer and the third is a **Price Research** spreadsheet. Use the latter to compare your prices against your competitors - it is a useful tool when you are launching a new product or service or revising your pricing structure.

I've also written a PDF file that explains how I created the spreadsheets - so you can do the same if you wish - and describes how to use them.

You can get your copy of these files; simply send an email to **excel-matrix@aweber.com**

You will be asked to confirm your request - I have to do this to avoid spamming problems.

To summarise...

Recession Proof Tip 2;

Don't miss selling opportunities

Make sure everyone connected to your business (including customers) knows *all* the solutions you deliver.

In tomorrow's tip [**Make Profitable Connections** on page 132] I'll explore the second point I made at the start of this post... how to find more warm prospects...

~ Carol Bentley

Date: Thursday, July 31st, 2008 at 1:31 pm

BUSINESS TIPS

URGENT Telephone Scam - Protect Your Card

This post is completely off-topic, but I felt it was so important I decided to add in an extra post so you don't get caught by this telephone credit card scam.

It came to me from the Federation of Small Businesses (UK), of which I am a member. It was an experience reported to them by a local member. It is a very worrying telephone scam designed to get confidential information from you about your credit card. It may even be happening in other countries.

Here are the details - please pass this to your friends and colleagues:

"This one is pretty slick since they provide YOU with all the information, except the one piece they want. The callers do not ask for your card number; they already have it.

One of our employees was called on Wednesday from someone purporting to represent VISA, and I was called on Thursday from MasterCard.

The scam works like this:

Person calling says, "This is (name), and I'm calling from the Security and Fraud Department at VISA. My badge number is 12460.

Your card has been flagged for an unusual purchase pattern, and I'm calling to verify. This would be on your VISA card which was issued by (name of bank) did you purchase an Anti-Telemarketing Device for £497.99 from a Marketing company based in London?"

When you say "No", the caller continues with, "Then we will be issuing a credit to your account. This is a company we have been watching and the charges range from £297 to £497, just under the £500 purchase pattern that flags most cards. Before your next statement, the credit will be sent to (gives you your address), is that correct?"

You say "yes". The caller continues - "I will be starting a fraud investigation. If you have any questions, you should call the 0800 number listed on the back of your card (0800-VISA) and ask for Security.

You will need to refer to this Control Number. The caller then gives you a 6 digit number. "Do you need me to read it again?"

Here's the IMPORTANT part on how the scam works the caller then says,

"I need to verify you are in possession of your card."

He'll ask you to "turn your card over and look for some numbers." There are 7 numbers; the first 4 are part of your card number, the next 3 are the security numbers that verify you are the possessor of the card.

These are the numbers you sometimes use to make Internet purchases to prove you have the card. The caller will ask you to read the 3 numbers to him.

After you tell the caller the 3 numbers, he'll say, "That is correct, I just needed to verify that the card has not been lost or stolen, and that you still have your card. Do you have any other questions?" After you say, "No," the caller then thanks you and states, "Don't hesitate to call back if you do", and hangs up.

You actually say very little, and they never ask for or tell you the Card number. But after we were called on Wednesday, we called back within 20 minutes to ask a question. Are we glad we did! The REAL VISA Security Department told us it was a scam and in the last 15 minutes a new purchase of £497.99 was charged to our card.

Long story - short - we made a real fraud report and closed the VISA account. VISA is reissuing us a new number. What the scammers want is the 3-digit PIN number on the back of the card. Don't give it to them. Instead, tell them you'll call VISA or MasterCard directly for verification of their conversation. The real VISA told us that they will never ask for anything on the card as they already know the information since they issued the card! If you give the scammers your 3 Digit PIN Number, you think you're receiving a credit. However, by the time you get your statement you'll see charges for purchases you didn't make, and by then it's almost too late and/or more difficult to actually file a fraud report.

What makes this more remarkable is that on Thursday, I got a call from a "Jason Richardson of Master-Card" with a word-for-word repeat of the VISA scam. This time I didn't let him finish. I hung up! We filed a police report, as instructed by VISA. The police said they are taking several of these reports daily! They also urged us to tell everybody we know that this scam is happening."

You can read more about this type of scam at Urban Legends on www.carolbentley.org/ccs.html.

Have you received any calls like this?

As I said at the beginning - please pass it on. Thanks.

~ Carol Bentley

Date: Tuesday, December 4th, 2007 at 3:30 pm

1 Response to "URGENT Telephone Scam - Protect your card"

1. December 4th, 2007 at 5:59 pm *Gail* Says:

    Hi Carol,

Thanks for the heads-up on this one. Having just passed this on to everyone in my inbox, I've also had a call from the FSB telling me the same thing!
Warmly
Gail Osborne

2008 and Beyond. . .

It's nearly that time of year again - *you know...* New Year Resolutions! And many experts will be advising you to review your business plans as well.

So what *are* your goals for 2008 and beyond? Have you got specific targets in mind? Are you focused on achieving them?

Here are a few tips on making realistic goals and, more importantly, increasing your chances of achieving them... You can use these steps for both your personal and your business goals.

The most successful people; whether in business or personal achievement, frequently have one thing in common; they write down what they want to achieve using the SMART acronym.

1. **What is your goal?** Write down what you want to achieve. Follow the SMART structure:

    - **S - Specific** e.g. 'Increase sales by 28%', rather than just 'get more sales' or 'lose 2 stone' rather than 'lose weight'

- **M - Measurable**. This is linked strongly with specific. If you have a specific goal you'll be able to measure how close you are to achieving it.

- **A - Achievable** or **Awesome**. Most people say this stands for achievable but I think the word awesome, given by my good friend Steve Pipe of *Added Value Solutions*, is much better. (http://www.avn.co.uk) Why?

- Because your goal must be *awesome* for you; fill you with excitement and inspiration. You see if it isn't an awesome goal for you to achieve the chances are you're not passionate about it and you are less likely to take the action needed to make it happen.

- **R - Realistic**. If they are realistic they are achievable. By all means stretch yourself; you don't want to be doing the 'same-old, same-old' but make sure what you set is practical. For example increasing your sales by 100% or 200% may be achievable - but can you handle that increase in business logistically?

- **T - Timed**. Set a date when you intend to reach this goal. E.g. 'reduce my working days to 4 days per week' is not as powerful as 'reduce my working days to 4 days per week by February 2009'.

2. **Why do you want to achieve this?** Is it a "it would be nice to..." or a passionate "I absolutely

must do this"? A weak reason for reaching your goal is not going to inspire you.

3. **What will happen if you fail to realise your goal?** What pain will you experience by not achieving it?

4. **What do you stand to gain when you succeed?** Will it light your inner fire? Give you less stress and worry? Make you feel happier? Give you a feeling of pride? Draw the admiration of your peers and superiors?

5. **What are the steps you must take to achieve this goal?** Write the key things you need to achieve this goal. Not the finite detail, enough to identify what action you need to take.

    For example if your goal is to increase your sales in 2008 by 28% you might decide you need to put your sales team through the latest sales training. At this stage you would not say it has to be training with 'such & such a company on this date'.

Repeat this sequence for all your personal and business goals.

Prioritise Your Goals

Some of your goals are more important to you than others. Some are dependent upon you achieving another goal before you can get started. For example if you have a goal that says 'increase the profitable response to my direct mailing campaigns by 300% by

June 2008 your goal to learn good copywriting skills would have to be achieved first.

And other goals may not, on reflection, be as important or inspiring as you first thought.

Decide which are your most meaningful goals and write those on a separate planning sheet. Constantly monitor your progress towards your goal as you take the actions needed.

Does Writing Goals Down Work?

In my personal experience; Yes! If I decide I want to achieve something but I don't write it down, following the SMART structure, it just doesn't get done or it takes an inordinately long amount of time to achieve a less than satisfactory result.

When I write my goal down it does 4 things for me:

1. It focuses my mind on the outcome I want and when I want it by.
2. It programmes my subconscious to find solutions for me.
3. It clearly identifies the actions I need to take and when they need to be done by.
4. Things happen! Unexpected opportunities that help me achieve my goal suddenly appear. Now some people will argue that's because I'm more focused and aware of what's going on

around me. So I see those opportunities more clearly. Maybe; I really don't care- it works!

Sometimes Sharing Helps

For some people stating a goal in public or sharing it with a mentor or valued colleague gives added impetus to achieving the goal.

Let me give you an example. In 2003 I decided I would write and publish a book. It didn't happen. Why? Because the goal, although stated, wasn't written down and wasn't specific.

In 2005 I committed to a group of business people that I would have the manuscript for my book on how to write sales letters completed for the next meeting, which was 1 month away. I did it!

So what was different this time?

I stated my specific goal (to write a book on how to write sales letters)

It was measurable (a completed manuscript ready for publishing)

It was awesome (I was very excited by the prospect of sharing my expertise in a book that would be available to other business people)

It was realistic (I had the knowledge, expertise and

material for the book content)

I said when it would be done (in 1 month)

And, for me crucially...

I stated the goal to people I respected. (My reputation was on the line. What would they think if I didn't achieve what I'd stated?)

If you find sharing your SMART goals helps you to achieve them feel free to share with me.

You can do so publicly (if you are very brave) by adding a comment to this post on my blog website at www.copywriting4b2b.com/archives/51 or privately in an email to carol@carolbentley.com. But *be warned* - I just might ask if you achieved what you set out to do when your stated time scale is reached.

~ Carol Bentley

Date: Wednesday, December 19th, 2007 at 10:00 am

Why Some People Never Learn From Their Own Experiences...

When you are planning your future goals for your business how much notice do you take of last year's achievements and disappointments?

Many people concentrate on what they *are going to do* without fully considering the experiences they have already had. I know I've been guilty of that over the years, even though I'm continuously building on what I've already produced.

But this post at Rich Schefren's blog (page 358) (or www.carolbentley.org/ystruggle.html) made me stop and think. He describes how to analyse your experiences, good and bad; how to learn from them and - more importantly - decide what action you're going to take so you benefit from those lessons.

Tie that in with my post on setting goals **2008 and beyond** (see it on page 169) (or read it online at www.copywriting4b2b.com/archives/51) and you have a powerful system for improving your business - and personal - success.

Take a look - even if you already do this in your business and life - Rich's explanation is worth reading.

~ Carol Bentley

Date: Thursday, January 3rd, 2008 at 12:30 pm

Does Your Business Pass the 'Charlie the Plumber' Test...

How much do your customers or clients value you and what you do for them? Do they really appreciate all the trouble you take to deliver the best possible service or product?

I saw this letter, talking about the 'Charlie the Plumber' test, in an email sent through a Yahoo group I'm a member of. And although it is written to copy-writers I think the essence of the letter and how you accept business is applicable to other companies, whether you are providing a service or a product.

It talks about choosing who you are prepared to do business with. Now I know a lot of business people believe they can't be choosy about who they deal with; they need all the sales they can get!

The only way to get out of this situation is to make sure you position yourself - as Charlie has - as the 'go to expert' who is selective about who you will do business with; someone who doesn't work with just anyone who might want to buy.

Here's the letter, in its entirety, reprinted with permission from Doug D'Anna.

Dear Friend,

Last week, I was pitched three jobs by three different companies and I turned them all down. I don't say this to be smug or arrogant; they simply didn't pass my three-rule test.

And I can tell you this with all honesty, they weren't right for you either, as I'll explain in a moment.

So why did I turn down these three new assignments?

Because none of them passed my **Charlie the Plumber** test!

What, exactly, is my Charlie the Plumber test?

Frankly, it's a simple test that every potential client I meet must past or I won't work with that person. I named this test after none other than own plumber, whom I affectionately refer to as Charlie the Plumber.

Charlie, by the way, is a great guy who has been doing work for me for nearly 10 years. He's an honest guy who charges an honest price for his work and whom I trust 100%. He never overcharges, never tries to sells you something you don't need, and always bends over backward for me.

What I love most about Charlie (other than that he's a big talker like me) is the fact that he not only treats me like royalty but also has come to a point in his life where he picks his clients.

You see, unlike most plumbers, who have full Yellow Page ads that scream discount, Charlie doesn't advertise. He works by referral only, and he's very choosy about whom he takes on.

As a client, I feel blessed that I have Charlie working for me!

Are Your Clients Lucky to Have You Working for Them?

If not, maybe it's time to separate the wheat from the chaff. Because having clients who value you for your knowledge and your experience is where you want to be.

And if you don't start picking your clients on that basis now, you could find yourself working with a demanding group of unappreciative people who see you only as a vendor at a price and not as the business builder that you are.

That's why before you accept any new work, I highly suggest that you put your prospects through my Charlie the Plumber test.

My Three Rules for Picking Clients Who Will Pay You What You're Worth

1. Got to Have Fun.

As I learned from Charlie, life's too short to work with a bunch of demanding jerks. You want to work with people who love their work and love life. When you find these people, as I have, you'll get up every day inspired to do your best to meet deadlines and exceed expectations, because you're having too much of a good time to do otherwise.

2. Got to Make Money.

Let's face it, copywriting is hard work. So there has to be an upside to bleeding all over the page. That upside in our society is known as money. Why bust your butt if the person only wants to pay you peanuts? No — you want to work with people who are fun and who will pay you what you are worth and then some.

3. Got to Be Appreciated.

Believe it or not, this is actually my first rule. I never work for people who are looking for just another copywriter. If the first question they ask is what do I charge, then it is clear to me that they are looking for another copywriter and not for the special something that I bring to the table.

Anyone who wants to hire me has to want *me*, Doug D'Anna, and have me working on his or her behalf. I say this not to be smug or arrogant, but only to drive home the point that you, too, are a unique individual worthy of the same appreciation.

When you think about it, why would you ever want to work for someone who doesn't appreciate you?

My Fourth Rule

4. Got to Learn Something.

Over the years, I have found that only half of my successes came from me. The other half came directly from the fine group of publishers, product managers, and business owners that I worked with–individuals whose knowledge was superior to my own and whom I could learn from.

That's why after a new client passes my first three hurdles, I always put them to this fourth and crucial test - especially when I have two or three projects to choose from at any one time.

You'll be surprised to know that I've chosen projects with far less immediate financial potential, simply because I would be working with an A-list marketer who could take my skills to the next level.

This fourth rule has not only allowed me to work with the top direct marketing talent in the country but also has resulted in much greater financial success as well.

Please Make Them Your Rules Too

When I started the A-list in 2007, I did it with one goal in mind: to bring you the NO BS, wealth-creating copywriting knowledge and marketing strategies you've been looking for.

Specifically, the knowledge to create more powerful, effective and lucrative advertisements, e-mails, and Web pages that could multiply your income exponentially - and without spending a dime.

These rules have worked for me. That's why I want you to make them your rules as well. I guarantee that if you follow them, you'll find yourself working with people who not only value and appreciate your knowledge and talent but just as important - pay you for it.

All good wishes for a successful and healthy 2008,

Doug D'Anna

PS If you haven't yet joined the A-list, go to www.dougdanna.com/joinmyalist.html

and you'll receive my best ideas on building your business in 2008 without a bunch of sales pitches or spam.

Doug has also generously offered a free copy of his **7 Proven Profit Triggers for Email Copywriters** at www.dougdanna.com/seven_profit_triggers_lg.html

Remember, you can position yourself or your company so you can be selective about who you work with. Simply demonstrate your expertise in articles, reports, presentations, audio programmes - oh, and of course - books.

And when you do refuse to do business with someone, for whatever reason, remember it can be done courteously. And if you can point them in the direction of a company that is a better fit for them, then they are still going to feel happy about their relationship with you.

~ Carol Bentley

Date: Thursday, January 10th, 2008 at 10:10 am

2 Responses to "Does Your Business Pass The 'Charlie The Plumber' Test. . ."

1. January 19th, 2008 at 7:16 am *Tip Diva* Says:

Thanks for this great post. I, too, have fallen into the trap of having clients who did not appreciate my work. I've printed this one out as a reminder.

2. January 21st, 2008 at 4:58 pm *Mike at Harbour Pilot* Says:

Thanks for passing this perspective along. Life is short and ... I have found that failing to apply those tests destroys your motivation, and damages your ability to do creative, high-value work. It can create a negative loop whereby soon, all you have are people who fail the 3 tests. It cost me a great deal about 15 years ago to learn this lesson. And it applies in both your business and your personal life. Mike

---

What Do You Think. . . Print or PDF?

In a previous post (**4 Easy Steps To Authorship** [page 100] at www.copywriting4b2b.com/archives/64) I explained how a tips booklet can be used as a highly effective marketing tool. A comment on that post asked about PDF (e-books) and how they fared. It is a valid question, especially with so many businesses expanding their web presence.

Creating and gifting a PDF tips booklet, report, 'how to' manual or book containing any valuable information is a proven method of attracting subscribers and enquiries via a web site. I have done that myself with free e-business reports and e-articles in the past.

I also know, as I'm sure you do too, many people who have successfully promoted their business purely through e-books.

The only caveat to a PDF is that it is relatively easy to create and is very inexpensive to produce and put out into the market place. Nothing wrong with that... except that in some circumstances the quality of content and presentation may not be as good as in a published document.

And for some reason people's perception of someone who has actually written **and** published a book - is an author - is quite different to any other sort of writer (at least that seems to be the case here in the UK).

So although the PDF allows you to get good and useful information out to your prospects, I personally don't think it gives you quite the same kudos as being a published author.

What I *do* recommend is that when you print-publish a booklet or book, consider creating a PDF version too and think about how it can be used creatively to improve your market strength.

And of course, once you have got a book (or books) published you can certainly just use PDF e-books to distribute further material or new books, as Steven

King has done.

Now - this is my personal view of the reasons for publishing a book. What do you think? Do you have a very different experience you would like to share?

~ Carol Bentley

Date: Tuesday, January 22nd, 2008 at 9:45 am

4 Responses to "What Do You Think. . . Print or PDF"

1. January 22nd, 2008 at 1:35 pm *John* Says:
   I agree with your reasons to publish a proper book. I'd always do both, generally you'll be creating a PDF for the printer anyway.

2. January 24th, 2008 at 7:36 am *Adam* Says:
   PDF will increase the circulations as online readers increasing rapidly. I saw a website www.pressmart.net providing similar services and most of the publishers use this website for their digitization work. By visiting this website I realized that PDF version is on full demand.

3. January 26th, 2008 at 7:23 pm *Tip Diva* Says:

   Thanks for answering my question from the previous post, Carol... very insightful!

4. January 28th, 2008 at 4:15 am *CG Walters* Says:

Thank you, Carol. I published my metaphysical novel, Sacred Vow, and got a national distributor (US). Then I decided to give away the full ebook/PDF. My perspective is that the reader of the ebook and those inclined to hold a book in hand are not the same. The ebook is a promotion for the paperback. http://sacredvow.dragonsbeard.com
Peace and wonder, CG

And The Best Question Is...

Well the result is in. Ed, who acted as my independent judge, has now chosen the question he felt was the one that best matched his judging criteria, although all the questions submitted gave us food for thought.

Was it your question? Or was it one that makes you think "That's a good question - *I'd* like to know the answer to that as well!"

Ed's judging criteria was:

- Does the question appeal to a wide business audience?
- Is it a question many people are probably asking? If not, is it something they *should* be asking?

- Is it a question he might have asked?

Here's the entry that Ed chose:

"Many small businesses are started by someone technically good at what they do, but not that hot on running a business. When are they better off writing "DIY" copy, and when should they outsource with an expert? As a rider to that, how should they (in your opinion) select a copy writer to work with?"

This was Ed's comment:

"Great question – and a tick in all the boxes of my judging criteria. THIS IS MY FAVOURITE because so many businesses need to know when to DIY or outsource, (How WHO and where) outsourcing, when to pay a little or a lot, split testing different copywriters' material versus your own etc etc. GREAT question."

It was sent in by John Holder from Ruskin Information Services. **Congratulations John**, here's what you've won...

The unabridged audio programme of my book on 3 high-quality CDs, plus a bonus Data CD containing additional document examples, checklists, a searchable PDF version of the book and more.

You also get an A5 workbook, with the PDF on the bonus CD so you can print out another workbook to help you with each of your writing projects.

I'm sure it will prove to be a valuable tool in your business.

Your prize will be rushed out to you for you to enjoy.

I'll be posting my reply to this thought-provoking question later this week. Look at **Outsourcing or When is DIY Writing Best** on page 237.

Thank you for sending your questions in, even if you didn't win the prize I trust you found my advice helpful.

~ Carol Bentley

Date: Wednesday, January 23rd, 2008 at 9:45 am

A Bit More On Outsourcing...

In Friday's post I shared my thoughts on when to go for outsourcing and some points to consider when appointing someone to do work for you.

One aspect I didn't cover is clearly described in a post I found on someone else's blog. And it is very relevant to a business person who is trying to develop a 'work **on** not **in** your business' culture.

The whole point is to make sure you don't undertake tasks that are not worth your valuable time. Hill Robertson gives a good example in his post **'You Must**

Spend Your Money and Time Wisely' (page 366)
(and at www.carolbentley.org/hrspend.html)

~ Carol Bentley

Date: Monday, January 28th, 2008 at 10:45 am

Cultural Communication Differences...

Do you export your goods or services? Do you have to communicate with people from different cultural backgrounds?

John Walmsley does and he asked:

"I have a great deal of overseas clients and worry about how I word my emails and newsletters in case I offend. Is there a rule for different Countries or should I just assume they relate to the Scottish wit."

First I'd like to say that I think it's great that you've thought about this John because many business people don't.

You see, it is very easy to think everyone we speak or write to understands what we actually mean and we understand them perfectly. But do we? And are the actions we take seen as disrespectful? There are distinct cultural differences - there are even subtle differences between regions in the same country!

You build a strong relationship by knowing and respecting those differences. By conducting your business in an acceptable manner.

But how can you be sure of what you should - or should not - be doing or saying, without asking them? You want to come over as professional, as understanding your prospect or customer. If you don't know their traditions and follow them you could come over as inexperienced or, in a worse case scenario, crass.

Now *I* do not know all the international differences... but I *'know a lady who does!'*

If you are dealing with overseas - or about to - check the free articles (over 26) on Deborah Swallow's website (www.carolbentley.org/swallow.html). And I strongly suggest you consider buying her book **Communicating Across Cultures**, which is on her products page.

The first article link opens a global map which you can click on to get information for different regions.

And John, two articles you might find particularly useful are:

- **10 Tips on Humour**
- **International Email Etiquette**

Her insights help you to avoid mistakes that could kill your customer relationships.

~ Carol Bentley

Date: Tuesday, January 29th, 2008 at 9:45 am

I Response to "Cultural communication differences. . ."

I. February 8th, 2008 at 4:22 pm *InvestorBlogger* Says:

Of course, we all can't learn all languages or learn all customs. Politely inquiring sometimes resolves problems that have arisen.

Most people are MORE tolerant of those unfamiliar with their culture(s), language(s), or custom(s) than they might otherwise be to people in their own country who make similar mistakes.
Kenneth

*How Appealing Are You?

Right - so you know all you need to know about your target market. You've got a fine-tuned understanding of your ideal prospect; you know their age; their gender; income range; whether they're employed or retired (for consumer marketing); where they're likely to live and what type of accommodation they have.

You know what interests them; hobbies; reading habits; beliefs and opinions, ethical stance and purchasing habits - maybe.

Pardon? Did you say you're selling to business and you don't need all this personal detail?

O-kay, tell me who makes the decision to buy from you? The 'business' or a person at the business; Owner, Director, Buying Manager or other decision maker?

Whoever makes that decision in your favour does so for a variety of reasons and one of the points that can heavily influence the outcome is do they think "I like [*your name*]; I feel I can trust his (or her) advice and I'm confident he / she has my best interests at heart."

I'm sure you've heard it dozens of times but it's true... you have to build a relationship in order to get the sale.

But let's say you can't get up close & personal with your prospect. How do you create a relationship then - how do you appeal to your target audience?

By reaching out in other ways; by freely giving good advice; advice that your prospect can use. Advice such as:

- Crucial facts he needs to be aware of before making a decision; whether that decision is in your favour or not. (Free reports or case studies are good for this)

- Clearly explaining what your product or service is suitable for - describing the features and how they work

- And just as clearly stating when it is **not** appropriate; be honest about limitations or situations where your product or service is inappropriate

- Recommending an alternative supplier you know and trust when you cannot supply anything that fits the bill, rather than trying to compromise

Now don't get upset about that last suggestion... at first glance it may look as if you're driving business away, but that is not always the case.

Think about it; when you recommend an apparent competitor you are demonstrating you're confident enough about what you supply to be absolutely straight and up-front about it. You're displaying a strong ethic of 'the customer's interest comes first'- that gives you kudos in your prospect's eyes.

Do you think there's a good chance your prospect will tell people they know about your honesty and trust-worthiness? And recommend you to people who *are* looking for what you offer? I'm certain it will happen because it has for me.

Plus - if you have a canny business mind I'm sure you can see the possibilities here...

You see, there's always a certain proportion of the enquiries you get that you are not able to satisfy; you don't match what the customer is looking for. Your 'competitor' does.

And your competitor will have enquirers they can't convert into business that you could make very happy.

Agreeing to direct those unconverted enquiries to each other can create a win-win situation for you both. And, if you agree an introductory commission beforehand for any business generated, it won't matter if there seems to be more traffic going one way.

Who in your industry or profession could you set up an arrangement like this with? Or perhaps you already have a similar understanding?

~ Carol Bentley

Date: Monday, February 11th, 2008 at 2:00 pm

I Response to "How appealing are you"

1.   February 29th, 2008 at 2:13 pm *JLB* Says:
     Greetings! Thank you for sharing your advice. I believe that another helpful way to reach out to potential clients is to make oneself accessible: I make it easy for clients to learn about me, my professional background, and my business services online to help match my services to their needs.

I agree with you that it is important to provide a customer with what s/he needs, even when sometimes that means pointing them toward other professionals and services.

Thanks,

JLB

Aiming at Corporates...

Is there a difference between corporate businesses and SMEs or entrepreneurs? Three questions asked in my recent survey raised this issue. My answer; Yes... and No!

Am I hedging my bets here? Maybe... but let's look into it a bit further.

First here are the three questions posed about dealing with big companies:

Q1: How to generate more interest in my business from larger organisations.

Q2: How do you adapt your copy if your targets are senior executives and buyers in major corporates? Most of what I read about copywriting proposes big, bold headlines with "huge" specific benefits. And I must admit that when buying myself, these offers can be very seductive. Yet I know from over a decade working with senior executives in major companies that this sort of hyperbolic language and copy tends to go straight in the bin - it's just not credible.

Corporate executives (in my experience) tend to react better to more conservative approaches. Is my experience out of touch? Obviously these people are human too - and have the same underlying psychology. Yet their experience and background (in my view) means they don't react well to over-strong selling messages.

Q3: How to find out who makes all the purchasing decisions in a large organisation.

Don't expect to do a bulk mailing to corporate businesses and get a great response. It's unlikely to happen. You have to work a little harder for those lucrative contracts.

I advise selecting 10 companies to target and work on, adding others as a rolling prospect line as and when you are able to deal with them properly.

Decide and Research

- *Decide which companies you want to do business with*. Define exactly what you are offering and which companies benefit most from your solutions. When you contact them talk about a specific 'niche' area. Don't give a smorgasbord of products and services that confuse your prospect and - in their eyes - dilute your perceived level of expertise and ability to deliver a focused result.

- *Do your research.* Research the company; the department or division your product or service applies to; discover the challenges the company or that division are currently facing. Check news releases (they are often shown on the company website); is something they have announced likely to give them logistic or 'knock-on' effect problems you can resolve?

- *Find your target buyer.* Don't go to the HR or purchasing department (unless your offer is for them); aim for the person who heads up the area you are targeting. Read the corporate website; some do give contact names in their 'about us' section, although this practice is dwindling. Use the phone; call and ask "who takes care of .... in the company?" (you fill in the blank).

Careful! You are in information-gathering mode NOT selling mode. One whiff of a sales pitch and the person you are speaking to is likely to clam up.

In her book, **Selling to Big Companies**, Jill Konrath describes how to make those important fact-gathering calls so you reach your prime target within the company. Steve Brewer also gives pertinent and easy to follow advice in his CD programme **High Impact Cold Calling**.

A Slightly Different Approach

- *Write individual letters*. I'd advise against using extremely large, bold headlines - it doesn't give the right impression for corporate correspondence. But that's the only change I would suggest to the structure of your letter. You are still writing to an individual who has challenges within his/her work life and is eager for a solution. So you do have to grab attention immediately.

Start your first paragraph with a compelling statement of what you discovered about the company or department's challenges. Then ask a question that is geared towards the problem he has - the one you identified in your research. Explain the value your offer could bring to his company; quoting case studies from other organisations rather than a general self-serving statement.

For example, instead of writing "*our QR2 system saves production costs*" say "*Xyz company discovered that 3 months after implementing the QR2 system, production costs had reduced by 2.8% which gave them a projected annual savings of £4.37million.*" Be wary of creating a general 'sales pitch' - it's unlikely to work unless you are extremely lucky.

- In her book Jill strongly recommends avoiding subservient language such as 'delighted', 'pleased' or 'honoured' and I agree with her. All of your contact (whether letter, email or phone call) should be from a position of equality and strength. Talk as a peer-to-peer. Treat your prospect with respect but expect respect from him too. After all, you *are* the expert that has a solution to the problem he wants resolved.

Realistic Expectations

- Don't expect to get an appointment with your first letter or phone call. Have a campaign of actions you will take to secure your appointment to meet. But make sure you deliver valuable information at each contact point; don't make a self-serving push to get through the door.
  - Let your prospect know about case studies from other companies.

  - Articles from trade publications.

  - Informative reports you can supply (make sure they are informative not just a sales brochure).

  - Gift a copy of a good book you've read that gives some good insights to their industry or business or helps address issues they are likely to come up against. (*Of course, if that book happens to be one you've written and published*

> *it gives you an even bigger boost in your pros-*
> *pect's eyes because you are perceived as*
> *knowledgeable; assuming you've included good*
> *content in your book).*

- If it's practical, be prepared to secure a small contract initially. Once you are delivering great results and the company is pleased with your service you can start negotiating the larger deals.

Share Your Thoughts...

Have experience with larger companies? Either as a provider or perhaps you work (or have worked) within one of these behemoths? Send an email to carol@carolbentley.com with your views.

~ Carol Bentley

Date: Tuesday, March 25th, 2008 at 1:10 pm

Don't Assume All is OK. . .

You've worked hard to make sure everything is working properly. Whether it's a process in your administration, in your production, in your marketing or on your website. Now it's time to relax, safe in the knowledge that everything is running smoothly.

Think again!

That's what I thought - but it was a false sense of security I shouldn't have slipped into.

Here's what happened...

You may have noticed that in the right panel of my www.copywriting4b2b.com blog there's an invitation to recommend the website to your colleagues and friends. When you click on the link you are taken to another web page from where you can send a message to the people you want to tell. After clicking the 'Send Emails' button you are **supposed** to go to a 'Thank You' web page where you collect your gift for taking the time to send those recommendations.

Now that system was working fine. So I didn't see any need to re-check it.

More fool me!

I discovered there was a problem when one of my readers kindly rang to let me know a *404 'Page Not Found'* error was coming up instead of the *Thank You* page. And there was a pretty good chance the recommendation emails were not being sent either.

Fortunately, thanks to the great IT support I get from my supplier, the problem was quickly resolved, and it is now working as intended.

Reviewing Systems

Of course looking at our systems doesn't just apply to

making sure they are still working - although that in itself is a good enough reason to keep a close eye on them. Improvements in our procedures and techniques are just as important. And that's where asking your staff, customers and even suppliers can reveal some extremely valuable insights.

How long is it since you reviewed your systems; the ones that run like clockwork? Are they in place because they are the most efficient and effective method? Or are they used because "we've always done it like that!" Is it time to dust off the cobwebs and see if there are better ways?

I Asked For Your Help

My main method of delivering information is through writing; books, articles, email messages... these blog posts.

But my previous profession was developing and delivering training courses - so I'm perfectly comfortable with talking to people and demonstrating how things work. It makes sense to incorporate all these coaching skills into any future materials or courses I create. But is that what people really want? Would using different presentation styles be better? Maybe, maybe not.

That's why I decided to ask your opinion in last Friday's post.

So... what areas in your business need a bit of oiling to

make them run more smoothly?

~ Carol Bentley

Date: Wednesday, April 30th, 2008 at 10:00 am

That All Important Rapport

In my book, and in previous posts, I've mentioned how you can create rapport in your writing by understanding how people communicate; whether they are auditory, visual or kinaesthetic. Knowing that helps with the words you use in your letters.

But how about verbal communication?

Yes, the words you use still count. But there is more to verbal communication than just the words or even the tonality I mentioned in my previous post Conversation or lecture. (See page 64).

People speak (and listen) at a different pace. Some people speak extremely fast, others have a slo-o-o-w drawl. It can make listening extremely frustrating if you don't happen to match their speed of communication. But, more importantly, if you don't recognise and take your customer's speaking (and listening) style into account you could alienate them.

Jill describes her experience with this in her blog post (online at www.carolbentley.org/konrath-blog.html)

and explains why it is so important to adjust so you match your prospect or customer's conversation style. (She also shows how preparation before making an important call is also vital!)

~ Carol Bentley

Date: Tuesday, May 20th, 2008 at 10:00 am

Giving Great Service

Giving great service is recognised by most businesses as a must. But what is great service? I think this experience related by my friend, Nigel Risner, is a good example. . .

"Last night I went to one of my favourite restaurants of all time, it has just reopened after many years.

What they have done so remarkably well, is to do exactly what they had done to make them one of the busiest establishments in the past.

Great service.

Great service; great menu and staff who actually want to SERVE.

They also have added some nice little touches, (kosher section) a booking service that lets you know they know you are coming. Valet parking, and many others.

Why am I writing about this with such passion? Because when times get tough, **get the basics right**.

Will I be returning? yes! Will I spend a lot of money? yes! Will I tell my friends **No** (only kidding.)

The Chicago Rib Shack is back and in my opinion EVEN BETTER.

I have also been asked to work with a very famous retail store. If I can get them to understand the messages from above I promise I can turn them around.

They had and have a great customer base, they had a great theme, but somewhere have lost their way.

Great service, great people, great choice.

I promise you if you follow that mantra business will come back

Remember the definition of a great organisation:

A product that doesn't come back and a customer who does

Nigel Risner (www.nigelrisner.com)

So how does your business stack up? Are your customers raving fans, like Nigel is of this restaurant?

~ Carol Bentley

Date: Monday, June 9th, 2008 at 1:00 pm

Asking For Help Is Not A Sign Of Weakness

Sometimes we forget that we can't be 'all things to all men'. And sometimes it is better to concentrate on our strengths and limit our apparent weaknesses by asking for help when we need it.

And it doesn't matter if the help we ask for is expert knowledge to achieve what we're aiming at or encouragement and belief from our family and friends to reach the goals we've set for ourselves.

Many businesses fail because the owner cannot be the expert in everything that is needed to make a business successful. Their passion is usually the service or product they are supplying; that's where their inherent knowledge lies. But sometimes a business fails because the owner does not know:

- how to create and implement a business strategy
- how to market their business
- how to get sales
- how to control their finances properly
- how to handle customer support effectively

- how to build a website and get it seen by their prospective customers

And a host of other related issues that crop up in business.

And the person that tries to handle all these on their own is creating a huge millstone for themselves.

Getting The Help Needed

The person who asks for help in the area they do not have experience in is showing wisdom. In the early days of a business the funding probably isn't there to opt for outsourcing.

That's where networking - talking to like-minded people, offering help and asking for help comes in. And networking can be online and offline.

Offline frequently takes the form of business clubs or groups, chambers of commerce, business support groups - different ones in different countries - and master groups.

Online help is available through forums, discussion boards and blogs, like this one. And sharing those resources can be your gesture of help.

Will you help others?

So - I'd like to ask your help for those people who read

this blog.

Which are the most useful online websites you've found? And why?

Share your experiences of where you've found helpful people who've answered your questions and given freely of their expertise - or maybe forums where you already contribute your expertise to help others. In fact if you have a business related blog that I haven't already discovered, now is the time to let me and everyone else know.

Use this contact link and tell us all about the support you've found, or given, on the net.
(Direct URL= http://www.carolbentley.org/ask.htm)

And, if I believe it is a valuable resource for my other readers, I will share it with my blog readers.

Thank you in advance for participating and sharing.

~ Carol Bentley

Date: Tuesday, June 10th, 2008 at 10:00 am

How Not To Run Customer Services

Reading about how other companies have handled customer complaints can act as a catalyst for us to review our grievance procedures because the end result and how it is reached can, sometimes, turn an unhappy customer into a voluble ambassador for us.

And equally - if it isn't handled properly - it can be extremely damaging.

This has always been the case - but in the past the 'bad news' didn't spread as quickly or as far and wide as it does in this modern, technology-focused age. And maybe that's why some less technologically-minded companies just don't realise how important it is to get their act together.

If your customer services is not all it needs to be then you could be leaving yourself open to the bad news spreading fast on the Internet - as is happening to the company I read about in www.modernselling.com's newsletter - in this particular case the company's staff completely forgot to act as if 'the customer is always right'. Visit www.modernselling.com to read **Hanging on The Telephone** (You'd think being a high-tech company they'd know better, wouldn't you?)

What examples, both good and bad, do you have of how companies handled customer grievances? Use the comments link below to share your stories.

~ Carol Bentley

Date: Tuesday, September 9th, 2008 at 10:30 am

4 Responses to "How not to run customer services"

1. September 9th, 2008 at 1:06 pm *Nigel West* Says:

    Hi Carol

    Had a similar problem recently with The Alliance & Leicester bank. The were fine 18 months ago when we moved from First Direct (because I objected to the £10 a month charge, even though we wouldn't have been charged) but now have a "To find out your balance press 1 to ...." and no option to speak to someone. And you need a telephone banking pin, which I don't have. After 2 hours I found a number where you can use your internet pin to speak to someone. Truly dreadful and we will be moving back to First Direct having learned that it's worth paying so that you can speak to someone when you need to.

    Regards

    Nigel

2. September 9th, 2008 at 1:28 pm *Frank* Says:

    Had a bad experience signing up with VirginMedia recently

    They're gushing all over you while they take your money, but when I called back to clarify part of a service I was getting, it soon got very bad.

They were stumped when I tried to explain the service they show on their website was different to what they had sold me. When I asked them to look at their website to check the details, I was told they didn't have access to their own website and didn't know what was on it!

I was left hanging on the phone for ages, then it was cut off. As I tried to explain my frustrations to two other 'customer service agents', they hung up on me (thank you 'Marcus' and 'Jerry').

My system is now installed, but I'm dreading my first bill and any ongoing service issues if it's not right.

3. September 9th, 2008 at 2:00 pm *Carol Bentley* Says:

    Nigel,

    It's awful when you change services (bank or otherwise) only to have problems like this.

    We changed our business bank to the co-operative bank last year because of the free-banking offer they had for FSB (Federation of Small Businesses) members.

    We had a few teething problems with the direct debits transfers (but we can't honestly say it was their fault, could have been from the bank we were leaving). And we've had problems with the online banking website.

But I have to say the co-op bank's customer service is absolutely BRILLIANT.

They were not in the least bit phased or upset about our complaints - which were mainly about the online system (now sorted and working smoothly). And their people bent over backwards to get our concerns sorted AND took the trouble to follow up to make sure we were happy with the final outcome.

Frank,

I think your experience rather connects with my post about 'linking up' your marketing activity (see post 'Do you have a (marketing) leg to stand on' page 137). Making sure everyone in an organisation knows what is on offer - so everyone is connected - is fundamental really, isn't it?

I use the Orange network - have done since my very first mobile phone which I took out in 1994 - still got the same number!

I did consider changing to Virgin a few years ago but Orange matched the deal so I stayed with them. Maybe I've been lucky 'cause I've had no problems at all.

I'll keep fingers crossed that your future dealings are a bit better for you.

Carol

4. September 11th, 2008 at 7:47 am *Nigel West* Says:

Hi Carol

I agree with you about the Co-Op Bank. We switched the business account via the FSB and have had no problems apart for their website going a bit wonky at times. Maybe I should switch my personal account there.

Thanks Carol and keep up the blog postings, Nigel

Customer Services - Wow Factor

Following on from Tuesday's post about bad (and good customer services) sometimes the service you get can be an experience with the wow! factor, which is what happened to me this week.

Actually, it made me smile because of the timing with the subject matter of my earlier post. . .

A week or so ago I took up the 'check it out' offer from Frank Kern (you may have seen some reference to it at various websites).

The package was a blatant continuity 'try my monthly material and I'll throw in DVDs of a successful seminar' subscription. I was asked to pay the P&P only and the subs payments wouldn't start for a month. No problem, I set up my reminder to review whether or not I wanted to take the monthly programme - as I shared with you on Monday in **How Not To Forget** on page 307.

The material arrived, I've started to look at it (and already got some great ideas both for me and my clients) but I've not got through the whole lot yet.

Yesterday morning I got an unexpected package from Frank. Another DVD.

Why did he send it?

Because he discovered one of the DVDs has a glitch on one of the tracks (probably some problem with the burning) and, rather than wait for people to report the problem and ask for a replacement, he decided to send everyone a new, re-digitalised copy of the damaged track plus a bonus session as a 'sorry for the trouble'. Because I haven't finished going through the material I wasn't even aware there was a problem.

Did he need to do this? Not really.

Has doing this helped his reputation with me?

Definitely - I'd decided, because of the value I've already got, to let the subscription continue so this attention to detail has confirmed I made the right decision.

Did Frank think taking this extra 'wow factor' step might help people who were undecided to give it a go for a while?

What do you think?

Has it turned me into an ambassador for his products? Probably, I'm certainly keen to see what else he's going to deliver in his monthly missives.

Offer a customer service that makes people say "Wow, I didn't expect that!" and you'll reap the rewards too. It's all part of building and keeping a good relationship going so people want to do more business with you.

Your Experiences

In my earlier post we talked about our bad experiences. Let's finish the week on a positive and share stories of good customer service experience. Use the comments link below to tell about companies who've given you good vibes.

~ Carol Bentley

Date: Thursday, September 11th, 2008 at 3:07 pm

BUSINESS RESOURCES

Your Blog Anniversary Gifts

I decided I wanted to celebrate my first full month of blogging by giving you a gift; but what? What would prove extremely useful and valuable to you?

Because I don't know exactly what business issues you are facing right at this moment, I had to think of something that would be useful to you regardless. And, of course, the other challenge I had is giving something that is valuable regardless of whether you provide a service or a product; sell online or offline; sell to other businesses or to consumers.

Which is why **I decided on 2 gifts** and I'm confident that you'll be very happy with at least one, if not both. You are welcome to take both.

Both gifts are downloaded as a zip file. Each contains a text file and a PDF e-book. The text file gives you an introduction to the e-book. The e-book itself contains the meat of the subject. Enjoy!

Gift 1

Service Sellers Masters Course - Because you visit my blog on a regular basis and you're probably comfortable using the world wide web, I'm guessing you have a website of your own. If you provide a service then your web site can (and should) be a clear source of new clients or customers.

This extremely easy-to-read 204-page e-book describes how to create a results generating website for service providers.

The e-book explains how your website should be set up to attract all the targeted traffic you need. And, even if you have a web company who designs and manages your web site for you, the insights this e-book gives helps you understand how your web site should be structured to give you the best results.

Get your *Service Sellers Masters Course* at www.carolbentley.org/ssmc.html

Gift 2

Make Your Price Sell - This shorter e-book (54 pages) describes how to establish the best pricing for your product or service. Although it is aimed at e-commerce sites, the underlying marketing premise applies to any pricing decision; whether online or offline.

Get your *Make Your Price Sell* e-book at www.carolbentley.org/myps.html

Enjoy your gifts and let me know how you get on with them.

~ Carol Bentley

Date: Friday, November 23rd, 2007 at 10:00 am

Refer, Refer and Be Referred

The lifeblood of many businesses is their satisfied customer base. These are the people who can act as ambassadors by recommending you to others.

Other people who can also refer you are the contacts in your business network circle. Which is why you attend business events; to meet new people.

So now, your network is growing. You know lots of different business people and you are getting to know what they can deliver. And, of course, they are getting to know you and what you offer.

But does everyone know **everything** about you and what your business provides? And do you know **all** there is to know about your contacts?

You need to know all this if you are going to seize every opportunity to build even stronger business relationships, which results in more sales...

Create Your Referral Matrix

The simplest way to keep an eye on what is developing is to create a Referral Matrix. The concept is very simple. The Referral Matrix gives you an 'At-a-Glance' picture of the progress of your business relationships.

Do this for your own contacts and services/products and another for your contact's products.

Let's start with your services and products:

1) Take a piece of paper.

2) Draw a grid shape. You need enough columns going across to list all your products and services in the top row; show one product/service at the top of each column, starting from the second column.

3) In the first column of the rows going down list your contacts or customers.

4) Choose 3 different, strong, colours. One represents 'Told', another for 'Sold' and the third for 'Referred'

5) When you tell a contact about one of your products; you have supplied information so you know he is fully aware of it, mark the colour for 'Told' against that company in the column for the specific product/service you've explained. (I suggest filling in a third of the box).

6) When a contact has bought that product/service from you add the 'Sold' colour – you now have two thirds of the box completed.

7) When a contact recommends your product / service to someone else; 'refers you', fill in the 'Referred' colour.

Some of the boxes may have the Told and Referred, but not the Sold colour.

Now you can see, at a glance, which of your contacts do not know about some of your products (in which case you can inform them) and, just as importantly, if they have been informed whether they have bought from you or referred you to someone else.

Create a similar chart for each of your 'Hot' business contacts – those you have a close working relationship with.

By doing this you take a pro-active stance to recommending their services to other people you know **and** you'll know if they offer something you may need in the future.

Taking such a close interest in your business contacts helps you build strong relationships.

What's more you gain a good reputation for being the 'person who knows who to contact' and your business networking circle grows.

A Free Gift For You...

This works really well on a spreadsheet, such as Excel,

using the conditional formatting feature. I have created a spreadsheet with the chart set up ready to use.

In fact the file, which I call the **Opportunity Matrices**, contains **3 spreadsheets**: 1 to use purely for referrals within your business contacts circle, another to use for checking what your current customers know about everything you offer and the third is a **Price Research** spreadsheet. Use the latter to compare your prices against your competitors - it is a useful tool when you are launching a new product or service or revising your pricing structure.

I've also written a PDF file that explains how I created the spreadsheets - so you can do the same if you wish - and describes how to use them.

Get your copy now, send an email to:
excel-matrix@aweber.com

You will be asked to confirm your request - I have to do this to avoid spamming problems.

~ Carol Bentley

Date: Thursday, November 29th, 2007 at 10:00 am

Is Socialising The Way To Go?

I've just read a 93-page report that made absolute sense to me.

It's a free report from a guy called Rich Schefren. Have you heard of him?

He's coined the phrase **Attention Age** and in his new report explains how trying to get someone's attention through the old 'in-your-face' sales and marketing methods is doomed in this high-tech, information overload age.

He says the most powerful marketing vehicle today is word-of-mouth; viral marketing. Specifically on the net through forums, blogs and social sites.

Giving information that people can use; sharing insights that help people before they've even spent a single penny with you is the most powerful marketing activity you can engage in.

Sound familiar?

He also warns about the power of these social sites and gives examples of how 3 different big corporate companies were brought to their knees by the 'man in the street'. That's worth the read in itself.

But trying to manipulate this type of marketing is a definite 'No-No'. You have to be genuine in what you do and what you give. And when you are the results can be mind-blowing.

Have I got you intrigued? If so, go get your own copy here:

Attention Age Doctrine Part 2 Released at
www.carolbentley.org/saad.html

Then come back and share your thoughts on the content.

~ Carol Bentley

Date: Tuesday, December 4th, 2007 at 10:00 am

How To Show Appreciation For Your Customers' Referrals...

For many businesses referrals generate a significant amount of new contacts. And businesses that actively seek out recommendations usually gain a higher benefit than those who just leave it to chance.

Think about it - even if you have provided the greatest service or product your happy customer may not think about telling other people or giving you information about other business people who are looking for what you offer. And it's not because he doesn't want to help you. . . it is purely because he is busy and it doesn't occur to him.

That's why it is up to you to have a structured, almost automated, referral generation system in your business.

When to ask?

The best time to ask for recommendations is when your customer has just experienced your product, or service. If you have a quality-check follow-through during which you make sure your customer got exactly (or perhaps more) than he was expecting then asking him who else is looking for the same good result is a natural step.

If you send out products you can include referral cards for your customer to complete and send back.

Offering an incentive

Depending upon your business it may be appropriate to offer an incentive - or as I prefer to think of it - a 'Thank You' gift. I'm sure you've seen companies who offer gift vouchers to you and to the person you recommend or a discount on future purchases.

Personally, I prefer to give a 'Thank You' gift that is linked with the service or product I supply - rather than something that is not related to my business and, therefore, may not be of interest to my customer or contact.

For example, if you decide to invite 3 people you know to visit this blog (using the link in the right hand panel) I show my appreciation of your support by gifting you an MP3 audio recording.

In the MP3 audio gift I describe some of the techniques high-performing direct response copywriters use to craft irresistible sales letters so they enjoy the highest profitable mailing possible.

It reveals:

- 4 Sales Letter Writing Rules That Persuade People to Buy
- How Answering This Critical Question Turns A Mediocre Sales Letter Into A Results-Generating Dynamo
- 8 Design Secrets To Compel Your Prospect To Continue Reading
- How Powerful Headlines Gain Massive Sales Increases: 10 Proven Examples for You to Adopt

As you can see the recording is closely connected with my products and services; writing for business sales and marketing.

Automating your gift

Now I'm sure you've already realised that delivering my gift is automated. With the web page being open 24/7 it is completely impractical for me to respond personally whenever a visitor decides to recommend this website. And besides, if you make a recommendation you want to get your promised gift of appreciation straight away, don't you?

How to automate?

You have a huge choice of tools you can use to automate delivery of electronic gifts like this. It can be rather bewildering which is the best option for you.

I looked at quite a few before deciding upon the tool I prefer to use: TAF Pro (Tell A Friend Pro) at www.carolbentley.org/taf.html.

I chose it because of the easy implementation and facilities it gave me - including checking that the email address is entered correctly; you know how easy it is to mistype an email address especially the more obscure ones (my brother's is xzavyaw@ - you can't get more obscure than that!)

Stunning Service

What I hadn't realised when I bought the product was that in addition to all the features (I've only used a third of them so far) there was also stunning service from the vendor, Paul Galloway. And I *do* mean stunning!

Let me explain. I bought the product last July to use on another website. About 3 or 4 days after I downloaded the program (and successfully followed the set up instructions) I got a phone call from the US. It was Paul Galloway.

He said "I'm going on holiday in a couple of days and I just wanted to be sure you were OK with the TAF Pro program before I left. Have you got any questions you need answering?"

Now *that* is service.

And on top of that... the service continues.

One of my blog visitors contacted me a few days ago to say that a couple of emails (which were valid) were being rejected by the TAF form.

So I popped an email over to Paul asking if he had any ideas why that might be happening. He tested the email addresses on his internal system and came back to me with suggestions within a couple of hours.

That's impressive bearing in mind he is in a time zone that is at least 5 hours behind us.

So what's my conclusion from all this?

1. Create a formal system for getting referrals & recommendations.
2. Decide when is the best time to ask for referrals and don't let the opportunity slip.
3. Consider giving Thank You gifts or incentives to encourage recommendations.
4. Automate your gift delivery wherever possible - especially if you have a web site you want people to visit.
5. Choose the delivery tool carefully; ease of use, reliability and support when there is a problem is vital.

Do you have referral systems that work well for you?

Are you willing to share? Send an email to carol@carolbentley.com and I may share with my blog readers. Don't forget to include your web URL for a live link. You never know, if what you share is valuable you may get some new visitors.

~ Carol Bentley

Date: Monday, January 7th, 2008 at 12:00 pm

Saying Thanks. . .

Within a business there are frequent occasions when a word of thanks is appropriate - and I'll be giving you my thanks a little later in this post. But first, I want to tell you about an inspired way of saying 'thank you' that makes your company more memorable, whether the thanks are to customers, business colleagues or a member of staff.

Many business owners are astute enough to realise that expressing thanks for business; for referrals and recommendations; for a job well done by a supplier; for an excellent result achieved by an employee is good business practice. It is also a canny marketing activity; showing you appreciate your clients and the support they give by buying from you.

How you express your thanks gives a different perception of your company; it's where attention to detail counts. So what are the ways you can show your appreciation - and how can you do it successfully without it becoming a burden on your budget or time?

- Send an ordinary email of thanks - this doesn't take much time and is certainly better than not doing anything; but I don't think it will really make you stand out

- Organise an impressive e-card (take a look at www.jacquielawson.com). These are beautiful animated e-cards, but if the person you are thanking has a spam filtering system in place the notification email may not reach him (or her) or he may not collect the card - it does need some effort on his part.

- Give a small gift of thanks - depending upon what you are expressing appreciation of - that may be appropriate.

- Write a personal letter of thanks. This does take more effort and for some people it can take considerable time, thinking of how to word the letter. Not everyone is comfortable about putting their thoughts into writing.

- Snail-mail a postcard. Although this is a little different, it's not very private and may not be appropriate in certain circumstances.

- Post a 'Thank You' greeting card - this is the inspired method I want to tell you more about. You see, at first glance it may seem as though it takes as much effort, if not more, than some of the suggestions above. But I found a brilliant website that sends a high quality card, complete with your personal message. The cards are sent from the US but, with the current exchange rates, the postage equates to little more than it would cost to send from the UK.

There is an incredible choice of card designs and the whole process takes just a couple of minutes.

Take a look at www.carolbentley.org/mrsoc.html where, for those extra special occasions, you can even add a gift (*but **before** you do that, have a look at my 'Thank You' message below*). I tested this service myself and can definitely confirm the high quality of the card that is supplied.

Marketing Thought: if you decide to use these cards as an alternative way of delivering your marketing message then the foreign postage frank may act in your favour if you are sending to UK addresses. It may intrigue your prospect enough to open the envelope - which is the first step we are aiming to achieve. It is something that is worth testing.

My Thanks to You

I have two Thank You's to say:

First: I'd like to say Thank You for the questions that were sent in. Some very interesting topics were brought up. Some of the questions have already been posted with answers; others - that are available for 'public view' - will be added over the next week or so.

Second: Even if you didn't have a question you wanted answering, the support you show by visiting, reading and recommending my blog; at www.copywriting4b2b.com, is really appreciated. That's why I'm always looking out for more information or resources that help you in your business and why I suggested visiting the SendOutCards website.

And whilst looking, one of the distinct advantages of interacting on the web is you come across some very nice people. And Martin Russell is one of those (check out his Word of Mouth Magic blog, it's listed in the blog roll on the www.copywriting4b2b.com website).

Martin has very generously said that visitors from this blog can test out 3 cards from his SendOutCards service at his expense. This gives you the opportunity to experience the service and test the quality for yourself.

Simply go to www.carolbentley.org/mrsoc.html

What other ways of saying 'Thank You' have you used or experienced?

~ Carol Bentley

Date: Monday, January 21st, 2008 at 1:14 pm

1 Response to "Saying Thanks. . ."

1. January 27th, 2008 at 3:12 am *Star Life Media* Says:

    Keep spreading the word Carol about the indispensable and often un-used law of gratitude -great article!

Carnivals and Useful Connections...

Useful business connections crop up in many different ways. When you're talking to people; when you're emailing people; when you're visiting other websites and at carnivals. *Really* - you will see why in a moment.

And when I find connections I think might be interesting I like to share. Before starting this blog I only shared with friends and colleagues who I frequently emailed. But now I can share with you. . .

And this post is not only sharing the links it is also saying Thanks (again!) because all of these links go to blog carnivals who have shown their support by posting a link to entries on this blog.

What Is A Blog Carnival?

Without getting too technical, a blog carnival is a collection of interesting blog posts on a subject or area of interest. If, for example, you have a specific interest (business or hobby) you can search for a carnival on that topic.

When you visit the website hosting the carnival you find links to interesting articles and blog posts the host has gathered together for you. It saves you trawling hundreds of different websites looking for good content to read.

The person acting as host invites people to submit their blog posts for the carnival. The host checks the content of the post to see if it is relevant to the carnival subject and would give valuable insights to the carnival visitors.

It is a useful source of information, thoughts and comments that is easily accessible to anyone.

In fact by following the posts from some of these articles I have discovered useful material; some of which I have already discussed in previous posts on this site.

Finding Blog Carnivals

You can often find blog carnivals by following the link in a comment below a post on your favourite blog site. (There are quite a few at the bottom of my earlier posts).

You can search on Google (or the other search engines) for blog carnivals. Simply type **blog carnival** followed by the subject you are interested in.

You can check out the blog carnivals listed below. These are all carnivals that have selected and shown posts from here. If the topics I write about here are useful to you it may be that some of the other contributors to these carnivals also have good material you'd like to read.

Let me know if you find anything interesting to share with your fellow visitors to this blog.

Thanking the Blog Carnival Hosts

Hosting a blog carnival is time-consuming. I'd like to express my appreciation to the hosts of these carnivals for their support.

If you host a carnival that has displayed one or more of my posts and it isn't shown here - please accept my apologies for missing you off this list - but rest assured your link is showing below the post you included in your carnival.

- Carnival of Making Real Money
- More Than We Know
- JustWriteBlogCarnival
- Web Business Marketing Blog
- Business and Blogging
- Tip Diva
- Success Part 2
- 4 Entrepreneur
- E3 Success Systems
- Today is That Day

- Uncle Joe's Leadership Blog
- Fiction Scribe
- The Writer's Block
- Carnival of Life, Happiness and Meaning

If you would like to check the other content on any of these carnivals you can search for them in your favourite web browser.

~ Carol Bentley

Date: Thursday, January 24th, 2008 at 9:45 am

3 Responses to "Carnivals and Useful Connections. .."

1. January 24th, 2008 at 4:20 pm *Aaron Crocco* Says:
   Carol thank you for linking to my site. I really enjoy the blog carnival and all it does to help promote my writing!

2. January 26th, 2008 at 7:20 pm *Tip Diva* Says:

   Thank you for submitting your post to Carnival Of Tips!
   And thank you for linking to my website, Carol. Blog Carnivals have done wonders for my site traffic and have introduced me to blogs I probably wouldn't have stumbled upon otherwise. Call me another believer.

3. February 5th, 2008 at 1:54 pm *therapydoc* Says:

It does seem as if people could spend their whole lives on-line, doesn't it, cruising these things? This is a nice post.

Outsourcing or When DIY Writing Is Best

Outsourcing can free up time, expand your resources and gain expertise within your business. It can also create an absolute nightmare if you choose the wrong person or company or don't clearly state your expectations.

And John Holder's winning question raised that subject specifically about copywriting.

This was his question:

> "Many small businesses are started by someone technically good at what they do, but not that hot on running a business. When are they better off writing "DIY" copy, and when should they outsource with an expert? As a rider to that, how should they (in your opinion) select a copy writer to work with?"

Let me split this into 3 elements:

- Business owner: Technically good
- When DIY writing is sometimes best
- How to select the ideal copywriter

Business owner: Technically good

A business owner, or entrepreneur, usually starts his (or her) business because he is passionate about what he provides - whether that is a service or product. Because of that passion he has a wealth of knowledge, experience, expertise and skill in his chosen field.

Ask a question and he can tell you everything you need to know about it; what to look for; why you should avoid this or that; different approaches; different uses.

Consider for a moment; your business... do you regard yourself as having a wealth of expert knowledge? Could you answer almost any question put to you about it? Are you immersed, heart and soul, in your business?

It's that in-depth understanding and vibrancy that shows through when you talk about your business - and it can shine through in your sales letters when you write about it.

Bottom line: *YOU* know *more* about your business and how it helps other people or companies than any copywriter simply because it *IS* your baby.

When DIY writing is sometimes best...

Because you know so much more about your business ideally you should write your own sales letters and marketing material.

You know every nuance, all the tips and insights that an outsider can never know. You know how to make your product or service deliver outstanding results for your customers and clients (you *do*, don't you?)

But there is one trap you have to be careful to avoid and that's becoming the 'business bore'.

You know what I mean, I'm sure you've met someone like that - you ask what he does and wham! you've opened the floodgates to all about his business; what he does; what he wants; how his product or service works - every little detail all told from *his* point of view... he will blah! blah! blah!

Yes - you do need to get your message across and you must show your enthusiasm for what you can do for people. But be subtle about it. Describe it from your customer's point of view.

Never forget the two questions your listener /reader is probably asking; "What's in it for me?" and "So what?" Keep that in mind when you write your letters (as described in my book '**I Want To Buy Your Product...**' available at www.carolbentley.com/offer) and you'll write compelling letters.

Having said that... for some people writing really *is* very difficult. They do not have a natural inclination to write - and that's probably particularly true for someone who is very skilled manually or technically.

For example my husband is mental about his business (sorry! I should have said passionate) but to me it seems 'mental' because he loves history, specifically military history, and in his business he buys and sells military collectibles (www.tigercollectibles.co.uk).

Personally I can't see the attraction, but by the same token he feels the same about the fact I love to write. He finds it very difficult to get his thoughts down onto paper.

Now it is a skill he could learn - as anyone can - if he felt the need or inclination. He doesn't (you can guess why).

And although it is a skill that can be learnt not everyone is willing to make that effort.

If you find it painful to express yourself in writing; if it takes you hours of blood, sweat and tears to write a sales letter and then you decide (or someone tells you) it's never going to get the results you want, then perhaps you need to consider the alternative.

Because those hours you're wasting trying to get a reasonable effort together could probably be better spent driving your business forward in other ways.

But, before you make that decision do make sure you understand the process because then you are better equipped to recognise good writing and to choose the right person to work with.

How to Select the Ideal Copywriter - 9 Points to Consider

Some of the suggestions I'm going to make here apply to any service you outsource - not just copywriting.

Decide what you want to achieve. Do you want...
- A powerful sales letter?
- A company brochure?
- Press releases?
- Feature articles?
- Reports or 'white-papers'?
- Copy for a website?
- An email marketing campaign?
- Advertising copy?
- A staff handbook?
- A procedures manual?
- A technical guide?

Many of these writing activities need different skills and approaches. When you've decided what you want produced you can look for someone who has experience in that particular discipline.

- Is he/she professional? By that I mean does he take the trouble to ask questions about your business, your goals and, if you are looking for a sales letter, does he ask about your offer and what other marketing you've already done and the response you got. Look for a copywriter who asks you to complete a project question-naire.

- And talking of professionalism, does he supply a contract and terms of business so you know exactly what to expect and what he is agreeing to do for you?
- Does he have a good reputation? Do you know his work? Have you heard good things about the material he has produced for other busi-nesses? Does his style match yours?
- How does he charge? By the hour; by the page or number of words; or does he charge a re-tainer? Be careful. Writing is creative work. It takes time to craft the documents you want, especially if it is a sales letter or marketing piece. Charges by the hour can mount up and storm past your budget before you realise it.

And be cautious about restricting the number of pages or words you want someone to write - unless it is a requirement for the project, for example when writing an article for a publica-tion that has to be a specific length.

Many professional copywriters quote a price for the project, which can make budgeting easier for you. Dependent upon the work you are asking for you may be able to negotiate a lower fee with a commission on results achieved. **Beware** - if the fees are very low, ask yourself why?

- Is he easy to work with? Some copywriters can be very autocratic. They can be opinionated and refuse to collaborate properly with clients. They regard requests for changes to what they've produced to be a personal insult to their talent.

  You want someone you can talk to; someone who matches your enthusiasm for your product or service; someone who is genuinely interested in what you provide and what you want to achieve; someone who listens and takes on board your ideas. And you want a copywriter who is willing to explain why he has taken a particular approach and why he thinks it will work for you.

- Does he do his own research? Obviously you need to provide as much material, information, insights and supporting documentation as you can. But the mark of a true professional is the copywriter who goes that extra mile by doing his own research to enhance what you've supplied.

- Is he reliable? Does he meet deadlines, deliver on time? There's no point having a good copywriter if he constantly misses deadlines. That's particularly important when you are sending out offers with a specific offer period or geared to anniversaries or seasons.

Take your time when choosing someone to provide an outsource service; whether that service is copywriting or any other. Ask the questions and make sure you are happy with the answers before making any commitments.

~ Carol Bentley

P.S. I have a couple more questions to share with you: Death of the Long Letter (from Ian Brodie) and Cultural Communication Differences (John Walmsley). Look out for these in next week's posts.

Date: Friday, January 25th, 2008 at 9:45 am

1 Response to "Outsourcing or when DIY writing is best"

1. February 3rd, 2008 at 5:04 pm *InvestorBlogger* Says:
   This is excellent advice. I'm sometimes just out of time to do the more mechanical writing for my blog... but there are times when I can't imagine why anyone could write what I want.... Good advice.
   Kenneth

How Do You Take Control?

This question came in from Chris Ingham asking how to take control...

"Do you have any info regarding Getting Things Done software? Might it be that you're already using such software yourself?

I'm interested in the different perspectives analysis (entering potential task information into a database, which can be filtered and viewed by perspective, at the click of a button. e.g.

- Context - listing tasks by nature, such as email, call, meeting or shopping, etc.
- Project - listing of current projects.
- Next Action - next action to be taken on each project.
- Waiting For - highlighting tasks waiting for an external event to occur before action can be taken.
- Urgent Now - literally can't be put off.
- Some Day Maybe - squirreling away possible tasks

A programme designed for work-life management and not just work. For business owners where the lines between work and life are often blurred .... like mine!"

There are so many different solutions available; some software based, some non-technical and others that are a mix of the two.

My system is a mix and is a process I've developed over

the years that suits my way of working (part of it is to do with having a brilliantly efficient PA!)

You might like to investigate Mark Joyner's ideas at www.simpleology.com which started off as a very effective off-line system and now has some software tools to go with it. It is a free programme and can be very effective if it suits your working style.

Apart from that I'm not really able to recommend a software solution as such - it's not my area of expertise.

Your Thoughts?

What advice would you offer Chris? Have you found an effective system you would recommend? Or are there solutions offered that you do not rate - for whatever reason?

Share your experience by sending an email to carol@carolbentley.com - I'm sure Chris will not be the only one who values your opinion.

~ Carol Bentley

Date: Friday, February 1st, 2008 at 10:45 am

Getting Your Thoughts On Paper

Your mind is buzzing, your senses are on fire as the ideas come to you thick and fast - you can't write them down quick enough and you just know that some gems are going to disappear into the ether.

Or you're listening hard, you want to capture every ounce of wisdom you're hearing but as you write you're missing other vital information. Sound familiar?

It was certainly a familiar scenario for me when I used to make my notes in linear form. When I discovered Tony Buzan and his mind mapping it opened up a whole new world. I could capture my ideas, brainstorm creatively and remember what I'd heard with simple keywords on a mindmap.

I remember attending a seminar in 2002 where Ivan Misner was speaking about business networking. I made notes; on a mindmap in a notebook that was no more than 10cm x 6.5cm - that was pretty small! I transferred my mindmap, complete with images to a larger map when I got back to my office. I still refer to that mindmap and in fact have written articles and given presentations to business groups using the material as my foundation.

But I'm not aiming to convince you about how wonderful mind mapping is as a business tool - you may already know that. No, what I want to share with you today is the mind mapping program that has been created by Tony Buzan and his team.

You see, up to now I've used Mind Manager from Mindjet. And I've got quite proficient at using it for most of my creative work. But today I discovered iMindMap, which has a more organic feel that ties in with Buzan's concept of mind mapping and the way our brains function.

So I downloaded the evaluation 7-day trial copy and gave it a whirl. And I *love* it! It is extremely easy to use and - for me - looks just right, completely organic like the mind maps you'd draw by hand.

And, just to show you what I mean, I created a mind-map to match one of my earlier posts: **8 Elements of a Compelling Sales Letter** (page 17). Here it is:

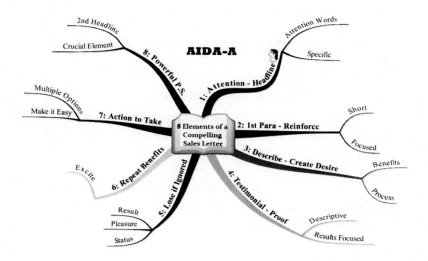

The other point that impressed me is the reasonable cost - just £58.69 per user license compared to £199 for Mind Manager. [*New releases priced from £49*].

I think I'm converted. If you like the flow of hand-drawn mind maps you'll love this software too.

You can download a free trial copy at www.imindmap.com/drwriter and test it for yourself. And yes, that is an affiliate link. If you'd rather not use the affiliate URL you can just go straight to www.imindmap.com

I'm off to get some more ideas down using my new mind mapping software, ciao for now

~ Carol Bentley

Date: Wednesday, February 6th, 2008 at 10:45 am

3 Responses to "Getting Your Thoughts On Paper"

1. February 6th, 2008 at 12:18 pm *Peter Kenworthy* Says:
   Carol - thanks for this blog - very useful. May be worth checking out FreeMind which I've found to be a good alternative for mind mapping and is Open Source (i.e. free).
   [Carol: You can download it from this website: www.carolbentley.org/freemind.html]
   Best wishes, Peter

   ### *Reply from Carol*
   Peter - thank you. I did download FreeMind a while ago but I never really got on with it, certainly not enough to entice me away from Mind Manager at the time.

2. February 6th, 2008 at 4:42 pm *Jeannie Monaghan* Says:
   Hi Carol, This looks great when you do it but I bought Tony Buzan's book years ago and thought he was a charlatan. Maybe I'll give it another whirl as clearly - you are writing and I am not!
   All the best, Jeannie

   ### *Reply from Carol*

   Hi Jeannie,

   to be honest - apart from buying Tony's book *Get Ahead* - I haven't had much to do with the guy himself. But I have found the mind mapping process very energising and stimulating. For example I use it when I'm creating headlines. I'm sure that without it I would never have come up with the 237 headlines I crafted for a client's new campaign a few months ago.

I also use it when developing new products, such as the book publishing guide I'm currently working on. For me, it just makes it easier to organise my thoughts and add ideas as they occur to me.

As I said, I really like the software they've developed but if you're not keen on dealing with the Buzan company then try the FreeMind program, suggested by Peter in the previous comment, before deciding if buying a software tool is the right step for you.

Regards, Carol

3. February 7th, 2008 at 4:08 pm *Katia* Says:

Hi Carol,

did you check out NovaMind? (get details at www.carolbentley.org/NovaMind.html) It has the best of both worlds - flexibranches give you the organic look, and you can move your branches around wherever you like, and they have great graphics libraries etc so you can make great looking mind maps. In NovaMind you also have the ability to make your mind maps really quickly with hotkeys or with their "branchstorm" mode, which is one thing I don't like about iMindMap - it's too slow to make the branches.

So you get great looking mind maps as well as quick and easy creation. I use the platinum version of NovaMind on Mac (they have a windows version too), and love the presentation system - much better than any other mind mapping prog.

All the best
Katia

Reply from Carol

Hi Katia,

Thanks for the info. It's great that so many people are sharing their experiences with the different mind mapping programs available. This is not one I've come across but sounds interesting from how you describe it. Certainly worth a look for anyone who hasn't yet decided.

New Business Tips Worth Looking At. . .

When a well respected UK business coach decides to share his knowledge and experience then taking advantage makes sound sense.

Brian James is just such a person... you may already know him. Brian has recently started his business coaching blog and I know, because I get his regular e-newsletters, his posts will be packed full of useful business tips.

If you don't know Brian then I strongly recommend you pop over to his blog, and browse his site, at www.business-coachinguk.com. You can start by getting 3 chapters from his book for free; he's gifting them just for letting him send you a notification email whenever he makes a post. Talk about something for nothing!

I'm looking forward to getting great ideas from Brian... you can too if you subscribe.

~ Carol Bentley

Date: Friday, February 29th, 2008 at 10:45 am

NETWORKING

Who Needs An Introduction?

In business you are personally at one of two levels:

1. You are well known within your industry, profession or generally. And your company is a household name. You need no introduction because people already know you by reputation. People such as Bill Gates and Richard Branson fall into this category.

2. You and your company are known by the people you deal with (suppliers and customers) and the people you target in your marketing (maybe). If you attend a business seminar or business networking meeting there is every chance you will meet people who don't already know you and don't know you by reputation.

If you fall into category 2 (as most business people do) then you owe it to yourself to know how to market yourself and your company as effectively as possible at meetings and events.

Meeting New Business Contacts

Business networking is a very popular way of spreading the word about what your business offers, finding new suppliers or even companies you can join forces with in your marketing campaigns. And, like any marketing activity, it needs to be properly planned if it is going to be effective.

Over the next few weeks, interspersed with other posts, I'm going to explore how to get the best results from these meetings and, if you are at all nervous, uncomfortable or just new to business networking, I'll give you some tips on how to make it less daunting as well.

Here's some of the posts you can look forward to:

- 9 tips to take the sting out of business networking meetings (specifically for newbies and people who are nervous).
- 8 rules for making business connections.
- Creating rapport with people you meet.
- You met new business people - now what? Getting organised.
- Refer, refer and be referred - the referral matrix - who warrants your valuable time?

These posts will include some useful tools to download, which I will be gifting to you, my blog reader. Make sure you don't miss these posts because even if you are experienced at business networking there are some copywriting gems and other valuable insights you can apply.

This blog is one month old on Friday 23rd and I'm

planning a special 'Thank you for your support' gift for you, as my regular blog reader - more details in **Your Blog Anniversary Gifts** post on page 217.

~ Carol Bentley

Date: Monday, November 19th, 2007 at 12:00 pm

9 Tips To Take The Sting Out Of Business Networking

Active business networking gets results for most types of businesses.

But when you are new to networking, either as a start-up business or as a responsibility in your new job, it can be very scary going to a meeting of business people. Here are 9 tips for networking newbies...

Make the meeting as easy as possible for yourself:

1) Contact the host or organiser, explain you are new to this and would like some help. Ask if you can have a copy of the attendee list BEFORE the meeting.

2) When you get the list, check if there is anyone on the list you know; or a business that your company deals with.

3) Then check who you would like to make contact with; who you would like to meet.

4) Arrange to be introduced: If you find someone (or a company) you know on the list, give him/her a call and ask if he knows the people you want to meet. If he does, ask if he would mind introducing you at the meeting. You now have someone you can talk to immediately you arrive (the person you've just called) and you have a goal to meet someone new, in a safe environment when you are introduced.

If you do not recognise any names on the list, call your host/organiser and ask if he/she would introduce you to the people you want to meet.

5) Arrive early. It is a lot easier to greet people as they arrive and have them join YOU, than it is to arrive later and then try to 'break into' conversations that have already started.

6) When you are introduced to someone make a point to remember his/her name.

7) Ask questions about him (or her); his interests; how long he's been in that business; what's his biggest challenge; what advice would he give to someone like you, who is new to networking (he'll feel flattered you've asked). And *actively* listen to his answer (look out for the post: Networking Meetings - Creating Rapport with People You Meet in a couple of days).

8) When you are asked a question, such as "What do you do?" have a succinct, but preferably intriguing, answer. Don't launch into a full presentation. (Look out for the post: Profitable Business Networking: Part 1 'The Power of The Elevator Speech' and Profitable Business Networking: Part 2 'Creating Your Elevator Speech').

9) Remember – networking is about creating relationships, so consider how you can help the people you meet – and that does not always mean by selling something to him (or her). Think about who you can introduce him to; people who need his services or products, or can supply something he has expressed an interest in that you are not able to supply.

~ Carol Bentley

Date: Tuesday, November 20th, 2007 at 10:00 am

---

8 Rules For Making Worthwhile Business Connections

Before I get into this morning's post, I'd like to say **'Happy Thanksgiving'** to my visitors from the US. I hope it's a good one for you and your family.

Moving on. . .

Do you attend business networking meetings? Yes? *Why?*

Most people, when asked that question, reply "To meet people I could possibly do business with." And yet very often these business people don't prepare before the meeting or make the most of the meeting itself.

Here are 8 rules for making connections at your business networking meetings...

Before the Meeting

1) Prepare before you attend. Is this the right meeting for you? Will the people attending be either your target prospects or target suppliers?

2) What's your purpose in attending? Do you want to find 3 new business contacts you can nurture for sales? Or do you need a new supplier for a particular product or service?

3) If possible get an attendee list before the event.

4) Go through the list and mark the people or companies you are interested in, either as a prospect or supplier.

At The Meeting

5) Learn as much as you can about the people you meet (see the article "Creating Rapport with People You Meet"). Find out how you can help them to find prospects (you create a feeling of gratitude and they make more effort to find contacts for you). Ask "Who/what is your ideal customer?"

6) When meeting other business people ask yourself "Do I know anyone who would be a useful contact for this person, as a prospect or supplier?"

7) Introduce people you have met to others you know at the meeting. Make it easier for them to meet people they don't know... again they appreciate you and warm towards you. And, of course, the other person also respects you for your consideration.

8) Collect the business cards of people who you want to create a relationship with; prospect or supplier. Make notes on the cards: the meeting or event name, date & venue, any comments the other person made that could be useful and, if it is not obvious on their card, what their business is.

Remember **it is more important to collect cards** rather than give yours out. When you collect cards you stay in control because you can make the next contact. If you give your card out, you have to wait for the other person to get in touch with you – and that may never happen.

(Some of these actions will be familiar to you if you read my earlier post - it's the same advice I give to people who are new to business networking).

The next most important activity is what you do after the meeting. Ah, but that's the subject of a future post.

I mentioned in Monday's post that tomorrow this blog

is exactly 1-month old. I also said there would be a gift for my regular readers.

Actually there are two!

Make sure you see tomorrow's gifts post - see **Your Blog Anniversary Gifts** post on page 217

~ Carol Bentley

Date: Thursday, November 22nd, 2007 at 10:00 am

You Met New Business People.. Now What?

You've had a successful business networking meeting. You've gathered dozens, maybe more, business cards. You remembered to make notes on the cards to remind you about the person you met. Now what?

In my early years in business I'd attend business meetings or events and happily gather up the business cards being handed out. When I got back to the office I'd follow up with a few people, who I'd spoken to specifically, but the rest of the cards were put to one side.

Because I went to so many gatherings I soon built up a huge pile of business cards - do you do that?

The problem was for the majority of them I hadn't got a clue who had given it to me (the names didn't really mean anything) or what the company did (I wasn't very good at making notes on cards then either).

Sound familiar?

Follow-up *is* important and before you do that... it helps to get organised... and that's what this technique helps with - I can't remember who told me about it - but it works really well.

1) Sort through your cards and split into 3 distinct piles; Hot, Warm and Cold...

HOT: These are the people who you have arranged to contact, either because they want information from you or you have thought of someone you can put them in touch with or you need something from them. They are the people you are probably more keen to create a business relationship with.

WARM: These are the people who you believe you could do business with, either selling or purchasing, in the future. But you have no strong reason to contact them immediately.

COLD: These are the people who have no direct connection with what you offer; cannot provide a service or product you need and do not easily bring to mind anyone you could connect them with.

2) Take action with the cards you've sorted:

HOT: Contact each person and arrange to meet for coffee or a more formal meeting. Or drop in with the information he/she has requested from you. Or ask for the information you need from them. Remember, if you are supplying information personal delivery makes a good impression.

WARM: Write a letter or email to each person, reminding him/her where you met and what you talked about (actually what THEY talked about is better). Make sure your message talks about him/her and, if you do mention what you offer, make sure you write from their point of view and highlight the benefits your service or product provides.

Have a look at the example letter (you can download it from www.carolbentley.org/mful.html) I give out when I'm speaking on this subject at a business event. Feel free to adopt it for your business.

By the way - because everyone uses email these days, **you really stand out if you send a personally written letter**. Plus you don't have to be concerned about whether or not your email will get through their spam filtering system.

COLD: There is no reason to keep these business cards – so discard them.

3) Keep a close eye on the progress you make with the contacts whose details you've decided to keep... create a chart that shows how you are developing the rela-

tionship. (See my next post: Refer, Refer and Be Referred)

~ Carol Bentley

Date: Tuesday, November 27th, 2007 at 12:00 pm

Do People Remember You?

Are you memorable? When someone asks "What do you / your company do?" is your answer instantly forgettable? Or do you find their eyes start to glaze over as they switch off because they think they've heard it all before.

If so, then it may be an opportunity lost for you.

Imagine - what if you say something that makes them ask *"Really? Tell me more..."* now you have a great chance to shine and maybe forge new, profitable business relationships.

This is where having a powerful, succinct – perhaps even intriguing – elevator speech works magic for you.

The idea is very simple, but extremely effective. Use your copywriting skills to give yourself a powerful or intriguing introduction. Get people to ask for more information – rather than 'switching off'.

The name; 'Elevator Speech' originates from the US

and refers to the time it would take to 'ride the elevator' to the top of a high-rise building – about 30 seconds.

And that's about the maximum amount of time you have to keep someone's attention after they ask "What do you do?" (sometimes even less, but I'll explain how to handle that in another post). If your answer is boring or long-winded he starts looking for a way to 'escape' from you.

There are many 'elevator speech' structures and theories around. I first came across this particular one at a Jay Abraham seminar in London in 1994. It was introduced by one of his co-presenters and the structure made it so easy for a beginner to use.

The 'speech' has 4 specific elements:

- "You know how..."
- "Which means ..."
- "Well, what I do is..."
- "Which means ..."

I thought this was such a brilliant way of introducing yourself I enthusiastically 'spread the word' amongst my own business colleagues.

And something suddenly struck me... an awful lot of them just 'didn't get it'.

Oh, they got the idea OK, and they seemed to understand the principle. But when they tried to put it into practice for themselves they either went on for too long (in some cases the lift could have gone up and down a dozen times before they finished!) or they missed the point of **highlighting a serious problem** and **demonstrating a solution** with a real benefit or an intriguing notion.

Let me tell you about one example...

I'd agreed to give a presentation on business networking with a good friend and business colleague of mine, who organises corporate events and exhibitions and offers training on how to get the most out of attending an exhibition.

Our presentation was at an important business meeting. Now, Chris is absolutely brilliant at networking, but he hadn't come across the 'Elevator Speech' before. We decided it would be a good tool to share with the delegates and Chris agreed to write his own Elevator Speech as a demonstration.

This is what he came up with...

> "You know how some business people attend exhibitions but don't know how to work their stands"
> "Which means they don't get the business contacts they need"
> "Well, what I do is train them how to work the stand properly"

"Which means they get new business from
the exhibition"

Although this was OK; it does actually describe what
Chris does for the exhibiting company, it is unlikely to
hit any 'hot buttons' for anyone listening.

You see, the first statement "You know how..." **must
reveal a hot problem** – whether real or perceived.
Chris' first attempt just didn't state a problem people
could identify with.

So what *is* the real problem businesses see in exhibiting?

Well, for smaller businesses there is a barrier to taking
part in exhibitions (at least there is here in the UK,
maybe elsewhere as well). Entrepreneurs and business
owners find it difficult to justify spending the money
and time on an exhibition.

And it is purely because they don't have a clue of how
to get the most out of it. Chris does – he and his asso-
ciates have over 50 years of experience between them.
So the 'real' problem here is not *'how to work the
stand'* it's *'how to justify spending the money on an
exhibition stand'*.

After talking it through, this is what we came up with:

"You know how some businesses regard exhibitions as a complete waste of time and

effort because they never seem to get any extra business, which means they don't exhibit and lose out on the opportunity to make a high number of business contacts in a comparatively short time, don't you?"

"Well, what I do is train business people on how to prepare for the exhibition beforehand, how to work their stand on the day and follow-up afterwards, which means they maximise their opportunity to make good contacts in a focussed environment, know how to follow-up and get good sales results by exhibiting, making the exhibition a cost effective way of increasing business and profits."

It needed more refining – but the perceived problem for prospective exhibitors had been established.

I'll show you how to create your own elevator speech and give you some important insights on how to make yours even more powerful... plus you can **download the template** to help you create your money-making introduction. That's all in **Your Wow! Introduction** on page 270.

~ Carol Bentley

Date: Wednesday, December 5th, 2007 at 10:00 am

I Responses to "Do people remember you?"

1. December 23rd, 2007 at 5:59 pm *Liz Fuller* Says:

Hi Carol

I found this article on COSBI - absolutely great. I linked to it from my site and recommended Part II as well. Thanks for the valuable information.
Liz

Your Wow! Introduction

In my post **Do People Remember You?** (page 265) I promised another example of an elevator speech and powerful insights to making your elevator speech 'hit the hot spot'- so here goes...

Have you ever been introduced to someone and when you ask what they do they've replied "Oh, I'm an accountant" or "I'm a solicitor/lawyer (attorney in the US)" or "I'm a financial adviser". Ya-awn! *Bo-oring!*

Did you know there are different aspects to accountancy, finance and the law that can be quite fascinating?

No, *really*! But only if they hit **your** hot-spot.

Because when someone says 'accountant' or 'financial adviser' it is *so-oo* easy to assume we already know all there is to know, isn't it?

But how about...

> "Well, you know how some business owners are just too busy to keep an eye on the financial aspects of their business, which means they are often paying too much tax or worse, missing the danger signs of the business heading for insolvency, don't you?"

> "What I do is keep an eye on the business finance, save on taxes and provide timely management reports, which means the business owner can still keep their finger 'on the profit pulse' whilst driving their business growth."

Don't you think that sounds more interesting than "I'm an accountant"?

And once you've got your main 'Elevator Speech' sorted you can distil it down into a 1-liner like this!

"I stop companies over-paying on taxes!"

Developing Your Own Elevator Speech

Find the answers to these questions and you have the start of your elevator speech.

Step 1: What is the *real* problem you solve for people? If not a problem, how do you enhance their life or experience – home, personal, health, wealth or business?

If you're not sure, ask your existing customers or clients what problem they were specifically looking to resolve when they purchased from you.

Step 2: What is the consequence of this problem or lack of something? Are they losing sales? Friends? Income? Home comforts? Experiencing embarrassment? Financial loss? Or loss of status? Again, ask your existing customers if you are not clear about the 'which means...'

Step3: What do you supply (product or service) that addresses this need? How can you resolve their problem?

Step 4: What benefits do your customers enjoy? What are the consequences of taking advantage of what you offer? Are they happier, richer, healthier, more profitable or more productive?

Now hone the answers you've got into short, succinct statements and precede each with the template words:

> **Step 1** "You know how...
> **Step 2** "Which means ...
> **Step 3** "Well, what I do is...
> **Step 4** "Which means ...

Use the template I've created to help you formulate your introduction speech - if you provide solutions for different problems or situations, craft a different speech for each one. You can get your PDF template at www.carolbentley.org/est.html

Nuances to Consider

A few things to keep in mind;

1) Always say "You know how **some** peo-ple/companies/businesses..." Nobody likes to be told they've got it wrong.

You have to be *subtle*; saying **some** people or **some** companies implies it's a problem **other** people or companies have – <u>not you or the person you are speaking to</u>. If he identifies with the situation you de-scribe he can ask questions and if he doesn't, you haven't insulted him by implying he has that lack.

2) Being an observant sort of person, you probably noticed in the examples I included the words "*don't you?*" at the end of the first 'which means', *didn't you?* Including these words gets the other person nodding his head (or thinking "Yes") in agreement with you. It involves him in what you are saying, starts to create rapport and opens him up for the 'solution' you are about to describe.

3) Be specific wherever possible. If you can quote fig-ures that catch people's attention it makes your speech more memorable and people seek you out to learn more.

The figures you quote, which must be truthful because

you may be asked to substantiate them, makes your speech far more credible and intriguing.

Develop and Practice

Work on the real solutions you offer, especially if you can identify something that is unique to you or your company. And use the speech whenever you can. At first you will feel awkward giving this little 'speech'. But after practising and saying it a few times it becomes more natural.

At this stage you might be tempted to change the wording. Apart from trimming it down to an impressive 1-liner, do be careful – the structure is important. You don't want to lose the opportunity to intrigue new people you are introduced to, and gaining the possibility of expanding your business contacts and your profitability. Creating a very 'woolly' version of this powerful technique could decimate your opportunities.

In the post **A Practical Approach to Business Cards** on page 275 I reveal your hidden marketing tool... until then keep working on your Elevator Speech and, if you would like to share yours, feel free to send an email to carol@carolbentley.com

~ Carol Bentley

Date: Thursday, December 6th, 2007 at 10:00 am

I Response to "Your Wow! Introduction"

I.   December 18th, 2007 at 8:13 pm *Adam Donkus* Says:

This reminds me of my sister in law who is a chemist and works for a 3M competitor. I always tell her to tell people she works on the forefront of adhesive technology.

A Practical Approach To Business Cards

The next time you go to a business meeting, where people are handing out their business cards, take a closer look.

Let's assume you don't know any of these people or their businesses in any great depth.

Does their card tell you what they do? And if it is clear, such as for an accountant or solicitor/lawyer (attorney for our US cousins), what makes them stand out from all the other cards you have for people in the same profession? Do you know instantly _exactly_ why they are different and what benefits you could enjoy by doing business with them?

Now look at **your** business card? What does it say about you? About your company?

Is there a clear message that describes what you offer and the results you deliver? If your answer is "No" you are missing a vital marketing opportunity...

Having said that, the content of your business card *depends very much upon how you use it*. If you only ever present it to clients or prospects you've spent some time with then the minimum amount of information is all you need. That's because these people already know you and the purpose of your card is purely to serve as a reminder of your contact details.

But if you attend business meetings, networking with other business people (as we've been discussing over the past few weeks of posts) then your card has to fulfil a completely different purpose. **It has to work harder for you**.

The challenge you, and your business card, is facing is making sure the people you meet briefly *do* remember you and are able to distinguish you from other businesses who apparently offer the same type of product or service. What makes you stand out?

You want to know that when someone else returns to their office or place of business and glances through the, possibly hundreds, of business cards they've collected, yours gives a complete picture.

Now I don't mean it has to be a vivid colour, or a garish design or have wacky graphics on it (although if this is appropriate for your business that's fine).

What it *does need* is information that clearly explains

why you are the 'go-to' company for whatever business you are in.

What Does Your Business Card Say About You?

- Does it clearly show what you do or offer? (Your Company name / logo may not be explicit enough).
- Does it give a testimonial from a happy client/customer?
- Is your photo on there?
- What's on the back of your card - it isn't blank - *is it?*

When I explained to a client the business card is a marketing tool and should include a photo, his response was "I don't want my ugly mug on there" (actually he's quite good looking, but modest). I told him being a 'shrinking violet' was not going to help his business to grow. The intention of the photo is to make your card stand out and make it easier for people to remember you afterwards.

Plus, if you send your card with your literature (and a letter) in the post it gives the person receiving it a sense of confidence they are dealing with a 'real person' – not an anonymous company. Remember 'people buy from people' no matter what size company they own or work for.

The Alternative to Your Photo

If, like my client, you really feel embarrassed about having your photo on your card – try this idea:

Get a photo of you with a happy, smiling client/customer. Ask their permission to use the photo and a testimonial from them in your marketing. Make sure the testimonial is specific, not "Great company, would use again" but something like

"I had problem with the manufacturing costs of our main product line, but the productivity solutions you provided reduced our costs by 31.6% and turned it into one of our more profitable lines".

Put the photo, with the testimonial underneath, on your card. (N.B. if you are a guy get a female customer to pose with you and vice versa).

Designing Your Card

You may decide to get a graphic designer to create the layout for your card. Regardless of who comes up with the design this is what your card should include:

Front:

- Company name
- Your name / position
- Your contact details
- Your photo*
- A descriptive strapline

Your descriptive strapline is a single 'headline' style sentence that encapsulates what your business does. (It could be your 1-liner from your elevator speech that we talked about in the post **Your wow! introduction**). And of course, this is where your copywriting skills come to the fore.

Back:

- Your marketing message: a description of what you offer.
- Testimonial(s) from happy clients/customers (with photo if you don't like your photo on the front)
- Key benefits you deliver

If you are planning to use your cards extensively at business and networking meetings include some space for people to make a note:

We met at................ On (date)............

We spoke about...............................

* If you decide to use a photo with a testimonial on the back of your card then you don't need the photo on the front.

Make Your Card More Memorable

Another way to make your card stand out from the crowd is to have a tri-fold card, just slightly bigger than the normal business card size, and include some useful tips or expert advice. People are more inclined to keep a card that has some valuable information on it and it demonstrates your expertise.

In my post **Another View on Business Cards** (see page 89) I describe things you shouldn't do with your business cards - especially if yours is a start-up company.

~ Carol Bentley

Date: Friday, December 7th, 2007 at 10:00 am

Twitter, Twitter

Have you come across Twitter? There's a lot of interest in Twittering; many people are getting involved. I can understand how it helps people communicate on a regular basis - especially socially. It certainly seems popular with younger people, almost as an adjunct to their mobile texting.

But how can that help in a business environment?

Well - it depends upon your business, how close a relationship you have with your customers or clients and how interested they are in what you are doing and vice versa. And, of course, it depends upon how open you like to be. I don't think twittering suits anyone who prefers to be really private.

But I see it as a natural extension to blogging. It is in effect a micro-blogging facility.

The idea is to post short comments on what you are doing. Or where you are, or something you've found that was interesting that you want to talk about. It is an effective way of keeping in touch with people you care about and sharing your discoveries.

Mind you - it is also a good test of writing concisely - you only have 140 characters for each post! Now *that* will be an interesting challenge

So I've just opened a twitter account at http://twitter.com/Carol_Bentley and popped a few people on my 'following' list.

I'll let you know how it goes... unless you want to experience it for yourself. If you do, simply go to http://twitter.com/Carol_Bentley and click the **Follow** button under my photo.

~ Carol Bentley

Date: Wednesday, April 23rd, 2008 at 2:24 pm

1 Response to "Twitter, twitter"

1. April 27th, 2008 at 2:11 am *Brad* Says:
    I'm following you now Carol. I love your blog and am curious to see what you think. I have done a few good posts in the blogs and forums on my site about Twitter and social media. So far my Twitter experience has been

awesome! I am a believer. I look forward to seeing what
you think.
    -Brad

WEB MARKETING

Blogging for Business Profit

"A lot of small businesses can benefit from blogging!" claimed my web marketing expert pal Ed. "How so?" I asked.

You see I must admit I was highly sceptical when he first said that - after all it's just basically someone pouring out whatever is in their head; a bit like a personal journal - isn't it?

But having watched how Ed has constructed his blog at www.edrivis.com and the immense wealth of information he gives each time he puts an entry in, I started to think a little differently.

After all it's similar to the articles and newsletters I send out; just it's all on-line in one easy-to-access spot. And of course, that means if you want to check back on an earlier article (blog) you don't have to go searching through your emails trying to find it - you simply visit this site to look it up (*or read this book*).

So how does a blog help you in your business? When you consider some experts claim up to 68% of business is lost through apparent indifference then it becomes obvious communication is key to keeping your customers (and prospects) happy. And blogging is a relaxed, informal and easy 'no-brainer' way to do that.

You can share information about your services or products - I'm not talking about your mainstream business marketing here; this is complementary to that day-to-day activity - I'm referring to the snippets you reveal to customers or prospects or discuss with colleagues during your daily business. The little 'aha!' factoids that people in your profession or industry regard as 'normal' but everyone outside thinks is a surprising revelation.

Want to know how to do it? Well the good news is Ed is about to launch a DVD/video called 'Ultimate Guide to Highly Profitable Small Business Blogging' as a stand-alone tutorial - I've already worked through it (I got a copy with his Shrink Wrap Your Brain programme) and he makes it amazingly easy to get started (believe me it has to be for me to bite the bullet as I have done with this blog!

www.carolbentley.org/rubb.html

~ Carol Bentley

Date: Thursday, October 25th, 2007 at 3:08 pm

A Magical Web Of People

I'm off to London for an Internet Seminar this weekend. Now why would I do that and how will it help you?

3 reasons:

1) The people: everyone attending is an entrepreneur - or an embryonic entrepreneur. They all want to know how to create a successful business on the web. There'll be a fascinating breadth of business ideas and people from all walks of life.

Imagine the rich source of stories, experiences and insights to what motivates people that gives me as a copywriter!

Remember, people like to know what others have done and how they've succeeded - especially when it reveals an idea they can adopt for themselves. You never know what tales I'll hear to give you and me a marketing gem or insight.

2) Additional expert knowledge: Although I've written copy for the web, which has been successful, and I have some working knowledge of internet marketing I am not an 'out-and-out' expert on search engine optimising (SEO).

- I know a little html code;
- I understand the concept of SEO to get websites to appear in the first few pages of search results;
- I understand the principles of how PPC (pay per click) advertising works (but not ALL the in-depth secrets to get the best out of it);

- I appreciate the thinking behind landing pages and how to use keywords and
- I already use article marketing to some degree of success (try typing Carol Bentley into the search box on Google).

So, as far as the Internet is concerned, I'm a bit of a 'jack-of-all-trades' - expert in none.

And that's OK, because in an ever-changing arena like the Internet keeping on top of everything is a full time job in itself and it's not my expert area - copywriting is *my* passion.

Of course it's useful to keep a 'finger on the pulse' and that's what I'll be doing at the seminar. Listening to the proven experts and picking their brains for the juicy titbits I can come back and use - and share with you!

3) **Connections:** meeting and networking with all those self-motivating people (they must be self-motivated to give up a weekend AND pay to attend) is rewarding in itself.

Who knows I might connect with an ideal joint venture partner; or find a great supplier for me and my clients (I found 2 champions at the last event I went to!) or even find people who want my copywriting products or services.

That's what networking is all about (I'll be writing

more about business networking skills in a later blog; having done it for over 20 years I've got some useful tips for you).

So I'm taking a short break - travelling up to London tomorrow.

Check back after the weekend - when I'll share any gems I've discovered.

And have a good weekend yourself.

~ Carol Bentley

Date: Thursday, November 1st, 2007 at 2:00 pm

Choose Your Words Carefully

The expert advice, if you are looking for a web domain name, is to find one with the specific keyword or phrase your target audience is likely to use in search engines. Plus, to increase your chances with search engine positioning, it's best (so I'm told) not to separate the words with hyphens or underscores.

As a copywriter I'd add another consideration to that... choose your words carefully! Let me explain:

I'm an avid fan of the TV programme QI and I watched the 'Children In Need' edition last week on BBC4. The host, Stephen Fry, asked the celebrity panel to describe what was being sold on four example websites which were:

- www.therapistfinder.com
- www.whorepresents.com
- www.penisland.com
- www.presentsexchange.com

You can imagine the ribald comments that came out of these names. I've capitalised the words to show the true intention of the domain names:

- www.TherapistFinder.com
- www.WhoRepresents.com
- www.PenIsland.com
- www.PresentsExchange.com

Words chosen perfectly innocently can take on a different meaning when they are run together as web domain names. So - before you settle on a web domain name - make sure it's not going to cause any embarrassment for you.

~ Carol Bentley

Date: Friday, November 16th, 2007 at 10:00 am

Does This Technique Work?

The biggest challenge when sending out a message is getting your reader to respond. That applies to email messages, advertising, direct mail letters and other marketing approaches.

That is the essence of the question Martin Russell from www.wordofmouthmagic.com sent in:

Q: "You send out blog notification emails with a bit of the post in it, so is there any evidence for which is better; title only, part of post, full post?"

A: I got my training on 'how to create a blog' from Ed Rivis' programme on business blogging for profit (read more at www.carolbentley.org/rubb.html). And, initially, I followed his email notification style of sending just the title of the post.

However, I noticed that in email notices I received from Dan Kennedy for his marketing newsletters, he always included the start of his article. Sometimes this intrigued me enough to go and have a look, sometimes it didn't.

And I wondered if giving a bit more of an idea of what a post was about would encourage more of my blog subscribers to visit. Effectively act as a teaser...

So I decided to test this and changed the notification style of my emails (if you've been a subscriber for some time you probably noticed the difference). It is still early days yet but the figures are showing an interesting trend. My average number of daily visitors has **increased by 31.65%** since sending the new style notice.

Now this is not scientific testing because the topics are different so it is not really a fair comparison. I shall keep an eye on the stats.

As regards sending the full post in the email, I'm not too keen on that approach. Not that I've tested anything – it's purely a personal thing because:

1. I would have to be more careful about the wording I use in the post to avoid triggering spam filter programs, which could prevent my messages getting through to you.

2. It would make some of the emails extremely long and I prefer to let you decide if you want to visit to read the full content.

3. If you got the full post in the email, you'd have no reason to visit this blog website. It would be more like an ezine newsletter. The idea of the website is to create a relationship, with the chance for you and me to interact. When you visit to read the post you can use the comment link to respond if you want to; effectively continuing the conversation I'm starting.

4. As this blog site grows, I'll be adding links to useful products I'm developing. If you never have any reason to visit you won't see the links and could be missing out on something that is important to you and your business.

So, on that basis, I don't have any plans to test sending the full post message.

What Are Your Thoughts?

Do you prefer to have an email showing just the post title? Or do you like having the introductory text that gives a hint of what the post is about?

I'd like to know your opinion - post your 2p's worth using the comments link below.

~ Carol Bentley

Date: Thursday, January 17th, 2008 at 10:00 am

2 Responses to "Does this technique work"

1. January 17th, 2008 at 11:45 am *Ed* Says:

    Hi Carol,

The one I prefer the most is the one you tell me results in most traffic! Look forward to hearing the results of your testing.

-Ed.

2. January 18th, 2008 at 12:18 am *Martin Russell* Says:
    There are a few problems with this.

1. The Hawthorne Effect - any change is likely to improve response, just because you changed. It may not be a response to the particular change itself.

2. The long-term training of readers. Training them to decide whether to click through or not based on what you write in the first bit may make it difficult in future.

3. All the points you identify for the full post, still apply to some extent for part posts.

How about a standard vanilla announcement, but with occasional variations to keep people on their toes.

Ahh, the limits of scientific testing.

Good News. . . I Got Rid Of It, You Can Too

It's the online marketing dilemma. You want to encourage people to subscribe to your newsletter, blog, reports or whatever other valuable incentive you've created for your web visitors.

You've studied the best way to encourage people to sign up - as I did - and took note of the experts' opinion about what works and what doesn't.

And then, with gritted teeth, even though everyone I talk to (and that includes me... yes , I admit it I *do* talk to myself) hates those annoying pop-ups I added one to my website. You may remember it.

Did you notice it wasn't displayed this time?

No, I haven't capitulated to the majority opinion (sorry, I do value you and hate the thought of upsetting you) but I've found a way to enjoy the best of both worlds. The power of the pop-up as a marketing tool **and** being able to stop the irritation you may have been experiencing.

Let me explain...

Once you've subscribed - whether it is through the pop-up or the in-line request in the right panel - you'll never see the pop-up box again. *Isn't that great*?

So how did I do it?

Well, I'm sorry to say it wasn't me!

Oh yeah, I implemented it... but the actual method came from a brilliant techie-geek (his words).

If you have a website using pop-ups (because you know they work) then take a look at Hill Robertson's post on page 424 and his offer page at www.carolbentley.org/nopopup.html

Is it worth the bother? Do Pop-Ups really work?

Now, if pop-ups really do annoy you, you might think

it's easier just to ignore using them altogether...

Not a savvy marketing decision based purely on my experience with this website. Here are my conversion stats, take a look and make your own decision:

Using pop-up displayed on every visit:

> Inline conversion (unique visitors to subscriptions): **6.8%**

> Pop-up conversion **16.1%**

Then I tested ***showing the pop up every 5th visit*** you made...

> Inline conversion **3.7%**

> Pop-up conversion **6.8%**

I think the figures speak for themselves.

It will be interesting to see how the new structure works...

~ Carol Bentley

Date: Thursday, January 17th, 2008 at 6:00 pm

Speedy Action Reaps Its Own Reward

Today's blog is a bit shorter and sweet - bet you're glad about that.

How many times have you heard someone say 'people who take action find the rewards' or something along the same vein? Well, it is a truism isn't it? And this post gives you a chance to take a quick and simple action that delivers a valuable (in my opinion) free gift.

You've heard me mention my good friend Ed Rivis on occasion. And you've seen my comments about the advantage of being a published author.

Well Ed is about to join the ranks of being a published author. He has taken his popular ebook, expanded and updated the topics and is about to launch his book; **The Ultimate Web Marketing Strategy** (more at www.carolbentley.org/ruwm.html) into the 'real world'.

And to celebrate he's gifting the unabridged PDF version of the book to everyone who is subscribed to his blog page **BEFORE** 1st Feb. So you see, a simple quick action and you get this informative book for free. Read more about the book on his blog: www.edrivis.com

(**Carol:** *Although this offer is closed you can still get Ed's book through his website or by visiting* www.carolbentley.org/ruwm.html).

Is it worth taking action for?

Well - actually - **YES!**

Ed is my go-to guru when I want to check anything about Internet Marketing. Whenever I get web marketing advice from someone else I go check it with Ed before taking any action.

Ed helped me get this blog set up - so you can thank (or curse) him for everything you've read on here because without his help it would not have been published. And *his* blog is full of good marketing insights - and not just to do with the web.

Pop over to www.edrivis.com and subscribe whilst you think of it.

~ Carol Bentley

P.S.   Ed has agreed to be interviewed about his journey along the road of being an author - which will give interesting insights if you're thinking of positioning yourself as an expert in this effective way.

Date: Wednesday, January 30th, 2008 at 9:45 am

Announcing A New Business Growth Book

This post is giving you very short notice - and I'm sorry if you don't see it in time.

I've mentioned previously about Ed Rivis publishing his book **The Ultimate Web Marketing Strategy** (at www.carolbentley.org/ruwm.html). If you took a look at his blog then you already know about his startlingly low priced 24-hour launch of his book which commenced yesterday (4th March) at 10.30 GMT.

As I write this post that means there is just over 2.5 hours before it goes from £6.99 back to its normal price of £19.97.

The description on the front of the book cover says...

"How everyday business owners can use the world's most tested and proven online marketing strategies to attract thousands of new customers, hyper-gear revenues, boost profits up to 2.5 to 25 times and grow their business or professional practice within the next 12 months or less."

I think that says it all - I've watched Ed testing and proving these strategies over the last year and, what's more, in his book he shares how he's discovered what works as well as explaining what to do.

(**Carol:** *Obviously this offer has now expired – but the book hasn't and is still great value at its full price*).

~ Carol Bentley

Date: Wednesday, March 5th, 2008 at 8:56 am

Landing or Floundering Page. . .

If you have a website and are familiar with the idea of online marketing you may have come across the term 'Landing Page'. An ideal web landing page is designed to target a specific audience with an end result in mind; that your visitor takes the action you want.

The design, structure and content of your landing page all have an impact on the outcome of any visit to your webpage. Are you creating a true *landing* page that makes your visitor feel they've arrived somewhere worthwhile - or do you leave them floundering; wondering why they are wasting their time?

- How exciting is your landing page?
- Is the headline so strong your visitor's eyes are magnetically drawn by it into your message?
- Is the offer you are making compelling? One that no-one in their right minds would dream of ignoring?
- Do you get high conversion rates; you know, the number of visitors who go on to take the

action you're asking them to? That's the *real* test of how successful your landing page is.

Testing each element of your landing page moves you closer to the 'perfect page' - *if there is any such thing -* but having a plan before you start also gives you a greater chance of realising your goal.

Get your landing page planner plus...

Ed (I know, I'm always mentioning him - but hey, why not when he's giving valuable info I believe you can use!) is gifting 3 useful tools for marketing on the web; Landing Page Flow Chart, Web Marketing Tactics and a nifty little tool that calculates the lifetime value of your average customer. And all you have to do is sign up for his blog posting announcements.

So - if you've not yet visited Ed's blog, or if you have signed up but haven't yet checked out your gifts, I suggest you pop over there and grab them now. Visit his post **Three Powerful Resources** (page 427) at www.edrivis.com/?p=227

~ Carol Bentley

Date: Tuesday, March 11th, 2008 at 10:00 am

Some (Web Marketing) Answers

If you asked a question about web marketing, getting

visitors to your blog etc. after completing my latest survey then please check the **Q&A's at this posting** www.edrivis.com/?p=233 on Ed's blog, which may give you your answer immediately [See pages 428 & 434].

I'll be covering the questions that were specifically for marketing and copywriting in my future blog posts.

~ Carol Bentley

Date: Friday, March 14th, 2008 at 8:00 am

Answers To Questions & 3 Gifts

When I asked "What's your most burning question you'd like answered on this blog" in my recent survey there were quite a few people who asked about marketing their websites. From making the website visible, so people could find it - to attracting visitors - to marketing the website on a budget.

And as I pondered the best way to answer these questions - which were very much on the same topic - I remembered I had done something similar quite recently for a new, private client who was not familiar with web marketing.

I created a mindmap showing a web marketing strategy and wrote a brief overview of the different aspects of the strategy. And, because my client is rather busy, I recorded an audio of the report as well.

"Ideal for you guys" I thought. So **I'm gifting the 3 files to you**; the mindmap - in a PDF file so you can open it regardless of whether or not you use mind mapping software; the audio (MP3) and the transcript (PDF report).

Now - let me just point out one thing. Web marketing, as a subject, is vast. And I do not profess to be an expert in all the different ways you can do it. *I'm sticking to my chosen area of expertise - the copywriting aspect - thanks very much.*

However, I do have a broad understanding of how things fit together, purely because I need to know it for my own marketing activities. And that's the approach you'll see in this overview. I hope it helps.

Obviously I need to edit the audio (and report) to take out anything that is personal to my client but the information it contains points you in the general direction of what you need to consider. So it will be ready for you on Wednesday (16th April) [See page 302].

Subscriber Only Gift

Oh, and it is going to be on a password protected post. You will get the password to open the post in your announcement email. Sorry, if you are not subscribed you won't get this. **This is a 'subscriber only benefits' post.**

Of course if you subscribe before the announcement

post then you will get the password too. Simply use the subscription box in the right panel or the one that appeared in the pop-over.

~ Carol Bentley

Date: Monday, April 14th, 2008 at 12:00 pm

*Your Web Marketing Strategy Gift

In the post I made on Monday I promised to let you have the web marketing strategy overview I created a little while ago. Well, here it is.

The download link is for a zip file, **WMS.zip** that contains 3 files:

- WMS-MindMap.pdf - contains the mind map graphic of the strategy
- WMS-Transcript.pdf - the written report of the strategy overview
- WMS.mp3 - the audio of the strategy overview. You can listen to this on your computer or download it to your MP3 player.

You will need Adobe Reader v 5 or later to open and/or print the PDF files.

Here's the download link:

www.carolbentley.org/wms.html

Please let me have your feedback; let me know how useful this overview is for you.

Would you like to see more multi-media sets like this? Send an email to carol@carolbentley.com to share your thoughts, thanks.

~ Carol Bentley

Date: Wednesday, April 16th, 2008 at 2:00 pm

*Finding Your Prospects

Questions asked in my recent survey included:

- "What's the best way to market to potential customers when starting afresh with no prior customer list or contacts?"
- "Increasing visitors to web sites"
- "How to drive visitors to web site"
- "What should I do to make a big impact on-line and off-line without spending a fortune?"
- "How to get more clients"

All of these questions, in one form or another, are asking about finding more people who are interested in what is on offer. It doesn't matter if your business is conducted on or off line; the challenge is the same - finding customers in the most effective and economical way possible.

And very often the way you can do that works well for both on and off line activities.

In his new report Ed concentrates specifically on finding new visitors, contacts, for websites. Effectively increasing the number of people you can market to. Many of his principles can be used in the off-line world as well.

In his FREE report; **'Who Else Wants More Traffic Than Their Site Can Handle'** (get yours at www.nobstraffictactics.com) Ed goes through a 6-part strategy starting with an old favourite of mine. One that has proven to be very successful - for both Ed, me and many other business people.

I strongly advise you to pop over and grab your copy of the report - it doesn't cost you a penny. You just have to agree to Ed giving you loads more valuable info when he makes it available.

Seems like a bargain to me!

Go to www.nobstraffictactics.com

~ Carol Bentley

Date: Tuesday, April 22nd, 2008 at 9:25 am

An Enjoyable Experience. . .

This year one of the most enjoyable projects I've worked on is a website for healthier chocolates. Yes - you read that right **healthier** chocolates.

It was a new product launch from a client who manufactures gorgeous Belgian chocolates in Surrey.

I have to admit writing copy for most of his products is exquisite torture for me... why?

Because I'm diabetic, but I love the taste of chocolate. And unfortunately the two don't really go together.

But the thing is, you cannot write passionately about something you have no experience of, that's why *you* are really the best person to write about *your* product or service.

But this new chocolate is different. It's an innovative antioxidant-rich chocolate.

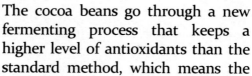

The cocoa beans go through a new fermenting process that keeps a higher level of antioxidants than the standard method, which means the chocolate retains 80% instead of losing 70% of the natural antioxidants found in cocoa beans.

And the better news for me... during my research I

discovered that scientific research had been carried out to check how antioxidants affect diabetics.

And it seems they are good for preventing the development of diabetes type 2 and can even help with blood sugar levels for diabetics. And that's in addition to all the other benefits of having your daily quota of antioxidants.

Now I indulge in my two small pieces of chocolate every day (they are just the size of an after-dinner chocolate you'd get at a restaurant). What's more I've noticed I have a lot more energy and clarity of thought (no bad thing for a copywriter) without upsetting my blood sugar levels.

So you can see why I enjoyed writing the website copy for my client. [www.copywriting4b2b.com/delvaux]

~ Carol Bentley

Date: Wednesday, December 12th, 2007 at 10:00 am

I Response to "An enjoyable experience. . ."

1. December 30th, 2007 at 1:16 am *CG Walters* Says:
   Thank you, Carol.
   Always happy to hear more information about healthier forms of one of my favorite foods....
   Good fortune and good chocolate this new year...
   CG

A Quick Tip - How Not To Forget

A trend I've noticed recently on the internet (well, it's being going on for some time really) is what is known as the continuity strategy. Which is closely connected to the old 'puppy-dog' appeal you may have heard of (especially if you've read my book).

You are invited to try out a subscription or newsletter for a month (sometimes up to 3) and, if you like it, you let the monthly payments start after that.

You and I know as business people we are extremely occupied with what is going on in our business and it is very easy to forget that we've taken up these offers, taken a look at the material, haven't quite decided whether or not it is really useful, intend to decide later... and then forget about it until the first payment is taken. You've got your subscription almost be default.

If the material you are receiving is something you can use and want to carry on receiving, that's fine - no problem. But if it was something that you weren't fully convinced about; you were uhm-ing and ah-ing about then you might feel a bit peeved that the decision was effectively made for you.

Sure, you can cancel - but you've still made a payment you might have decided against.. if you'd remembered to reconsider it.

So here's my tip - if you think it's a blindingly obvious one that you already use, no problem. But if it gives you an 'aha moment' that might save some frustration... and might let you try more offers without worrying about having to remember to make your own decision, then that's great.

What I do...

- 1. Check when the paid subscription starts (1 month, 2 months, 3 months).
- 2. Put a reminder in my Outlook tasks (it could just as easily be a note in your diary) usually 1 to 2 weeks prior to the subscription commencement date.
- 3. When the reminder comes up I review the material I've received and make my own, informed decision.

Simple, eh? But it does save unexpected charges and it saves me scratching my head thinking 'What the heck was that charge for?' when my accounts lady asks.

~ Carol Bentley

Date: Monday, September 8th, 2008 at 3:00 pm.

3 Responses to "A quick tip - how not to forget"

1. September 8th, 2008 at 10:39 pm *Nigel West* Says:

Hi Carol

Good post!

Another method is to use Google calendar, which sends out free SMS messages of events, so there's no excuse for forgetting. We have a calendar for me, one for my wife and one for the kids, all linked so we can see who is doing what. Plus I bought some software that syncs my very old Palm Pilot with Google calendar, so I can see what's going on even when I'm not near my computer.

Everything goes in the calendar, from MOT expiry, with a week's notice, to everyday appointments with 30 minutes notice.

Highly recommended and best of all free (except the Google/Palm software, but that was quite cheap).

Regards

Nigel

2. September 9th, 2008 at 12:27 am *Ian Brodie* Says:

Hi Carol,

I've fallen foul of this one a couple of times - I always think I'll remember, then I don't - so it's a great tip.

Personally I don't like these continuity strategies - essentially they're often designed to make money from your forgetfulness rather than adding real value to draw you in as a customer via the giveaway.

Ian

3. September 9th, 2008 at 11:42 am *Carol Bentley* Says:

Nigel...

Thanks for the additional suggestions - I'm sure people who don't use a PC/Outlook will appreciate the alternative.

Ian...

I understand what you mean Ian. I suppose it depends upon your view and the true intention of the supplier.

The idea of 'try before you buy' is a pretty old selling concept designed to take away the risk for the buyer. So I suppose for many the idea of being able to see the material before deciding if it is right for them is reasonable.

Those who make this offer with good intentions want to make sure you don't accidentally miss an issue - which could hold vital information for your business - so having the subscription start automatically does that.

For the unethical seller then yes, they are relying on people not remembering.

For me I have taken up many of these offers - some I've kept on others I haven't. But those I've kept I don't think I would have gone for at all if I hadn't been given the opportunity to check it out first.

And, in my experience, some suppliers will refund the first payment if it was taken unintentionally - the buyer meant to cancel. If they offer to refund I rarely bother taking it up because I'm happy that the original subscription wasn't set up with any intention of just grabbing the money.

Just out of interest... if you were supplying valuable information for a monthly subscription how would you get people interested and start the payment cycle off?

~ Carol

INSPIRATIONAL

Creating Rapport With People You Meet

How do you feel when you meet someone, perhaps a business person, who you've only seen once before at meeting... and they remember you AND your name?

It feels great doesn't it? And, be honest, rather flattering too. And because of that you probably have more rapport with them.

Now let's turn that around and say it's *you* who always manages to remember people and their names. Do you think they just might be more interested in doing business with you? Or recommending you to their business colleagues who are looking for what you offer?

Here's how to make remembering people easier...

When you are introduced to someone make sure you hear their name clearly.

- Repeat the name and ask if you've got it right.
- Check the spelling with them if it is unusual... they will be flattered that you consider them important enough to take the trouble.

- Repeat the name at least twice, silently in your mind, to give yourself a better chance of remembering it.
- Ask a question and listen

Listening is a Skill – Take Time to Develop It...

The challenge we all have is to silence or ignore our own thoughts. Especially whilst other people are talking.

How often have you drifted off in your mind whilst someone is talking?

Perhaps, like I used to be, you are guilty of finishing people's sentences for them? It took me a while to stop that one, I can tell you! Especially with people who were more precise in their conversation and took their time to finish a sentence, it could be agonising for me.

Or if you don't interrupt, perhaps you are busy thinking about what you are going to say just as soon as they stop to take a breath. Yep, been guilty of that too!

Guilty, that is, until I found this neat trick. Peter Thomson told me about it in the late 1990's and it's a real gem. He calls it **Active Listening**, which is a pretty good description.

It's great for group meetings; presentations; 1-to-1 meetings; in fact any conversations at all.

Here's what you do...

Repeat, internally, everything the other person is saying. I think you'll be surprised at the unexpected benefit you get; here's 7:

1. You don't miss anything important that is being said.
2. You understand the communication better.
3. You give the impression of being very interested in what the other person has got to say (well, you are, *aren't you?*)
4. Your reply, which you won't be in a position to make until the other person finishes speaking, appears considered and relevant because of the slight pause.
5. Your reply is more appropriate because you have completely understood the previous part of the conversation.
6. You do not annoy the other person by interrupting them, ***and the biggest bonus...***
7. You can recall the conversation and important details more clearly, when you need to, at a later date.

By the way, it is a good idea to practise this technique in private or with a group of friends or business colleagues before 'going live'. The other person will find it a bit disconcerting if you stare at them with a glazed look in your eyes. And they certainly will not be flattered if you move your lips whilst repeating their words internally!

~ Carol Bentley

Date: Monday, November 26th, 2007 at 10:30 am

The Power Of Words. . .

Do you ever have a conversation in your head? Do you sometimes criticise yourself - perhaps harshly?

Have you ever stopped to consider the power the words you use have over you?

Because words *do* have power. If they didn't we wouldn't bother writing sales letters using words to persuade people to buy from us.

So what do you say to yourself when you're mulling things over in your mind?

Do you berate yourself for your mistakes, rather than acknowledging you've just eliminated another way that doesn't work for you?

Do you tell yourself you cannot possibly achieve what you see others doing, especially in business? Are the words you use negative and degrading - putting yourself down?

Or do you think of the glass as being 'half-full'? Do you expect to achieve what you plan; use words that are uplifting, encouraging and supportive?

Your thinking affects the way you feel as well as what you achieve, which is why on my office wall I have this favourite reminder...

Watch your thoughts, they become words
Watch your words, they become actions
Watch your actions, they become habits
Watch your habits, they become your character
Watch your character, for it becomes your destiny
Anonymous

If you look at any successful person, whether in business or some other field of achievement, they all have one thing in common - they do not regard themselves as a failure that will never get anywhere. And more importantly, they ***expect to achieve*** what they set their heart on.

Do you?

~ Carol Bentley

Date: Friday, November 30th, 2007 at 10:00 am

6 Responses to "The power of words. . ."

I. December 15th, 2007 at 8:18 pm *theskinnyonjanuary.com*
    Says:

    I do and I agree wholeheartedly. I know I will succeed in my business ventures without a shadow of a doubt. Our words are powerful enough to not only control our success, but our health and everything around us.

Great post!

2.   December 15th, 2007 at 10:01 pm *CG Walters* Says:
    I agree, Carol....words are very powerful.
Words become or reinforce belief, which create reality.
Peace and wonder,
CG

3.   December 17th, 2007 at 6:13 pm *mentalmosaic* Says:
    Good point! Catching yourself in the middle of nega-
tive self-talk is so important. For some reason, we are
often so much harder on ourselves than we are on others.

    You might enjoy my post entitled **"Write Yourself
a Permission Slip"** (read it on page 384 and at
www.carolbentley.org/permission.html)   which
explains a simple and fun way I use to encourage positive
self-talk.

4.   December 18th, 2007 at 1:37 am *Carol Bentley* Says:
    I popped over to look at mentalmosaic's post and it is
worth reading. The post talks about giving personal
permissions - I think it is just as relevant to our business
activities.
    So I'm off to give myself permission to take a break
and enjoy myself over Christmas
5.   January 7th, 2008 at 9:38 am *sara* Says:
    Great advice!

6.   January 13th, 2008 at 6:49 pm *CG Walters* Says:
    Thank you, Carol....I agree.
    "Sacred begins at the tip of your tongue. Be careful
when speaking. You create the world around you with

your words." (Navajo Elder Traditionalist; Two -
Spirit People)
    Peace and wonder,
CG

Failing Is Not An Option

In my last post I mentioned how negative self-talk can
be a hugely demotivating activity. And it reminded me
of what my good friend Max Eames said in his
presentation at a seminar I attended the weekend before last (you can read it at www.maxeames.com);

**"Failure is not the falling down, it's the not getting
back up!"**

...and that really sums up what business, and especially
being an entrepreneur, is all about.

Having the confidence and self-belief to stick at it; as
some people would see it, being pig-headed and stub-
born about making your business work, is crucial to its
success.

So - expanding on from that thought - do you think
about what you could do? See the opportunities as
they arise? Or do you say *"that's impossible - I can't do
that!"*

Have you heard the phrase **"You cannot conceive
what you cannot achieve"**? As Max, who is a psy-

chotherapist explained, "You cannot dream of achievement without having the inherent ability to do it."

Isn't that a liberating thought?

Yes, we may have to study and work hard to reach that goal, but it's not impossible for us because *we* came up with the idea in the first place.

(Having said that, there may be some practical restrictions - I don't think dreaming of flying without a means of doing so - as in para-gliding - is counted as a possibility).

Keep your eyes open for the chances that are out there for you and your business and eliminate the negative thoughts that turn those golden opportunities into impossibilities.

Become a 'possibility thinker'.

~ Carol Bentley

Date: Monday, December 3rd, 2007 at 2:05 pm

How Positive Are You About Your Success?

Just how positive are you about your success or failure - in life or business? Have you noticed the way people think seems to support the outcome they experience?

So tell me, are you a *'the glass is half-full'* or *'the glass is half-empty'* type of person? And does it really matter?

For many years experts have encouraged us to 'think positively' in order to be successful. But some people find that far more difficult to do than others.

And thinking about it, I realised that the worriers in this world; the people who get stressed; the people who agonise over what's happening when things don't go quite to plan are often those who have a 'glass half-empty' approach.

So why have I brought this up? I'll tell you.

I recently received an ezine with an article that gave a very interesting - and quite different view - of positive thinking. In fact it started off by saying **'Positive Thinking Does Not Work'**.

Have you had people say that to you? Maybe that's the experience you've had.

The author went on to say:

"And, not only does positive thinking NOT cause transformation but it could actually be a root cause of people living life in a vicious cycle."

Now *that* caught my eye because I'm one of those

positive, 'glass half-full' people and this seemed to be heresy!

But I'm also open minded and, after reading the remainder of the article, I concluded it not only makes sense, it is also an insightful explanation for anyone who has tried positive thinking with disappointing results.

It might be just the refreshing start you need for the New Year and, even if it isn't, it certainly helps to understand why positive thinking doesn't work for some people.

You can read the full article at **Positive Thinking Doesn't Work** (page 387) (www.carolbentley.org/silbert.html)

My best wishes to you for a prosperous 2008 and good luck with all you aim to achieve this year and beyond.

~ Carol Bentley

Date: Wednesday, January 2nd, 2008 at 11:00 am

I Hereby Give You Permission To...

Many business people are good at putting pressure on themselves to succeed and beating themselves up when it doesn't all go quite to plan. I know I am pretty good at doing that to myself .

In spite of the fact I ***absolutely love*** what I do.

Then, whilst browsing the Internet I saw. . .

> "One day as I was venting to a friend about a
> job I despised, she interrupted and grandly
> proclaimed, 'I hereby give you permission to
> quit your job and do what you truly want!' I
> had to laugh. Her words made me realize that
> the only thing keeping me stuck was that I
> hadn't given myself permission to do other-
> wise."

. . .that was the start of the blog post that caught my
attention; enough to share with you.

You see, as well as sometimes being a little too hard on
ourselves, I wondered how often do we do the opposite and shy away from success. Or avoid doing
something because we feel silly about it; are scared of
the consequences or nervous about what other people
may think?

This post expanded on the idea of giving yourself permission to do or be something different; to - maybe -
get outside your comfort zone and experiment.

And I thought... how about applying it to our business
and career aspirations?

After all - if you own a business - why shouldn't you give yourself permission to fail and learn by your mistakes; to relax and enjoy what you are creating and, ultimately, be outrageously successful?

You can read the original post on page 384 and online at: www.carolbentley.org/permission.html

~ Carol Bentley

P.S.   And how about giving yourself permission to relax and enjoy your family and friend's company this weekend?

Date: Friday, January 11th, 2008 at 10:00 am

4 Responses to "I Hereby Give You Permission To."

1.   January 11th, 2008 at 11:45 am *mentalmosaic* Says:

Hi Carol,
Thanks so much for featuring my article, "Write Yourself a Permission Slip" on your blog. I like your perspective on it, too.
Giving yourself permission to succeed (as well as fail) is so liberating. It's definitely a lesson I learn and re-learn.
Tui

2.   January 13th, 2008 at 3:21 am *Carol* Says:

How about giving yourself permission to only work part-time, to turn away certain clients/jobs/projects and to say "enough is enough"? Sometimes I struggle with being able to say "no" or "not yet." We live in such a high-pressure, do-it-all society; I want permission to define success my own way...Thanks for the thought-provoking post

   (another) Carol

3. January 13th, 2008 at 2:53 pm *Carol Bentley* Says:
   Thanks for you thoughts Carol, I think it is certainly something that a lot of business people aspire to although I suspect that many do not achieve it. It ties in rather strongly with Tim Ferriss' 4-hour work week (check out http://fourhourworkweek.com)

4. January 21st, 2008 at 12:36 pm *CG Walters* Says:
   Thank you, Carol.
Permission to enjoy and grow...is there any better success?
Peace and wonder,
CG

Brainstorm a Result. . .

A little while ago I explained why I migrated to iMindMap from Mind Manager. Chris Ingham sent a message describing the surprising result he gained when he decided to give mind-mapping a try - here's Chris' full message (with his permission to share):

   "Good Morning Carol,

   We'd like to thank you for promoting Tony

Buzan's **iMindMap** (information available at www.imindmap.com/drwriter).

In an exciting and 'full' weekend, we've re-thought our Business Plan totally <u>and</u> committed it to paper.

It's certainly something that I've been procrastinating over for a long time and I've had some great reasons for delaying: waiting for various marketing to run its course, still running a particular ad., not being able to get everyone focused and on-site, etc., etc.

We've found the iMindMap Blue-Print can easily be passed around for input (or not) and with time-limits in place, a speedy result can be on the table in next to no time. I particularly like the fact that the team feel and are involved.

Heading up the particular project is exciting; I (we) can visualise the business growing along with the map. Interestingly, with projects in the past, it's always been an effort to refocus and concentrate on the job to hand; with iMindMap, you just know what's down on the paper and you're (your brain is) in-tune with the content immediately.

For just £58.69 our harnessed, collective brainpower is now a permanent team member."

Thank you for sharing Chris.

If you'd like to get the 7-day free trial you can download it at iMindMap

www.imindmap.com/drwriter

And for those of you who are using a MAC check out NovaMind at www.carolbentley.org/NovaMind.html

~ Carol Bentley

P.S.   My thanks to everyone who sent their best wishes following my earlier post explaining my 'absence'.

Date: Thursday, February 21st, 2008 at 10:45 am

TIME MANAGEMENT

Can You Really Do More In Less Time?

Applying the Pareto Principle to your activities is the way to truly achieve more in the time (or even less time) than you currently have is the claim from some experts.

Although not an exact science, many studies frequently seem to show 20% (or thereabouts) of effort generates 80% of the results achieved.

OK - hands up (mine are already waving high in the air) how much of your time is not as productive as you'd like it to be?

Gary Bencivenga (have you heard of him?) gives a great description in his Bencivenga Bullets newsletter of how this principle applies to copywriters and marketers; how he discovered it for himself many years ago and what action he took to turn it around so he didn't continue to waste 80% of his time.

If you have ever looked back over your day and thought "Where the heck did the time go today? What have I got to show for it - nothing!" then some of the insights Gary shares in this bulletin (and his next one) may give you back a feeling of being in control.

Read ***Bencivenga Bullets*** at
www.carolbentley.org/bencivenga.html

~ Carol Bentley

Date: Thursday, March 6th, 2008 at 10:05 am

3 Time Management Tips And Recommended Reading

I've been taking a peak at some of the questions people have been asking in my blog survey that's currently
running.

And 'how to find the time to do things' whether copywriting, marketing or other activities has come up a
few times. So I thought I'd share with you just 3 effective tips I've discovered and also recommend a book
that I got some good pointers from.

Change Your Mind...

We all have just 24 hours a day (yes, I know you've
probably heard that from *every* time management expert) and I believe that changing how you think of
'time management' is probably the first step towards
using that time effectively. I don't think of 'time-man-
agement'; no - I tend to regard it as 'activity management'; deciding what activity you want to do and
complete in any given workday.

So here's 3 of the tips I've picked up over the years. I bet you've come across them before or you'll say "well, that's just common sense!" True - but does that mean you're using them to make yourself more effective?

1) Get Rid of The 21st Century Time-Thief

Emails! Go on, be honest - how much time do you waste every day on your email? Which of these do you find yourself doing...

- Sorting & deleting spam emails - even with filtering software too many still get through
- Checking your spam-filtered emails in case anything urgent has been caught by accident
- Checking your inbox regularly throughout the day - especially when you're expecting a reply to an email you've sent
- Stopping to read and reply to non-urgent emails - effectively getting distracted from what you are meant to be doing

Guilty as charged m'lud!

Yep - given the chance, I'm a confessed email junkie! And it was draining valuable hours of my time. So what did I do? Simple...

1. I decided on a timeframe when I would check incoming emails, e.g. 11a.m. for morning emails and 3p.m. for afternoon missives for just half-an-hour or less.

2. I had numerous email addresses. I redirected ALL my incoming emails, except those coming to a personal, unpublicised address, to Kelly, my P.A. (Yep, this is one of those solutions where you need someone to delegate to. If you aren't in a position to employ a P.A. I suggest you seriously consider a virtual assistant). Kelly checks the content and forwards the emails I need to attend to personally. You wouldn't believe how much time that has grabbed back for me.

The second action took care of the spam controlling and the distraction problem because I only see emails that are important.

2) Organise and Prioritise

Different people do this in different ways... blocking time in my diary when I intend to do something specific... like working on a particular project; write posts for this blog; work on products; studying (yes, that is continuous for me) and so on works for me.

I prioritise my tasks as I set my time blocks. By the end of the day or week I have a clear picture of what I've achieved and what remains.

I must admit I do get a real sense of satisfaction and achievement as each activity is completed and 'ticked off'.

3) Stop Those Rude Interruptions

The rudest interruption you suffer every day, without fail, is the telephone. Think about it - if you were in the middle of doing something or having a conversation and someone barged into your office and started shouting at you "*Listen to me NOW!!*" you'd be understandably extremely annoyed. And yet that's exactly what we tolerate with incoming phone calls.

The phone is a rude and distracting interruption.

And it is something that, as the business owner or an entrepreneur you need to take control of. Here's my advice...

- *Don't answer the phone yourself.* If you haven't got staff to take the calls organise a top quality, personal telephone answering service. Dependent upon your business I would suggest you do not rely on an answering machine or voicemail. It may not give the right impression to prospective clients. After all, if you call a business number and get an answering machine what do *you* think?

- *Use gatekeepers.* This is obviously part of the previous point. Make sure that whoever is answering your phone doesn't just put callers through without checking with you first. In fact I tell my PA at the beginning of the day if I'm expecting any calls I need to take. All others are a definite "No" and she deals with them appropriately.

- **Make telephone appointments with clients.** If they want to speak to you set a date and time when you will take their call. You'll find that clients are far more respectful of your time if you start your relationship this way.

- **Don't give your mobile phone number out too readily.** I have the same mobile phone number that I started with back in 1995. I have never had to change it. And that is because I do not tell anyone - other than private clients, family and close friends - what the number is. And even with private clients I'm selective about who gets the number. I only ever give it to people who I trust not to abuse it by calling me at ridiculous times of the day. They respect my time and privacy, whilst knowing they can get hold of me in an emergency.

- **Set a time of day when you will follow up on any incoming calls that need your attention.** Perhaps, like with emails, a half hour in the morning and/or afternoon.

- **Set a time of day when you will take calls**, for example from your team or work colleagues, let them know when they can call you and expect to get through. Explain you are not available at other times because you are working on projects and cannot be interrupted.

I appreciate that for many people some of the pointers above may seem to be impractical - but you'd be surprised at just how readily people accept your working method and respect your time.

Worth Spending The Time On Reading...

There are many books, courses, seminars and systems that seemingly offer a solution to this age-old problem of time management.

One of the easiest and most entertaining to read, as well as the most useful, I've found is Dan Kennedy's **No BS Time Management for Entrepreneurs**. Dan's thoughts on the time-wasters we all face every day are sometimes colourful - but I think you'll probably find, like me, that you're frequently nodding in agreement. I'm sure you'll find some good tips in there.

~ Carol Bentley

Date: Thursday, March 13th, 2008 at 10:00 am

Avoiding More Time-Wasters

In the post I made on 13th March I talked about how we can control what we do and perhaps regain some much needed time for ourselves (read **3 Time**

Management Tips (on page 330) or see it online at **www.copywriting4b2b.com/archives/101**) .

Tim Ferriss (author of **The 4-hour Work Week**) describes another time thief in his blog. And d'you know. . . this is one that might be more difficult for some to handle because of the associated guilt certain people are good at creating!

See what you think...
The danger of expectations and the beauty of duty (at www.carolbentley.org/duty.html)

And here are a few pertinent quotes on time management that a business colleague (Nigel Risner – website www.nigelrisner.com) sent to me in his last newsletter...

"Time has a way of getting away from us, because we never have a grip on it during the day..."
— *Doug Firebaugh*

"Learn to use ten minutes intelligently. It will pay you huge dividends." – *William A. Irwin*

"Lost time is never found again."
— *Benjamin Franklin*

"Don't mistake movement for achievement. It's easy to get faked out by being busy. The question is: Busy doing what?" — *Jim Rohn*

~ Carol Bentley

Date: Monday, March 31st, 2008 at 1:00 pm

How Much is Your Time Worth?

Would you like to grab hours of your time back and still get through all the material you need to read, listen to or watch? I share 3 **time-saving tips** to help you do that on page 330!

With so much information; articles, videos and audios swamping us our time is becoming more and more precious, don't you think?

Yes, we *do* want to keep up to speed with anything that can help us in our business, our careers or our hobbies/interests – but sometimes it can get overwhelming. There are just not enough hours in the day!

So how can we keep on top of all this; absorb **all** the material we want without sacrificing the hours we need to do other things?

It's a challenge isn't it?

You see, for me, it was important to find a way of minimising the time I spent absorbing necessary information because I'm carrying out huge amounts of research for new products I'm currently working on.

I'm talking about checking hundreds of hours of audios and videos; thousands of pages of written material; that's only a *slight exaggeration*; I totalled up the pages of the book and articles I've researched for one project and it comes to 2,336!

Fortunately I discovered another 3 tips to save my time and still get through it all; some you'll already know about, others may be a welcome solution.

Here they are...

3 Time-Saving Research Tips:

1. *READING* - I'm pretty certain you already know this one. Speed reading.

Now I'm a pretty fast reader anyway – or so I always thought. Mark, my husband, and I have similar reading tastes when it comes to fiction. So when we buy a new book by a favourite author I always read it first because he takes far longer than I do to finish it.

But I was surprised to discover that my reading speed was only just above average – I say *'was'* because after going through a program with Patricia Hutchings of Unique Perspectives Un-limited Inc. I've **boosted my reading speed 2-fold**. That has been a huge help. (The training is part of Rich Schefren's Strategic Profits program - check it out at Strategic Profits). www.carolbentley.org/ssp.html

If you have a mountain of reading material you need to get through and you've never tried speed-reading training, then give it a go.

Think about it, if it only takes you half or a third of your normal time to read those articles and books what does that mean in saved time for you and your business?

2. *WATCHING VIDEOS* – More and more self-study and information material is delivered by video these days, especially online. And frequently the delivery mechanism is through Quicktime movies. The problem of course is you are stuck with the presenter's delivery speed.

Well, actually *No* – you're not! I'm watching hours and hours of these videos so I was delighted to find a way of speeding up the Quicktime movie-playback:

When you are playing the Quicktime movie:

Press **Ctrl+K** to display the A/V Controls (on the menu **Window, A/V Controls**).

Drag the **Playback Speed** indicator to the speed you want to play it at.

When you close the

Quicktime file it will ask if you want to save the changes. I usually choose **Save** so I don't have to reset the playback speed next time I watch the video.

3. LISTENING TO AUDIO - speeding up audio (or video) can give the sound-track a chipmunk effect, which can be irritating to listen to. So I was really chuffed to get a software package that lets you increase the speed of the audio; MP3 or WAV files - anything up to 3.5 times faster (I haven't tried it *that* fast!) without the high-pitched chipmunk sound.

What I really liked about this software is it converts and saves your speeded-up MP3 audio file into a new file (leaving the original intact) so you can transfer it onto your MP3 player or even create an audio-CD if you have Nero-Burner or similar CD recording software.

The program is called FasterAudio and *Yes!* - this is a blatant plug for it - because I've saved so many research and study hours with it. That's why I think anyone who listens regularly to informational audios needs this in their time-saving arsenal. The online URL is www.carolbentley.org/fa.html

Up to now there was a restriction on the distribution of the program. It is shortly due to go on general release. The good news is I persuaded the developer to let me **tell you about it first**.

It's Not A High Cost

I asked at the beginning 'How much is your time worth?'

Is saving hours of your listening time **worth an investment of £67?**

For me it is a definite **"Yes!"** - but this guy is based in Canada, so he priced FasterAudio in US dollars!

$67!

That means you're only looking at far less than £67 for a must-have, easy-to-use, time-saving audio conversion program.

Will I understand speeded-up audio?

That was the question I first asked myself, and I was surprised at how much I actually do.

But why not listen for yourself? On FasterAudio's website there are audio testimonials from 15 different people - each with different 'normal' speaking speeds. You can listen to them speeded up from 100% to 125%, 150%, 175% or 200%. Find the speed that works for you and then calculate how many hours you could save.

OK, 'sales pitch' over - but seriously it is worth considering the FasterAudio program (visit www.carolbentley.org/fa.html).

An added bonus... FasterAudio also has a slow-down

facility if the presenter you're listening to talks too fast!

I hope these tips help you keep on top of the material you need to know in a lot less time. I'm off to do some more listening - I'll catch up with you again next week.

~ Carol Bentley

Date: Thursday, May 22nd, 2008 at 3:41 pm

FUN STUFF

A Fun Spinner

Just a quick fun post for the weekend... although it might send you crazy trying to figure out what's going on.

I found this post on Lindsay Polsen's blog site, which displays a spinning girl, have a look for yourself at www.carolbentley.org/spingirl.html

The direction the girl is spinning in is supposed to show which is the dominant hemisphere in your brain. I only saw one direction. When I got my husband to look he saw her going in the opposite direction and then, after about 15 seconds, she reversed direction!!

Someone in the comments said it was a flash display - but the blog author said it was a GIF graphic image. And it is. I copied the image onto my desktop and popped it into an Outlook email to see if she stopped spinning (hadn't got a GIF viewer to hand). She didn't - it's definitely a GIF image.

Have fun with it... oh, and if you're curious, yes my creative side *showed dominant* - but when I looked again she had reversed direction which means I rely on realism and words... and you'd expect that from a copywriter wouldn't you?

~ Carol Bentley

P.S   Lindsay's blog shows a collection of advertising and promotional ideas he's gathered – well worth a look. Visit http://stuff4business.com

Date: Friday, November 9th, 2007 at 3:00 pm

Christmas Fun And Looking Forward...

Many businesses are closing over the next week or two for the Christmas & New Year break. For me it's an ideal opportunity to catch up on projects; catch up on reading and - surprise, surprise - do some writing. No, not marketing writing; writing the content for a product I'm crafting - all will be revealed in 2008.

In the meantime I'd like to say a huge **'Thank You'** for visiting this site. I've enjoyed sharing with you over the last few months and look forward to exploring more with you next year.

And to finish off - here's a bit of Christmas fun for anyone who does email marketing...

If Santa was an email marketer... (page 368) (and at www.carolbentley.org/santa.html)

My favourite...

In roughly 10% of houses, Santa would emerge from the chimney to find himself in the trash can and not the fireplace. This despite a squeaky-clean sender reputation.

~ Carol Bentley

P.S.　I might not be able to keep away from you though... so I might slip in a post or two over the holiday period, when no-one's looking!

Date: Friday, December 21st, 2007 at 10:03 am

A Play On Words

OK - it has been an extremely busy week so a few minutes light relief is welcome. Especially something that makes me smile as these did...

The Washington Post's Mensa Invitational asks readers to take any word from the dictionary, alter it by adding, subtracting, or changing one letter, and supply a new definition.

Here are the winners:

　1. **Intaxication:** Euphoria at getting a tax refund, which lasts until you realise it was your money to start with. (my personal favourite)

2. **Reintarnation:** Coming back to life as a hillbilly.

3. **Bozone (n.):** The substance surrounding stupid people that stops bright ideas from penetrating. The bozone layer, unfortunately, shows little sign of breaking down in the near future.

4. **Giraffiti:** Vandalism spray-painted very, very high.

5. **Sarchasm:** The gulf between the author of sarcastic wit and the person who doesn't get it.

6. **Inoculatte:** To take coffee intravenously when you are running late.

7. **Karmageddon:** It's like, when everybody is sending off all these really bad vibes, right? And then, like, the Earth explodes and it's like, a serious bummer. (second favourite)

8. **Decafalon (n.):** The gruelling event of getting through the day consuming only things that are good for you.

9. **Dopeler Effect:** The tendency of stupid ideas to seem smarter when they come at you rapidly.

10. **Arachnoleptic Fit (n.):** The frantic dance performed just after you've accidentally walked through a spider web. (oh, I *sooo* relate to this one!)

11. **Beelzebug (n.):** Satan in the form of a mosquito, that gets into your bedroom at three in the morning and cannot be cast out.

Which is your favourite? And can you go one better and come up with a word and definition of your own? Share your word inventions, hit the comment link.

 **Happy Independence Day** to all my American readers - have a great holiday.

And have a good weekend.

~ Carol Bentley

Date: Friday, July 4th, 2008 at 9:00 am

I Response to "A play on words"

I.   July 7th, 2008 at 8:16 pm _Tom_ Says:

Taken from the Categories section on your blog 😊

Inspirrational - False prophet/guru blindly leading unquestioning followers with unfounded faith

Web Murketing - Pornographic sleazy content visible only through squinted eyes

Business Trips - Pithy advice handed out by marketing gurus who either should know better or will never know…

Copywrithing - Ecstatic convulsions induced by the pen

Fun Stiff - Corpse who's the life and soul of the party

Natworking - Social inept attempting to ingratiate themselves to procure business (Silent eponymous prefix of 'G') ☺

GENERAL

Daily Dose? What d'You Think?

Keeping in touch with people is important. But so is making sure you're not annoying them with an excessive overload of information. And although Internet experts say that daily blogging is a good thing, I'm not so sure.

Do you think a daily post on this blog is too much? If you like getting these snippets daily let me know using the blog question contact form you can find at www.carolbentley.org/ask.htm. (Why not send your most burning copywriting or marketing question at the same time?)

If I don't get a deluge of messages saying "Keep going - I love what you send" I'll temper my posts and do just 2 or 3 per week, with an occasional flurry if something important crops up.

Look out for my post announcements on Tuesday, Wednesday or Thursday. Oh, by the way tomorrow's post is '**The 8 Elements of a powerful letter**' (page 17).

~ Carol Bentley

Date: Tuesday, November 6th, 2007 at 10:21 am

Reasons to Unsubscribe...

Sometimes stopping a subscription is the right thing to do. If the information offered is not useful to you, or it doesn't supply valuable insights to what you need to know then making that decision should be your choice - and your choice alone.

Which is why you have complete control over the notification emails from this blog website. In every email notice you receive there is an unsubscribe option. If you use it you get a chance to say why you are leaving the group, which is good feedback for me as the host.

One gentleman did that when he dropped out last Friday. His reason? "Too many emails"

I wasn't sure if he meant he was *generally* getting too many emails or if he was specifically referring to the number of emails about this blog.

Either way I totally understand how he feels and I'm sure you do too! Does cancelling his subscription mean he will miss out on the future posts? Maybe - but not necessarily.

Keeping In The Loop Without Emails

So what do you do if you want to know about the posts made so you can choose what to read, but you don't want the daily email?

You can use the RSS feed in the bottom right panel. If you are not familiar with RSS feeds you can read Ed's description (printed on page 425 for you or read it online at www.edrivis.com/?page_id=17). It can feed each new post through to your desktop without sending emails.

Disadvantages of Subscribing

In the early days of this blog I was undecided about how frequently I should post; daily, couple of times a week, weekly or even monthly. Although my subscriber numbers at that point were quite low - were you one of them? - I asked those readers what they would like to see. The feedback I had was very positive and the content of most of the messages was similar to Gail's comment:

"I don't think there's anything wrong in blogging every day as long as the content is useful and informative to the readers! With your blog, every post so far has had something worthwhile in it!"

(Gail is still a subscriber, thanks for sticking with me Gail).

So I went with the majority opinion and I've continued the daily blog since - of course that means you get a *daily* email. Actually it's only sent out on weekdays, I take the weekend off.

However, I appreciate for some it may be too much

with all the other emails bombarding their inbox.

Disadvantages of RSS Only

On the surface there may not seem to be any real disadvantage to using an RSS feed to get your notifications. You can still see when a new post goes up and choose whether or not to read it.

Where you *do* lose out with an RSS feed is accessing any private posts I make. Why? Because these are password protected. And the password is only released to email subscribers.

"So what? Will I really miss anything by not being able to read the private posts?" you might be thinking.

Well, actually, *yes*!

I've only used the private post once so far when I shared a birthday gift. But there are more in the pipeline. They will include more valuable information, sometimes in the form of a free report or audio or video and the only way you can get it is with the password supplied in the post notification email.

What Do You Do?

It's a dilemma isn't it?

If you don't subscribe you don't get the extra goodies I gift from time to time.

If you do subscribe you get a daily email when a post is published.

The **good news** is - it's purely your choice. And it's instantaneous - subscribe and you are immediately 'in the loop'. Unsubscribe and you never get another email about posts on this blog again.

I hope you choose to stay subscribed, but I fully understand and respect your decision if you decide to use the RSS feed instead.

~ Carol Bentley

Date: Thursday, January 31st, 2008 at 10:45 am

I Response to "Reasons to Unsubscribe. . ."

1. January 31st, 2008 at 9:40 pm *Brad Trnavsky* Says:
   Great post Carol.
   I have struggled with many of the same issues on my blog and am wrestling with them again as I launch my new site. I learned more in 5 minute on this site about how to get traffic to stick with me than I have in a year of blogging!
   Thanks! —Brad

Things Do Not Always Go To Plan...

No matter how well we plan ahead sometimes things just don't go as we'd hoped. And that's what has happened which is why I'm sending an apology and asking for your patience and understanding.

Let me explain; when I started this blog I made a commitment to you, my reader, to make a daily (well, week-daily) post. When I had days out of the office scheduled I simply wrote up the posts in advance and set a date and time for publishing. That way I kept my promise and you got your daily dose of my thoughts.

If you are a regular reader you may have noticed I've missed a few days this week. The reason for that is a completely unexpected absence from my office (actually I'm still away). That is because my Father has had a sudden, serious stroke which the Doctors do not expect him to recover from.

I'm sure you appreciate my family must take precedence. So, please forgive the erratic posts that may happen over the next few weeks. I promise my usual daily post will resume as soon as possible.

Thank you for your understanding.

~ Carol Bentley

Date: Friday, February 15th, 2008 at 9:30 am

2 Responses to "Things do not always go to plan..."

1. February 17th, 2008 at 12:53 pm *Jirel* Says:
   Hi Carol,

I discovered your blog from Carnival of Inspiration and Motivation. The problem you are facing may happen to any one and I think it will not have much effect with your readers even if you post after some days. You have clearly   explained   the   reason. Anyway, help your father in his hard time.

2.   March 2nd, 2008 at 2:18 pm *InvestorBlogger* Says:
Yes, it's best to be with your father at this time, for sure. Don't worry about us, we'll still be here!
Kenneth

OTHER BLOGGERS' INSIGHTS

In this appendix I have included the contents of blog posts where the author has given permission for me to do so.

I deliberately decided to ask these authors about including their articles so you can enjoy, and benefit from, the insights they share in their articles without having to sit at your computer to read their post online.

I've shown a smaller URL for their post so you can use it to visit their website to explore their other posts and I strongly recommend you do that. There is a wealth of sparkling, innovative and thought-provoking articles written by these people, which is definitely worth reading.

All the material in this appendix is the copyright of the original author as indicated at the end of each post.

You can learn more about each author in the short bio at the end of their post (if there's more than one contributing entry from an author I've included the bio at the end of the first post). Because some of the authors are offering you free gifts, I've also created a **Bloggers Biographies** section where you can quickly check back for their website addresses.

Category: Business Tips

*Why Almost Everyone Struggles More Than They Should

Published by Rich Schefren on January 2, 2008
at www.carolbentley.org/ystruggle.html

It's great to be back. The time off was fantastic but I'm ready to dive back into work. I hope you are too.

Taking time completely away from work is a necessity for many reasons. But before pressing on here's a reason you probably never thought of, and more importantly what it can tell you about yourself and the business you are in...

If your business is the ideal business for you - you should've noticed a certain feeling over the break. With each passing day away from work you should've felt a tension drawing you back to work. It keeps building with each passing day away until you just couldn't take it anymore. Finally to simply keep your sanity you NEED to get back to work.

If you have no idea what I am talking about, odds are you are in the wrong business. If you took a (long enough) break and weren't itching to get back - you need to evaluate your business and determine if it's right for you. If your business is not calling you back while you're away, it's likely you're not playing to your strengths.

I've written about playing to your strengths often, so I am not going to dive deep today - but hopefully the whole reason you decided to go into business (aside from the money) is do something you love doing daily.

To put this issue to rest, here's a plug for our product that gets great reviews from our clients - Strengths Mastery (at www.carolbentley.org/ssma.html) - It's designed to help you know exactly what your strengths are. This way you can build a business designed to leverage your strengths - so you make more, and you love what you do (because you're good at it).

Too many entrepreneurs find themselves in improperly designed businesses and it's a real shame. If you're not sure what your strengths are, and how you should build your company around it, you should really check out Strengths Mastery.

(visit www.carolbentley.org/ssma.html).

Alright, enough plugging, let's get back to the real purpose of this post: Why almost everyone struggles more than they should and how to easily fix it.

I discovered long ago if I wanted to continually improve my company and my own performance I need to leverage my past experience for all it's worth.

Stated more simply - To make 2008 the best it can be, you need to analyze what took place in 2007. You need to identify every nugget of knowledge your past performance offers and leverage it for all it's worth. If you do, you can count on 2008 being the best year of your life.

Unfortunately the vast majority of people and companies don't learn enough from their mistakes or their accomplishments. It's like everyone is simply plugging along with their heads down. Similar to the pattern Bill Murray's character, Phil Connors, in the hilarious movie Ground Hog Day.

But, instead of repeating the same day over and again, both companies and individuals seem to repeat the same outlook, approach, and strategies.

Look, no matter how good or bad your results - we can always do better. Yet, the single biggest key to improving both your performance and your results seems to go ignored by almost everybody. If you want to be at the top of your game you absolutely must learn from what has already happened.

I am going to share with you how I do it, this way you can make 2008 your very best year (so far).

All you need to do is answer five questions. If you're serious about your success then you should do this today!

Ready, set, go....

Q: What Were Your Greatest Accomplishments In 2007?

Even if 2007 was the worst year of your life, odds are if you look close enough there's something somewhere to be proud of.

If 2007 was a great year for you, then this question is even easier.

Here are a three business ones from my list this year:

1 Writing both the **attention age doctrine 1** and **attention age doctrine 2**
(visit www.carolbentley.org/saad.html)

2 Creating the **business acceleration program** (visit www.carolbentley.org/sbap.html)

3 Developing the **strengths mastery program** (visit www.carolbentley.org/ssma.html)

Now, if you were to see my notes you'd see several takeaways under each of these. You should do the same.

So, after you've identified each and every accomplishment, go back to each one. This time through identify what you learned or were reminded of by each of them.

Q: What Were Your Biggest Disappointments Of 2007?

Practically every company and individual resists analyzing their mistakes. That's a shame because this is where the best learning comes from.

No matter how great everything in life is going - we all make mistakes. The trick here is to really analyze them, what preceded them, what could you have done differently, and how can you prevent them in the future.

Even though 2007 was the best year of my life so far - I still had my share of disappointments both personally and professionally.

I won't bore you with the details but once you have your list - once again, identify the big takeaways.

Q: How Did You Limit Yourself Last Year and How Can You Stop?

Were there certain actions you took or didn't take that came back to haunt you? If you're even the least bit honest with yourself you'll be able to build your list.

In order to make sure you don't limit yourself again - you need to bring these self-defeating actions to the surface, shine light on them, and most importantly determine what you must do differently to make sure you don't make the same mistakes all over again.

Here are just a few of mine...

1 not reviewing my goals daily
2 not sticking to a daily sleep schedule
3 hoping things would work out well in a few situations where my gut told me not to

Of course, just like you did with the earlier questions, identify the takeaways.

For example, one of the big takeaways for myself (even though I know better) is when I don't review my goals daily I get sucked into what's currently happening and easily get distracted from what's most important. That caused me to miss the mark on a few goals I had set out for myself in 2007. I now know I won't make the same mistake this year. What about you? In what ways did you limit yourself and what can you learn from it?

Q: What Did You Learn from the Last Three Questions?

This is where it all gets interesting. Remember the goal of this exercise is not simply to know yourself and your business better but to actually to use the information to make certain 2008 trumps 2007.

What are the big takeaways from answering the first 3 questions. What do you know about yourself or your business that you didn't realize or weren't thinking about?

Here are two random nuggets (from my complete list of 62) I gleaned from the exercise...

1 Creating products, programs, and free material to help entrepreneurs and their businesses grow consistently gives me my greatest feeling of accomplishment. Therefore I need to spend time daily on creating these materials and not let the fast growth of our business pull me too far away from what I do best.

2 For strategic profits to positively impact even more small business owners we have to religiously stick to our schedule of introducing new front end products. We cannot allow ourselves to deviate from the schedule no matter how great things are going, because client acquisition is the lifeblood of any business.

You should shoot for as many distinctions as possible because it's here that the rubber meets the road. It's these distinctions that'll practically guarantee that this year is the best year of your life.

Obviously, having this list isn't going to do it all (although it'll do a lot all by itself). You still need to take this new knowledge and USE IT!

Fortunately, that's what the last question is centered around. And here it is...

Q: How Can You Use This Information to Make 2008 Unrivalled?

The idea here is to build in to your schedule, your interactions, your management style or whatever else you've surfaced in question 4 and build yourself a new better approach.

For example, I've already scheduled into my daily routine 2 hours a day of content creation, and 10 minutes every morning to review my goals.

Plus, I've already slotted on my calendar a weekly 20 minute appointment with myself to surface and then analyze whatever concerns I have.

Of course, I have a lot more - but you get the point. Besides, it's not important what I am going to do to make 2008 great - it's what you are going to do yourself to make 2008 great.

So, once again the questions are:

Q: What Were Your Greatest Accomplishments In 2007?

Q: What Were Your Biggest Disappointments Of 2007?

Q: How Did You Limit Yourself Last Year and How Can You Stop?

Q: What Did You Learn from the Last Three Questions?

Q: How Can I Use This Information to Make 2008 My Best Year?

OK, now that we've ensured 2008 will be the best year of your life, here's a quick update:

The **Business Acceleration program** was a smashing success (visit www.carolbentley.org/sbap.html). We hit our projected sales targets in just 32 hours.

What do you think of the process I just shared with you and what new observations did it spark for you?

They call Rich Schefren the "Coach to the Internet Gurus".

His unique philosophy about how to build real businesses online gets big money results for his clients. And that's the reason he formed Strategic Profits in 2004. Read more from Rich at www.carolbentley.org/ssp.html

~ © Rich Schefren

You Must Spend Your Money and Time Wisely

Posted by Hill Robertson on January 19, 2008
at www.carolbentley.org/hrspend.html

To run a successful internet business, you need to value your time and understand what it is worth to you. If you really take time to think about it, you are probably spending a lot of time on "business activities" that you can better outsource or otherwise take the load off your own plate.

It can be easy to get in this trap because you feel like you are working on your business and taking the next step. You may very well be doing that. However, can you spend that time on something more productive that you can't outsource? Let's look at this in more detail.

When I started my internet businesses, there were many services I could have outsourced easily. There was also software I should have bought to be able to do certain tasks of my business.

Instead, I looked at the cost involved in outsourcing the services and purchasing software. So, in order to "save" money, I would write my own software that would accomplish the same goal as the services and software. But did I really save?

I would find a software product that would help me do a certain business task that I needed to do. It would cost $200. I knew I could write my own software to do the same thing. I would code it up myself so I wouldn't have to spend the $200.

However, it would take me 40 hours to complete the software. Let's see, that is $200/40 hours. That works out to $5/hour. That is less than minimum wage! I haven't worked for minimum wage since I was 16 years old. I certainly wouldn't want to work for that today. Yet, that is exactly what I was doing. In addition, I lost that 40 hours that I could have spent with my family. That 40 hours is gone forever. All for a measly $200.

Of course, if you are starting out and don't have any money, you may have to go this route to some degree.

But really think about the value of your time compared to what it would cost to accomplish the same task through outsourcing in some way or another.

There is a cost to everything whether it costs money, time, or both. You can always make more money but the time is gone forever. Think about how you are spending both and then spend your money and time wisely.

Hill Robertson is the ultimate geek when it comes to creating websites.

He got started building websites from scratch in the early days of the Internet just for the fun of it. His fanatical hobby evolved into several successful internet businesses. He loves to share his success principles about the Internet, business, and family on his blog at http://hillrobertson.com and what's more, he talks in plain English!

~ © Hill Robertson

Category: Fun Stuff

If Santa Was An Email Marketer....

Posted by Mark Brownlow on December 10, 2007
At www.carolbentley.org/santa.html

1. Nobody would get any presents unless they wrote to Santa explicitly asking for them.

2. The gift wrapping would have a little transparent window in it, so recipients could see the contents of the parcel without having to unwrap it.

3. He would pack each gift twice. Once in colored gift wrapping and once in plain brown paper.

4. Some people would insist on just the plain brown paper version, citing the pre-color printing origins of gift giving as justification.

5. The message on the accompanying gift tag would be limited to 50 characters.

6. In roughly 10% of houses, Santa would emerge from the chimney to find himself in the trash can and not the fireplace. This despite a squeaky-clean sender reputation.

7. He would address the problem by getting Rudolph whitelisted at major urban conurbations.

8. He would still get 100% open rates, despite the fact that his delivered content is often low-value or irrelevant.

9. Nor would he get many people reporting his gifts as unwanted (even though some of them are) and opting-out of future deliveries.

10. He would not need long to work out the "best time to send."

Mark Brownlow is an independent web publisher, writer and accredited journalist. With the emphasis on independent. He published his first email newsletter in 1998 and has been in and around the business of email marketing ever since. His 2001 book on creating e-newsletters that have influence and impact is available for free at www.carolbentley.org/bnewsletter.html

~ © Mark Brownlow

Category: Copywriting

How to Craft a Compelling Headline

Hubpage posted by Carol Bentley on Feb 9, 2008
At www.carolbentley.org/hub1.html

Your headline can make or break your promotional piece, whether you are doing on or offline marketing. I know - you've heard it all before; "You must have a compelling 'grab-them-by-the-throat', 'can't-look-away' headline if you are going to have any chance of your reader responding."

Think about it. When you're browsing the web or scanning a magazine or newspaper, or even reading your mail are you concentrating absolutely 100% on what you are reading - unless it pulls you unrelentingly in?

If that headline doesn't make you exclaim "How the heck did you know that?" when it asks the question that's been bugging you for ages. Or "This solution is *so* what I want - it's almost uncanny!" then your interest may easily slip away.

And *your* reader is no different!

It's a challenge we all have no matter what our line of business or how we go about our marketing.

Is there a 'no-brainer' way to come up with the most

outrageously effective headline that grabs your reader's attention? Not really - there are techniques; there are attention words that help to make your headline stand out; but it still takes practice, experience and skill to find the one that pulls no punches, hits the mark dead on and delivers the best measurable results.

But hey, we've all got to start somewhere so here's a few tips for you, starting with a mindmap you can download and keep as a reminder. Simply use the link after the picture to view full size/colour in your web browser, then right-click and choose **save image as**.

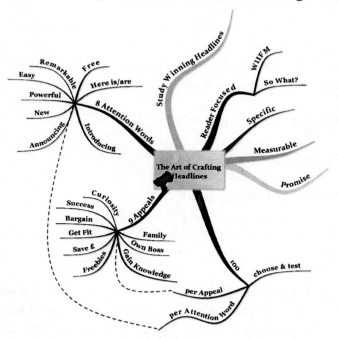

View & download at **http://hubpages.com/u/200409.jpg**

Get Your Creative Juices Flowing...

Don't fall into the trap of writing one or two headlines and thinking "That's it!"

Sorry, I doubt it!

When you start crafting your headlines you are only just getting warmed up - your creative performance is still in first gear. As you write more - allowing each headline to act as a catalyst for the next - they begin to flow, like sliding into the higher gears in a high performance car.

That's why I recommend writing as many headlines as possible before deciding which ones to test. Personally I aim to write at least 100, if not more. I'll show you a simple process to help you do that in a moment.

But first prepare your mind...

Study Winning Headlines

Search out winning headlines.

How do you recognise these? Look for these attributes:

1. It's a headline for a direct response advert or sales letter. You can tell if it's a direct response marketing campaign because there is a reference code. You are asked to quote it or it is printed on the response

form or in the advert. It is measurable and is being monitored.

2. You see the same headline all over the place and it's a direct response advert or letter or webpage; these type of headlines are only used if they are continually successful.

Study the headline.

Is it specific? (Being specific makes your headline more believable)

Does it contain the promise of a result or benefit that appeals? (People are only interested in results; 'What's In It For Me?')

Does it intrigue without being obscure? (Curiosity can hold your reader's attention provided your first paragraph is strong).

What is the appeal; envy; greed; pride or status; generosity; well-being or health; peace of mind or something else? (You need to know what your target market is looking for - and you may have to test different appeals to see which is the strongest motivator).

Here's 9 Proven Appeals to test:

- Crave success
- Love a bargain
- Want to get fit

- Dream of being your own boss
- Want to gain knowledge
- Anything that helps or protects the family
- Curiosity
- Anything that shows how to / does save £
- Freebies

Is it short or long? (Your headline should be long enough to get your message across).

Is it using any of the attention words that magnetically draw the eye and catch attention? (See the short list of example words below).

Attention Words

Using specifics, identifying a benefit or result your reader will enjoy, or a problem they have that you can solve, makes your headline more compelling. Including one or more attention words increases the attraction because certain words are proven to draw the eye - just like a magnet.

Here's 8 to get you started. Look for others in the headlines you're studying:

- Remarkable
- Powerful
- New
- Here is/are
- Announcing
- Free
- Easy
- Introducing

The Secret of How To Make Writing Scores of Headlines Easy

When I said to aim at writing 100 headlines to give you the best chance of finding the winner, did you think "*No Way!*" or something similar? It seems like an insurmountable task - doesn't it?

Try this:

Grab a pen and paper

Look at the first attention word in the list above

Now look at the list of appeals

Think about a descriptive headline about your product or service; the result you can deliver or the problem you can solve, using that word and write one for each of the appeals. Follow the headline advice I've given you earlier in this article.

Wow! You've already got 9 headlines!

Now take the second word and do the same again.

Continue down the list - by the time you've used each word **you have 72 headlines**.

They won't all be fantastic - some may even be ridiculous, but the point is your creative juices are starting to flow and...

You've written over two thirds of your 100 headlines!

Think you could repeat the exercise again? Do it and you've flown past the 100 headlines target! Not bad going eh? Now you've got your headlines you can start working on your letter or advert.

Comment on Hubpage (printed with permission)

Cari Adamek **says:**

I thought you were nuts about trying so many different headlines. After coming up with 25 or so, I changed my mind. Several of my later ones were much better than my first few. Thanks for the tip!

My reply:

Hi Cari,

LOL - I know what you mean 'cause that's what I thought when I was told the same thing 'way-back-when'. Since then I've frequently found it is the later headlines that hit the mark, which is why I devised this way of making writing so many headlines a bit easier.

I usually set up a mind map with the attention words and then add each headline as I think of it. It means I can jump all over the place as new ideas come to mind without losing the flow.

Good luck with your writing projects.

~ © Carol Bentley

Outline of a Winning Letter

Hubpage posted by Carol Bentley on Feb 28, 2008
at www.carolbentley.org/hub2.html

Busy people often 'scan' through a sales letter (or website) that has attracted their attention - they want to gather the essence of the content and offer so they can make an instant decision; *"Is this sales letter interesting enough to read through or shall I just dump it?"*

Provided your offer is strong and very relevant, people who are interested, and who like details, may well read every single word of your letter, provided of course it is not boring.

Other people, who are not so 'detail orientated', read as much as they need to understand exactly what is being offered, how it benefits them - what it does for them - and what it costs.

They may not read every single word after they've gleaned the relevant detail - and this is where your sales letter sub-headlines help because they draw the reader into the important sections they also need to be aware of.

Either way, to be successful, your letter has to marry

with both types of reader.

To help me do this I often create a 'skeleton' or outline of my letter and offer and then 'flesh it out' with more detail, anecdotes, examples, testimonials, facts and figures.

Start with a skeleton outline of your sales letter

Outline of a Compelling Sales Letter

Creating your 'skeleton outline' also helps you to be clear on what you are going to include in your sales letter and how you are going to make your offer 'come alive' for your reader.

This is what your skeleton represents; use this picture as an at-a-glance reminder of what your winning sales letter - whether on or offline - should include.

The skeleton gives structure to your sales letter...

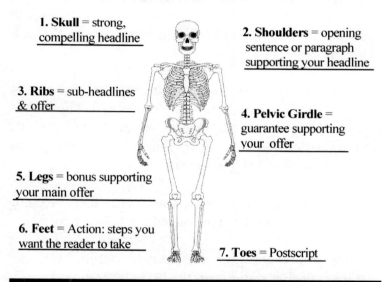

Outline of a Compelling Sales Letter

1. Skull = strong, compelling headline

2. Shoulders = opening sentence or paragraph supporting your headline

3. Ribs = sub-headlines & offer

4. Pelvic Girdle = guarantee supporting your offer

5. Legs = bonus supporting your main offer

6. Feet = Action: steps you want the reader to take

7. Toes = Postscript

The **skull or headline** - as you already know - is the most important element of your letter.

The **neck and shoulders** 'support' your headline and are the opening sentence or paragraph of your letter. It should expand on the promise you made in your headline.

The **ribs** represent your sub-headlines and the offer itself. These give your letter its shape. Think of them as short 1-liner sentences, similar to what you would put in a telegram. The gist of the offer or message can often be gleaned from these short sub headings.

Your **guarantee** is supporting your offer - it is your demonstration of your confidence in your product or service. It is taking away the purchasing risk from your buyer and in your skeleton is represented by the **pelvic girdle**.

One good way to encourage your reader to respond to your letter is to offer bonuses or a free gift. The **legs** of your skeleton are the **bonus** or gift you're offering your reader if they act and follow the **action steps** (which are the skeleton's **feet**).

And finally your **P.S.** is the **toes** of the feet. 'Keeping you on your toes' - by writing a good P.S. or two.

Once you've got your skeleton, or outline, you can start to flesh it out; create the body by adding descriptions, testimonials, case studies to fill your letter out.

Use These 8 Techniques to Make Your Letter Attractive

When you've got the content sorted here are a few techniques you can use to make your letter attractive to look at and easy to read.

Most of these tips apply to both on and offline sales letters...

1. Keep your sentences short. Use simple words that are easy to understand. Unless you are writing to people who speak the same technical language as you do, don't use jargon.

Think about how you would describe your offer if you were talking to your best friend. This is the language you use in your letter.

2. Use short paragraphs - 6 lines or less. Long paragraphs give a 'solid' appearance, which does not encourage your reader to tackle it.

It is perceived as hard work and creates a barrier for your prospect. Aim to cover just one point in each paragraph.

3. Don't finish a sentence or paragraph at the end of a page. (This is specifically for letters you are sending offline). You want your reader to continue onto the next page... a split sentence or hyphenated word entices them to turn over so they can finish the word or sentence. People rarely want to stop mid-sentence!

Plain is Best...

4. Don't go overboard with fancy fonts or colours. Adding too much colour and large, fancy fonts screams 'sales brochure' at the reader. It's a little different for the web, but you must still keep it easy-on-the-eye for your site visitor - too many stylised fonts looks amateurish.

5. Use bullet points (in printed letters use indented paragraphs) to make your points stand out. Don't be tempted to use fancy symbols for your bullets; just a simple • gives the best effect.

Link Your Paragraphs to Create a 'Flow'

6. Link your paragraphs so your letter 'flows'. These links are known as transitional phrases - sometimes called 'the bucket brigade'. They lead the reader smoothly from one paragraph to the next.

Use links such as:

>'The thing is...'
>'But that's not all...'
>'Now - here is the most important part'
>'And in addition...'
>'Better yet...'
>'You will see for yourself why...'
>'What's more...'
>'But there is just one thing...'
>'Make up your mind to...'
>'Take advantage of this opportunity to...'
>'Now - for a limited time only -'
>'Think about it...'
>'Interestingly enough...'

'To help you do this...'
'What you do next...'
'Now - here's an added feature...'
'So - let me ask you...'
'But first...'
'The Result?'

These are just a few of the hundreds you can use - you'll find some work better than others - it depends upon your target audience.

Keep It Personal...

7. Write your letter to a specific person. Have a picture in your mind of your ideal prospect or reader. Start your letter with the person's name; "Dear John" or "Dear Mrs Allen". When you've finished your letter, go through and replace the name of the person you've written to with someone else's. Does the letter still work? If not, scratch it and start again.

8. Always, always, *always* sign your printed letter with a hand-written reflex-blue signature. Never use a computer generated 'handwriting' font and do not get someone to p.p. your letters. Both of these give the recipient the impression they are not important enough for you to take the trouble.

Even using a signature graphic on you web sales letter may help lift response if it is appropriate to your target audience... it's worth testing. BUT - don't use a real signature image, I'd suggest just your first name or a nickname - rather than your full signature which could be downloaded and mis-used.

This article is adapted from Chapter 10 of my published book **I Want To Buy Your Product... Have You Sent Me A Letter Yet?** which is a step-by-step, easy to read and follow instruction on how to write your own winning sales letter.

~ © Carol Bentley

Category: Inspirational

Write Yourself a Permission Slip

Posted by Tui Bijoux on April 7, 2007
at www.carolbentley.org/permission.html

One day as I was venting to a friend about a job I despised, she interrupted and grandly proclaimed, "I hereby give you permission to quit your job and do what you truly want!"

I had to laugh. Her words made me realize that the only thing keeping me stuck was that I hadn't given myself permission to do otherwise.

So now, whenever one of us is hesitant about the next step in our lives, the other will say, "Would you like a permission slip?" It's our playful way to remind each other that the only real limitations come from within.

Since then I have made it a habit to write up a "Cosmic Permission Slip" for myself from time to time. Here's what I do:

I create a new file in my word processor and begin with the phrase, "The Universe hereby grants me permission to..." and then quickly fill the rest of the page with anything - and I mean anything - that comes to mind, "...sleep in, stay up late, buy new pants, write a novel, feel whatever I feel, paint my toes, make mistakes, snore, follow my heart, create artwork even if it sucks, be as happy as I want, be cranky, say goodbye to toxic friendships, be a hermit, go dancing, contradict myself, have fun, change my mind, do what makes me feel the most alive," and so on.

It's important to fill up the entire page, because often, about halfway through, I will hit upon areas that make me feel uncomfortable. It's tempting to stop at that point, but it can be very enlightening to push on through your resistance.

It was while writing up a Cosmic Permission Slip, for instance, that I realized how many issues I had around the idea of whether or not I deserved the kind of life I desired.

I encourage you to try it for yourself. Quickly fill up a page granting yourself permission to do anything that comes to mind, then slowly read back through your list and observe your feelings.

Does any of it make you feel embarrassed or uncomfortable? Do you catch yourself thinking, "how selfish?" or "how silly?" Those are the items to explore. Those are the places you are stuck. Ask yourself, "Why haven't I given myself permission to do this particular thing?"

Now go back to your list and choose five or six items that feel especially important to you and your current situation. Write or print them onto a piece of paper.

I have even laminated one the size of a business card to carry in my purse before. After all, a Cosmic Permission Slip is just as important - if not more so - as a driver's license or credit cards.

In case the idea of making a Cosmic Permission Slip still sounds silly to you - why not give yourself permission to try something silly?

And perhaps it will help you to know that Albert Einstein once said, "If at first an idea is not absurd, there will never be any hope for it."

So, go ahead. Make yourself a Cosmic Permission Slip. You have my permission!

Tui Bijoux divides her time between Italy, London and the Pacific Northwest. When not battling jet lag, she enjoys composing music, writing, photography and blogging at her website www.mentalmosaic.com.

~ © Tui Bijoux

Positive Thinking Does Not Work

Posted by Cindy Silbert at
http://www.carolbentley.org/silbert.html

Recently, a client told me about a conversation she had with her brother. She shared the personal transformation work she was doing with him and how it was helping her business. He responded with, "You know...this positive thinking stuff doesn't work." And then he went on to say that no matter how "positive" he had thought in his past, he still experienced limitations in his career.

My reaction was to feel sorry for this poor man who obviously doesn't "get it". I discussed it with my client and we completed our call. The next day, I had an epiphany as I realized that my client's brother was absolutely right.

"Positive" thinking doesn't work. And, not only does positive thinking NOT cause transformation but it could actually be a root cause of people living life in a vicious cycle.

The act of thinking positive to overcome negative thoughts adds a layer of confusion to a person - taking them further away from personal clarity which is one of the keys to manifesting what you desire. And in turn, positive thought to overcome negative thought leads to positive action to overcome negative action causing a person to take two steps forward and three

steps back not leading to anything but frustration, irritation, stress and more confusion.

Many people are looking to the Law of Attraction as
the answer to fulfilling their desires. The Law of Attraction says that by thinking positive you create a
positive vibration and attract positive things in your
life.

What most people don't realise is that if you are
thinking a positive thought to overcome a negative
thought or are trying to change your life out of need or
fear, your efforts are cancelled out.

Your mind weeds through all of this effort and puts
out a vibration aligned with the source, which is fear
and thoughts about what you don't want.

In addition, most people aren't prepared for the fact
that when you try to change undesired thoughts and
break free from what your mind has determined a safe
and familiar place, your so called negative or non-de-
sired thoughts get louder and louder.

People like my client's brother can't take the self-in-
duced mental abuse and give up trying to improve
their thoughts.

So, what DOES work if positive thinking DOES NOT?
The real secret is connecting with your desires in a
way that they are not something you think, they are
actually who you are and a foundation for how you

live. So how do you connect with your desires? Shifting from thinking to creating is the key.

During the act of creating there is no place for positive or negative thoughts. Creating connects you with your desires and puts your mind to work in a different way. Creating propels you forward and negative/positive thought patterns fall away. When you are creating, you naturally connect with your inner self so your mind is active but it is free of pre-conditioned thought.

Positive thinking does serve a purpose. Revealing your positive thoughts can reveal your negative thoughts and revealing your negative thoughts can reveal your fears and revealing your fears can reveal your desires and revealing your desires can provide the foundation for shifting from the unproductive negative/positive thinking cycle to creating.

By revealing these layers of thought, you welcome them rather than resist them allowing you to let go and create something new. The more you shift to creating the more your thoughts will follow what you are creating - replacing the vicious cycle with manifestation of your desires.

This is part of an article by Cindy Silbert.

Read the three-step process, for shifting from the negative/positive thinking cycle to creating a life that fulfils your desires, in the remainder of the article at www.carolbentley.org/silbert.html

Cindy Silbert is the ultimate guide for successful women who want to thrive in all areas of their life from home, work, love, body and soul. She is an Author, Coach, Speaker and Creator of Life Cultivation, a fusion of eastern and western practices that transforms your personal or business life through one-on-one coaching, books, workshops and online programs.

She founded Bring U to Life, Inc.. and www.cindysilbert.com to inspire and guide women across the globe to full self-expression and lasting personal fulfilment.

~ © Cindy Silbert

Category: Marketing

The Word of Mouth Dentist

Posted by Martin Russell on November 27, 2007
at www.carolbentley.org/womm.html

One of the first people I ever came across who had really mastered the art of 'Word of Mouth' was an Australian dentist named Paddi Lund.

In fact in "Word of Mouth Magic", the whole of Chapter 4 is devoted to just a few of Paddi's ideas and leverage points. It's that powerful.

Paddi is famous for such quirks as:

- not having a front counter, but instead having individual private booths with your name on the door

- serving 23 types of tea (on a menu) in Royal Doulton tea cups
- having a "V8" cappuccino machine in the entrance way
- giving his clients "dental buns" to take away which are delicious but good for your teeth
- having a locked front door
- doing zero advertising
- being unlisted in the phone book
- saying he is not in dentistry but in the "happiness business".

More importantly, and the reason I followed Paddi's material, is that he had found a way to make his solo practice By-Referral-Only, AND make 6 times the money of the average Australian dentist only working 3 days a week AND have fun too.

That's a model worth copying! So I dove head first into Paddi's stuff.

First his small book "Building the Happiness Centred Business" which is actually about his personal transformation from pathological depression to happiness, in business and in life.

Then I took on his complete series of workbooks on all aspects of his business.

No I did not follow all his methods in my own practice. In fact I discovered many ways in which I either couldn't, or more often, didn't want to mirror what he had done. However some things did stick.

One of these is in fact one of the biggest WOW! factors in my practice. That is having a "Welcome Book".

I already had introductory information that I sent, but I restyled it to more match Paddi's suggestions and took the name "Welcome Book" to heart.

To this very day I use it in my counseling practice and it still receives admiring comments and guides people into my practice, even though I have updated it only in minor ways since my first development phases back in 2001.

Any business can use the idea. When people first come to you they are thirsty for more information about you, and your best word of mouth advocates will want you to tell them more.

It was hard for me to set it up initially, but I began with a simple template and let it grow, and now it such a vital part of pre-educating people about how I run my practice that, as Paddi says, "I wouldn't work without it."

Want a simple WOW!?

Make up a Welcome Book. Hey, copy mine if you wish, from my consulting section at www.DrMartinRussell.com, or get Paddi's full How-To package which currently costs Aust$599 (about US$550)...

Whatever you do, make sure you have some way to educate your best clients right when they want to learn more about you.

But I was reminded of Paddi's stuff because I was sent an email from the publisher of his books. Yes, that's right. They have been following me up by email and by mail for 6 years now!

Is your follow-up system that long and that reliable?

It was about his book on referral systems he calls "Mobilizing Your Customer Sales Force" aka Secrets to a By-Referral-Only Business.

I highly recommend you check it out at **Solutions Press** (www.carolbentley.org/mobilising.html)

It now has a convenient downloadable version that wasn't available back when I bought it.

Martin Russell is a medical doctor with a difference. After creating his own counselling practice in 2001, he decided to share his experience of building his business through referrals. www.WordofMouthMagic.com is the incredibly successful result.

Martin's passion, in both his counselling and in business, is helping people get access to incredible tools that make their lives easier and their efforts more rewarding, both in business and their personal life.

~ © Martin Russell

Write Press Releases that Sizzle

Posted by Ed Rivis on February 5, 2008
at www.edrivis.com/?p=199

Part of my book launch strategy involves submitting press releases - lots of them.

Now many people don't bother with press releases. I've been one of them. But recent research has proven that even Internet only businesses can benefit immensely from frequently submitting press releases.

One example of such research was conducted by Marketing Experiments (find out more by visiting www.marketingexperiments.com).

They ran a 6 month trial where they submitted seven press releases, relating to specific items on either their own or third party owned web sites.

The content of the press releases were mostly announcements about things like changes in pricing structure, mention of third party press coverage, and even basic announcements like new team members.

Through careful tracking they measured an extra **3,000 new visitors** as a direct results of those free press releases. Not bad.

Would you like to attract up to 3,000 or more extra, and highly targeted visitors to your site, for free? By responding to press releases prospects are pre-qualifying themselves — anyone who visits your site from one is more likely to respond than someone who clicks on a single link or small Google Adwords advert for example. That's also been proven.

Other benefits they reported include an extra 12,500 incoming links to their site.

(Explained in the section of my book – The Ultimate Web Marketing Strategy - about link building.)

Given that the major search engines count the number of links to any web site as an indication of it's authority — which has a direct impact on search engine rankings, having an ongoing press release strategy as part of your business systems could be highly beneficial.

But all this leaves us with one, ahem, 'minor' issue. **Writing them!**

What on Earth do you write about?

Obviously for the kind of results reported above you need to write press releases that sizzle.

Terry Dean has just written what I think is one of the best free courses about press releases anyone has written on the Internet. (**Author Note:** *see the following included post from Terry*)

It's a fantastic resource, as is Terry's blog. Highly recommended.

Ed Rivis has been in the web industry for more than 10 years. He's learnt all the strategies and tactics in his book, **The Ultimate Web Marketing Strategy**, through extensive training, experience and - most importantly - testing. His straight forward approach brings you an easy to read, jargon busting and fully comprehensible book that delivers web marketing techniques you can start implementing immediately.

Ed also shares his expertise in regular posts on his blog at www.edrivis.com

~ © Ed Rivis

*21 Ideas for Hot Press Releases

Posted by Terry Dean starting on January 30, 2008 at www.carolbentley.org/deanPR.html

Step one to generating publicity is coming up with a hot story. After you come up with a hot story, then you'll learn how to deliver it to the media. This is the first post about 21 idea generators to help you come up with hot stories the media will love. The hot story could be compared to your business USP. It is the basis of everything else that happens. In fact, one of the hot story ideas could be your USP!

As you read through these methods, pay attention to ways you could combine multiple ideas into one press release or story. You could have an outrageous claim which piggy-backs on national news while giving away free information. You could give away a free report revealing the 5 scams perpetrated in your industry (combining 3 techniques).

You might have discovered a solution to a problem and tie it into the human interest story of one of your clients. Most of the hottest ideas are combinations of multiple ideas. What other ideas could you come up with?

Hot Publicity Idea #1: Traditional

You can send out the "normal" press release about the new person who was hired or how you became a member of the million dollar club. You can let people know you're opening a new office. You may have hired 13 new people. You could have released a new product or started a new service. You might get a short blurb from these releases, and a few people might even see it.

Just don't limit yourself to this type of release. Let's say you send out 12 press releases this year. You're allowed a couple like this. They won't be big winners, but they can get you a little publicity. They're also easy ones to create in between your big ones to make sure you stay in the habit and in the news.

It's also possible local or small media might pick up a release like this and add to it or save it for later. If you haven't been sending out press releases, this is an easy way to get started (just don't get discouraged when it doesn't produce incredible results overnight).

Hot Publicity Idea #2: Outrageous Claim

Now we're cooking. What kind of outrageous claim or promise can you fulfil? What is the ultimate benefit you deliver to your clients and customers? Two great examples of this type of release come to mind. Robert Allen originally built his information empire on the outrageous claim, "Send me to any city in America, take away my wallet, give me $100 for living expenses and in 72 hours, I'll buy an excellent property using none of my own money."

That's an outrageous claim. The LA Times eventually took him up on this, and he met the challenge by buying the properties in less than 72 hours. His publicity immediately took off and his "Nothing Down" book sold like hotcakes.

The second example is an offer Paul Hartunian makes. The headline on one of his most popular press releases is, "I Can Help Anyone Find the Love of Their Life in 90 Days or Less!" He then sends out the release just before Valentine's Day. Do you think that is popular? He says the media call him like crazy when he sends out the press release. People are lonely and always looking for love.

Some media people will want to immediately do a story on it. Others will want to put him to the test by finding him the biggest loser they can for him to test it out on.

What kind of outrageous claim can you make? What are the big benefits you help people achieve? And how quickly can you do it? The one condition with this is you must be able to back up your claim. Eventually the media will call you on it and you better be able to produce the goods. If you can't make it happen, then don't make the claim. You'll be exposed as a fraud in front of their entire audience. That's the one kind of publicity you don't want!

Hot Publicity Idea #3: Share your Unique Selling Position

If you've done a good job creating a unique selling position, it's a pretty incredible claim on its own. You can use it as the basis for your press release. This is especially true if you guarantee your focus statement in some way. You're essentially issuing a challenge to all the other businesses in your market niche. Just like the outrageous claim, you had better be able to back it up.

The idea behind this type of story is that you're offering something totally unique in the marketplace. The reporter or interviewer will be doing their entire audience a service by sharing your information. Just follow the rule that you're telling, not selling.

You're providing information on what you can do for people, not trying to sell everyone on it. This is accomplished by being lower key in your presentation. You're an educator, not a salesperson.

Focus on the facts and cut out the adjectives. Your press release must simply answer the question of why their audience would be interested in what you offer. The more unique you are, the better this works.

Hot Publicity Idea #4: Piggy Back on National or Local News

Find the hot story and get in front of it. Listen to local radio stations and read the local newspaper. Use the Internet and list www.cnn.com as one of your favorite places. You can also use Google News at http://news.google.com.

Both of these sites will allow you to quickly scan the top breaking news of the day. Even if you do business exclusively in your local area, world news is still valuable to your market.

The media you'll be contacting use these sources themselves. If you can tie your local news angle into a hot story of the day, you've got it made. The same rules apply if you're promoting a product in a larger area or simply want traffic at a website. Piggy-back your story on what's already going on.

If oil prices are high, how can you tie in your story to that news? If you're a car dealer, it means that the cars which get high miles per gallon are hot. If you're the furnace installer, it means clients who buy your new energy efficient furnace will save 37% more this winter.

If you do pizza delivery, it means people save more buying from your delivery drivers than going out to eat. If you're a travel agent, maybe people should book their trip now before rates go up.

If the hot news of the day is that interest rates are rising, how does that affect your audience? If a new medical breakthrough occurred, how does that affect your clients? If the IRS just announced they're doing more audits, what does that mean in your business?

Begin looking at all news as an avenue for more publicity in your business. On election night, prepare a press release which is ready to go no matter who wins (just edit it with the name of the new winner when it's announced).

If you're a real estate agent, the press release can be about how the new president is likely to affect home prices. The accountant might discuss tax laws. The lawyer may discuss laws. How does whatever happened affect you and your clients?

Hot Publicity Idea #5: Expose Scams

What kind of scams go on in your industry? This one is an exciting topic to get into because it has a two-fold effect. Not only do you generate free publicity, but you're also seen as the good guy. You're exposing all the dirty rotten tactics for what they are.

This strategy might not make you real popular with certain business people in your industry, but you don't need to be friends with people pulling scams anyway. I wouldn't ever mention names because then you bring on a lot of legal liabilities, but you can talk about the methods used to scam people.

The real estate agent could talk about scams listing agents do to get more business. Or they could talk about deceitful tactics used on buyers. The dentist could talk about how some dentists get you to pay for unnecessary work or do poor work on your teeth. The doctor could talk about health or nutritional scams.

The personal trainer could talk about fitness scams. The person who wrote an ebook on learning the guitar could talk about overpriced guitar sellers or how to spot a fraud instructor. The list here is endless. Any type of business can point out scams which take place in their industry.

The keywords are, "How to spot a Fraud in..." Or, "How to Spot Deceitful Tactics Used By..." "How _____ Rip You Off." What goes on in your business that's pretty scummy? What would a show like Dateline or 20/20 love to do to expose your industry? This is what you're dealing with here. This is a hot topic. It can be controversial. And it definitely benefits the media's audience.

Hot Publicity Idea #6: Free Information

Give away free information. If you've created a free report for lead generation in previous weeks, here is a perfect place to use it. Your press release can be about the free report and then the call to action at the end of the press release could be for people to contact your office to receive the free report.

Make sure you're using a real free report in this instance. While the information in the report can lead them back to buying your product or service, it must have valuable information in it by itself. Even if they never contact you again, the report must still make their life better in some way.

This shows how you can get multiple use out of one of your marketing techniques. The report can be used for lead generation in your advertising. It can be used to build an opt-in email list on the Internet. It can be used as your publicity hook to get free advertising.

You could also pull out a section of the free report and offer it as an article for newspapers, magazines, ezines, or websites. Can you see why I like those free reports so much?

Hot Publicity Idea #7: Lists

This is similar to the last publicity idea, but it goes one step further. You're providing free information here, but you're actually placing that information in the body of the release itself (this makes it easy for someone to publish an article). In the above idea you were essentially teasing the audience to call for a report.

Here you demonstrate your knowledge by giving the list of information.

You could build a tip sheet such as "7 Best Ways to Generate Traffic to a Website," or "3 Secrets to Improving Your Child's Education." We're following the model I already gave you of a specific number of tips to achieving a benefit. You could also talk about myths in your industry. Examples of this may be "5 Myths About Going to a Dentist," or "7 Myths About Furniture Buying."

Since press releases need to be short (1 page with 1.5 spacing or double spacing is normal), you have to keep your lists very concise. Don't try to give too many tips at once. This is not the place for your "13 Ways of Building a Doghouse" report. You also don't give much supporting information. Each tip or myth only gets one to two sentences about it. So make sure all the information is easy to understand.

Hot Publicity Idea #8: Charity

How can you tie in your business to a charity? Maybe

you're the sponsor of the newest charity fundraiser. You may have closed your office early to have your staff all help out the charity. You may be hosting a special charity sale for an entire weekend.

All proceeds from the sale go directly to the charity. Perhaps one of your lead generating products is being sold with all profits from that sale going to charity all month. The grocery store could donate food for the homeless shelter. Maybe you're appearing at the new charity fundraiser where you're giving away free massages.

Notice how you can work with charities again here in publicity.

Last week we discussed working with charities on joint ventures. Anytime you setup one of these deals, you need to contact the media about it. They can help drive the success of your deal. The "halo" effect of the charity you're working with becomes doubly effective when the media begins talking about it.

Hot Publicity Idea #9: Contests

Run a contest. Give away a car. Give away a free $2,000 package. Give away a gift certificate worth $500 off anything you offer. Come up with something for a contest and then run it. Your contest could be a simple sign-up, but that's a little boring for publicity.

How about a pick the score of the upcoming high school basketball game contest (that's tying into local news)? Run a "Dumbest thing you've ever done with _____" contest. If you sell cars, this could be the dumbest thing you ever did with your car.

Or you could run a, "Name the New Burger" contest. If your restaurant just released a new monster burger, you could have people give you the best name for it. You pick the best name and give them a prize.

Radio programs are always giving away prizes. You could offer your product or service as a prize they can give away. It gets you free publicity on the air while taking advantage of the contest interest. This is an easy way to run a contest, but it has one big weakness to running your own contest. You don't get to collect all the leads. You get the mention, but not the follow-up.

Hot Publicity Idea #10: Events

Are you having a special event? Maybe Friday night will be kid's night and a magician will be in your restaurant. Rent costumes and let all your employees play dress-up for the day in your retail business. Try to earn a spot in the Guinness Book of World Records for something. Let someone else try to earn a spot in Guinness at your location.

Hire a band. Hire an Elvis impersonator (or some other impersonator). Create the world's largest taco, cookie, hot dog, or hamburger. Hold a free advice day at your business.

Most business people are boring. Come up with ways to make buying from you an experience or an adventure. You don't want to compromise your integrity or your business image, but you do want to be interesting. If your business isn't fun, then you're not doing something right!

Some people are wound up so tight they haven't had an interesting idea in decades. Be willing to be different. If you try something and it doesn't work, try something else!

Hot Publicity Idea #11: Awards

Create an award to give away. It could be the "Best Teacher in New Castle, Indiana" award. It may be an award for a police officer or fireman/woman. It could be the Hero award for someone who's rescued someone (great way to tap into local news again). Maybe it's an award for the fittest person in the city. How about a, "Most Inspirational" award? How about an award for the person who has done the most to help the poor or homeless in your area?

There are numerous awards you could come up with (both serious and humorous).

The publicity can be generated in multiple ways. Maybe you need people to sponsor someone for the award (contest). That needs to be in the news. Then once you pick the award winner, you can have a ceremony (event publicity). Give them a prize which will help them and identify with your business.

You could even turn your award into an annual event where you pick a new individual each year. Reward someone for good work while building your business.

Hot Publicity Idea #12: Human Interest Story

This is one of my favorites. Do you have a strong human interest story? Did you start with nothing and build a successful business? What caused you to start the business you're in? Did a salesman inspire you and you have to go into their field? Maybe your mother or father did what you do, and you've followed in their footsteps. Has your business been in your family for 3 generations? Tell the story.

Did you come to America to start your business? Did you overcome a childhood disability? Were you orphaned as a child? Is there anything you've overcome in your life? People love a "Rocky" underdog story.

I didn't keep it a secret that I delivered pizzas for Little Caesar's before I first started my very successful Internet business. I started with nothing back in the day before anyone knew you could earn a profit from the Internet.

Everything I built was through simple trial-and-error of what worked...and what didn't. It's an interesting story whenever I tell it. People are excited to learn I didn't come in with a business degree. I didn't graduate college. I didn't apprentice to some successful marketer. I delivered pizzas. Then I became a success on the Internet. It's a human interest story.

Maybe you can't come up with an exciting story of your own (or you've already used it to death). Do any of your clients have an interesting story to tell? Are they using your products or services in an unusual way? Have you helped them overcome anything in their lives? Who in your client list has a story to tell?

How can you help them tell their story while creating publicity for your business? If none of your clients has a story either, then you definitely have a boring business and life.

Hot Publicity Idea #13: Solutions to Problems

Running a business is all about finding problems and solving them. This is a more straight approach than many of the other methods. You tell the problem and the solution to the problem. Many non-fiction book authors use this simple model. Their book explains how to solve a problem in your life. Then they discuss this problem and solution in press releases, interviews, and articles.

What problems do you solve? What problems have clients recently presented to you that you've helped them solve? Are there any "interesting" problems you've ran into that you've solved? Have you seen any problems discussed in the media lately that you know how to solve?

I'm going to beat the rule into you over and over again until you're moaning it in the middle of the night, "What's in it for me?" What problems does the media's audience currently have, and how can you or your business solve those problems for them?

Hot Publicity Idea #14: Niche Your Solution

The last idea was simply to find a problem and solve it. Now we're going to do the same thing, but we're going to get specific. For example, chiropractors solve problems with pain. This publicity idea is for them to go after people who have tennis elbow. Or they could focus on runners or bike riders. Or they could just target people with migraines. Or they could focus on children.

The essential idea behind this method is you take the overall problems you solve and you niche them to be more specific.

I could take some of my information and niche it to just one business industry. The real estate agent could niche to only discussing condos in their press release. The car dealer could niche to only discuss people with credit problems. The carpet cleaner could niche to discussing homes with dogs. Or they could talk about homes with smokers who have children. The women's clothing store could talk about their executive women's special day. The men's clothing store could talk about their niche just for managers.

Any of the ideas given throughout these tips can be niched into a more specific sub-section of your clients. You may only have one or two press releases you do that target this niche, or you might make it your overriding publicity goal. Send out a release or two and see how the project turns out. If it's wildly successful, run with it. If it only produces meager results, try something different.

That's what makes publicity so exciting. You can test an idea for less than $100 (try to start any normal business for $100). And you'll know quickly whether the idea is a winner or not.

Hot Publicity Idea #15: Controversy

Start a fight. The media loves controversy. Watch TV any night and you'll realize quickly people love controversy. Challenge something everybody believes to be true in your industry. Find something that will cause a debate with differing view points.

It could be as simple as doctors discussing different ways of treating a patient – each one believing their way is the best, of course.

The idea on exposing scams is part of the controversial approach as well. Expose some scams people don't know about or that the industry will defend and you've just created a world of controversy.

If you really want to go full bore, pick something that is a very emotionally charged issue if you can stand the heat. This would include anything that discusses religion, politics, sex, etc. If you do go this route, you'd better be prepared for the backlash.

If you have clients who are on the other side, be prepared to lose them. If all or the major majority of your clients are on your side though, it may be worth it.

You also have to be prepared for the possible lunatic fringe which may threaten you or your family. Don't jump into the emotionally heated debates if you're not ready for the fire you'll create. But if you do jump in one, you're pretty much guaranteed publicity.

Hot Publicity Idea #16: Educational Class

Hold a class or seminar providing people with free

useful information about your subject. You could teach an adult education class at a local college. You could hold a free or low cost seminar at the library or large book store. You may even create classes at your place of business.

Speaking on your topic at association meetings and community groups is another way to generate publicity. You'll simply teach something about your business which people can pick up and learn quickly. This is following the same free informational approach which has been covered multiple times throughout this course.

I understand you may be afraid of speaking in front of a group, but these classes aren't what you imagine them to be. You could design them to be a type of workshop and have your students doing something. For example, the mechanic could show people how to change their own oil or something else minor.

Any professional could explain a few things and then have worksheets for their class to fill out.

Having a class doesn't mean you have to actually talk for an hour or two. Ask questions. Elicit feedback. Demonstrate. Have them practice. Answer questions. Participation is much more fun and a better way to learn anyway.

Most of your teachers in school weren't very good! So don't look to them as your guidance. If you had a good one, they would stand out in your mind as someone who got the class to participate. Do the same for anyone you teach.

Hot Publicity Idea #17: Holidays

Tie your offerings and press release to the holidays. Paul Hartunian always talks about how he sends out his press releases for, "How to be Outrageously Successful with the Opposite Sex" during the Valentine's Day season. Obviously anything involving romance will work well during that week. Run a romance event for your store, restaurant, or practice.

Give away Christmas gifts to clients from your business or website. Have a special on all your green items only on St. Patrick's Day. Run a costume contest with great prizes a week before or after Halloween just to be different. Discuss stress over the holidays and how to deal with it. What holiday could you tie your offerings into?

Go on the radio and discuss why every child should see the optometrist before going back to school. Send out a press release about how every football player needs to see a chiropractor as soon as the season's over.

Create your own holiday as Dental Awareness week when you give away free information packets at your office. Celebrate Columbus Day by announcing a new discovery in your industry. Announce that every home should hire a maid service for Mother's Day. Or create a do something special for mom sheet where hiring your maid service is one of the items on the list.

Hot Publicity Idea #18: Weather

Does the weather affect your business or industry in any way? How can you turn this into a news angle? It's getting cold outside so now is the time to prepare your car for the winter. Have free booklets printed up which tell someone how to do it all themselves, but also include a coupon for the full service at your automotive facility.

It's getting warm out so this is when people begin participating in sports again. Here's how to ease yourself back into activity (useful for chiropractors, doctors, nutritionists, and personal trainers). Here's how to keep your pipes from freezing (plumbers). How to look great even in the rainy season (stylists, nail salons, and clothing stores).

Your business may not be seasonal, but there are seasonal effects you can discuss in any market. This idea is based on educational marketing. Give vital information that helps the media's audience while leading them toward your product or service. You could use the booklet method.

Or you could simply write the tips in the release itself. Or you could run a class about it. What do you know because of your expertise that the average person out there doesn't know? This could be based on proven statistics or stories which have occurred in your business.

Hot Publicity Idea #19: Predictions

Make a prediction. It doesn't even need to be a good one. Make enough predictions and some will eventually end up correct simply by accident.

Does anyone really believe the groundhog can predict the end of winter? There are books about how the stock market will crash and books about how it will soar.

The beginning of the year is full of predictions for what the next year holds in _____. The movie critic predicts top movies. The accountant predicts upcoming tax changes. The real estate predicts home prices. The doctor predicts the flu season.

Everybody is full of predictions, and the surprising thing is we all want to hear more!

The prediction is even better if you can create a controversy over it. If everybody is talking about how such-and-such will occur, you'll get publicity by predicting the opposite. You might even get to debate about it.

All the time you're building your business all the way to the bank. If your prediction comes out wrong, explain what went wrong...and make more predictions. Watch major analysts and you'll quickly realize this is the way to go.

Hot Publicity Idea #20: Be Funny

Stop being so serious. I've been around business people who I've wanted to title the "Sourpuss marketer." I haven't done it yet, at least not out-loud.

Humor can be a little dangerous in sales copy because it can be misunderstood, but it is a great tool for publicity. Have you ever heard of the "pet rock?" Gary Dahl created a manual, "The Pet Rock Training Manual" and sold it along with a ROCK. He sold millions of these things as the answer to the perfect pet which didn't cost much, didn't make messes, and didn't misbehave. He created a fad and became famous selling a rock!

Has anything interesting, exciting, or funny ever happened in your business? Have you ever had a wacky idea? Is there anything you sell which has an unusual story behind it? Gary Dahl sold a ROCK because he created a story to go with it (it was your pet). Did you take a funny picture? Do your employees have a funny story to tell? Do your clients have a funny story to tell about your products or services?

Can you hold a funny contest? Create an award that's funny. Run an unusual sale like a sale only for people who are left-handed (have them prove it with the left-handed test).

Ask some of your clients what they find funny. Ask a few of them if they think something you're planning on using is funny. The key principle here is you don't want to drop your client's perception of your expertise while being funny.

It doesn't matter what other business people in your industry think of you. They're not your target market. It only matters what your target market thinks of you. So be a little silly. Be unusual. Be attention getting. But don't go totally off the deep end where you lose your clients.

Hot Publicity Idea #21: Be a Resource

You receive publicity because you help the media do their jobs better. They need interesting stories and you provide them with those. They need an interview and you give them one. If they need photos, you provide those. You're there to make their jobs easier for them.

One of the great ways you can do this is by calling reporters and editors who deal with your subject on the phone. Either ask them over the phone or take them out to lunch. Ask them one simple question. "How can I help you?" What is it you can do to make their jobs quicker and easier?

Suggest that you're available if they ever need a comment on your subject. Give them your personal phone or cell number to call you if they need a quick quote on a story they're writing. If they do interviews, tell them you'll fill in for any guest who doesn't show up when scheduled.

Whatever it is they need, you're the person they can go to in your industry. A little bit of relationship building with the key people who cover news in your market goes a long way to generating the kind of publicity you want for your business. If they continually come to you for quotes and information, you'll soon be seen as the "expert" by all their audience.

Terry Dean is offering you his Free Report, "10 Key Strategies to Earn More, Work Less, and Enjoy Life!" Discover how you too can have a profitable business, spend more time with your family, and concentrate on elements of your business you truly enjoy. Check out his free report and blog today at: www.terrydean.org

~ © Terry Dean

Category: Selling Tips

Trash Talk & Delete Buttons: A Candid Letter from Your Prospective Customer

Posted by Jill Konrath on September 23, 2007
at www.carolbentley.org/konrath-letter.html

Dear Seller,

I only have a few minutes, but I understand you're interested in what you can do to capture my attention and entice me to want to set up a meeting with you.

> Let me say this loud and clear right now -
> **you have no idea what my day is like.**
> You may think you do, but you're missing the boat. Until you understand this, my advice to you makes no sense.

I got into the office early this morning so I could have some uninterrupted time to work on a major project - something I can't seem to squeeze into the normal business day, which is filled with back-to-back meetings.

But, by 9 a.m. all my good intentions were dashed. My boss asked me to drop everything to get her some up-to-date information on a major reorganization initiative. Product development informed me that our new offering won't be available for the upcoming tradeshow. Sales is already in an uproar because they have customers waiting for it. Then HR tells me that one of my key employees has been accused of cyber-stalking.

Starting to get the picture? **Welcome to my world of everyday chaos where, hard as I try to make progress, I keep slipping behind.** Right now, I have at least 59 hours of work piled on my desk, needing my attention. I have no idea when I'll get it all done.

Did I mention my how many emails I get daily? Over 100. Everyone copies me in on everything. It drives me crazy. Then, add to that at least 30 phone calls - many from vendors who want to set up a meeting with me. And the pile of junk mail I get each day is ridiculous.

In short, I have way too much to do, ever-increasing expectations, impossible deadlines and constant interruptions from people wanting my time or attention.

Time is my most precious commodity and I protect it at all costs. I live with the status quo as long as I can - even if I'm not happy. Why? Because change creates more work and eats up my time.

Which gets us back to you. In your well-intentioned but misguided attempts turn me into a "prospect," you fail woefully to capture my attention. I'm going to be really blunt here: **I could care less about your prod-**

uct, service, solution or your company.

I'm not one bit interested in your unique methodologies, extraordinary differentiators or one-stop shopping. Your self-serving pablum, while designed to lure me into your clutches, has the exact opposite impact.

> **It's trash talk! I quickly scan your emails or letters looking for those offensive words and phrases that glorify your offering or your firm.**

The minute they jump out at me, you're gone. Zapped from my inbox or tossed into the trashcan. When you talk like that in your voicemails, I delete you immediately. Delete, delete, delete.

That's the most expeditious way to handle bothersome telemarketers. Use those same words on the phone with me and I'll quickly raise an objection you can't address.

> **I'm a master at sniffing out trash talk and deleting** it. I have work to do and refuse to waste even one iota of my time on something that's irrelevant or self-promotional.

You need to know though that I'm not always like this. Occasionally a savvy marketer or seller captures my attention, gets me to raise my hand asking for more information and even entices me to request a meeting.

What are they doing? **They're completely focused on my business and the impact they can have on it.** That's what's relevant to me - not their offering.

> I'm always interested in ways to shorten time to market, speed up our sales cycles and reduce our supply chain costs. **Notice that this is business talk, not marketing speak!**

When you get even more specific and tell me how much impact, now you're really talking my language. I guarantee that if you mention you've helped organizations similar to mine increase sales conversion rates by 39% in just 3 months, I'll be on the phone to you in no time flat.

Do you have any good information or fresh insights about the challenges my company is facing? How about how other companies are addressing these issues? If so, I'm interested in that too.

That's the good stuff. It stems from a focus on the difference you can make for my company, instead of how you're different from everyone else. When you emphasize that, I'm interested.

> **But you can't rope me in with the good stuff, then slip back into that trash talk.** If so, you're gonzo as fast as I can hit the delete button.

I pay attention in about 5 second increments, too. I don't have time for fluff. If it's relevant info, you've got me; start meandering and I hit delete.

Get the picture? I hope so, because I'm late for a meeting and while I've been writing this, the phone's been ringing off the hook.

Hope this helps!

Your Prospective Customer

Jill Konrath, author of **Selling to Big Companies**, is an internationally recognized sales strategist. As a frequent speaker at national sales meetings, she helps salespeople crack into corporate accounts, speed up their sales cycle and win more contracts. Jill also publishes an industry-leading newsletter, hosts a widely read blog and has written hundreds of articles on sales success

For more articles like this, visit Selling to Big Companies article library. Also, download your free BONUS ebook on *Can LinkedIn Increase Your Sales?*

Read more about Jill's insightful book, **Selling to Big Companies** at
www.carolbentley.org/konrath-book.html
Check out Jill's article library at
www.carolbentley.org/konrath-articles.html
Can LinkedIn Increase Your Sales?
www.carolbentley.org/konrath-report.html

~ © Jill Konrath

Category: Web Marketing

Email Scheduling – How Soon is Too Soon?

Posted by Marc Kline (aweber) on November 8, 2007 at www.carolbentley.org/awblog.html

Somewhere in the back of my mind I was waiting for it – the first Christmas song of the year. This time I was at a local coffee shop (OK, it was the local Starbucks).

John Lennon and Yoko Ono's "Happy Christmas (War Is Over)" made it through about 10 seconds of play. Then, the stereo went silent for about another 10 and we were back to quiet, singer-songwriter cafe music.

From a back room I heard someone scream "It's too early for Christmas!". It might seem odd at first, but this got me to thinking about email marketing and how we schedule our messages.

Holiday Business Has Awakened

I got a laugh from this event then quickly forgot about it until today, when I was reading a periodical report from RetailEmail.Blogspot covering their index of re-tailers and how many were sending holiday messages (see the report at www.carolbentley.org/retail.html).

I couldn't help but picture scores of people with silent thoughts screaming, "It's too early!" upon opening their inboxes.

But now that I'm sitting down to write this, I can't help but think about how big a boom the holidays can provide for some businesses. And who can argue with an early start?

How Should We Schedule Our Emails?

Holidays aside, scheduling is something we think of every time we write messages, especially the type that focuses on some type of time-sensitive information.

Our Education Team thinks about it every time we announce a live video seminar on our blog (see it at www.carolbentley.org/aweber.html) and in its corresponding email updates.

Too late and our readers can't clear their schedule for the event. Too early and there's no sense of urgency.

Clearly, there's a balance to be found between procrastination and being overzealous when it comes to getting information out to our readers. Where do we find it? Is it ever "too early for Christmas"? When?

While we're on the subject of holidays, be sure to take advantage of our Free Holiday Marketing Calendar (at www.carolbentley.org/calendar.html) for reminders on both common (e.g. President's Day) and uncommon (e.g. Yellow Pigs Day) holidays you can use for your campaign.

~ © Marc Kline, Aweber

Stop Pop-Ups

Posted by Hill Robertson on January 5 & 15 2008
at www.carolbentley.org/popblog.html

As we start out the New Year, I am launching my first product on this blog. It is for those of you who have a blog or website of your own and use <u>aweber</u> for an opt-in popup. (See more about aweber at www.carolbentley.org/aweber.html)

When someone subscribes to your blog, they shouldn't have to keep putting up with the popup window any more. I know I wish blogs that I subscribe to didn't keep bugging me to sign up.

The product is an online video procedure where I show you how to set up your blog or website to stop the aweber popup window to new subscribers after you implement the procedure. It may even be a good incentive for your readers to sign up knowing that they won't get bothered anymore.

It is only $10 for the next 72 hours (until 11:59 PM EST Monday Evening). You have my full money back guarantee if you are not satisfied. If you are satisfied, please post a testimonial as a comment on this post so I can use it on the sales page. (**Author Note:** *The special price has now expired but it is still worth having at its full price of $35*).

Here is the link:
http://hillrobertson.com/aweberNoPopup

Now get rid of those popups to reward your subscribers for signing up.....

~ © Hill Robertson

How to Stay Informed with Simple But Powerful 'RSS' Technology

Posted by Ed Rivis at
www.edrivis.com/?page_id=17

If you visit a lot of blogs like EdRivis.com you may have noticed a small icon like this ▣ in orange, or a button with the word 'RSS' in it.

Those icons give you the ability to subscribe to the blog and automatically receive fresh content — soon after it's added — and **directly** to your computer or into a web browser.

Meaning you don't even have to *visit* this blog in future to stay informed of the very latest ideas and techniques for using the Internet to increase your small business sales and profits.

How to Get Started

All you need is a small piece of software called an RSS Reader and then you're up and running.

Best of all - unless you go for a premium service, RSS readers are free – like for example **FeedReader** (www.feedreader.com/).

There are two types of readers available; the one you choose depends on your circumstances. If you work in front of a computer all day then you'll probably go for a desktop software news reader. I use one called Newsgator (www.newsgator.com/) which integrates directly into my email software.

If you're frequently on the move you can also sub-scribe to online RSS newsreader services that allow you to connect through any standard web browser wherever you are in the world.

In a nutshell, RSS technology saves you time and keeps you informed of critical updates to both EdRivis.com and many other web sites.

It's worth your time to check out RSS because it could well be a critical addition to your **own** small business web strategy in future. (And of course I'll explain ex-actly how that is so in a future blog entry!)

Happy RSS'ing! ~ © Ed Rivis

Three Powerful Resources

Posted by Ed Rivis at
www.edrivis.com/?p=227 on March 8, 2008

I just created a new special resources area containing...

1. Landing Page Flow-chart.

Landing pages transformed my business, and they probably can yours too. The flowchart allows the beginner to quickly identify the steps involved in setting up and launching a landing page campaign.

2. Lifetime value calculator.

When you know how much each newly acquired customer is REALLY worth, small gains in conversion achieved through split and multi-variate testing take on a whole new perspective.

The calculator is an easy way to determine how much muscle you can put in your web marketing (or ANY type of marketing).

3. Web Marketing Mind-Map.

It's non-exhaustive, but the mind-map shows some of the most critical tactics you can use to drive traffic to your web sites (especially landing pages).

Sign up to the blog if you want access to these resources (plus the first 3 chapters of my new book if you don't already own it) - **The Ultimate Web Marketing Strategy** at www.carolbentley.org/ruwm.html

~ © Ed Rivis

---

*Answer Time: Overcoming 9 Big Challenges; part 1 (of 2)

Posted by Ed Rivis
at www.edrivis.com/?p=233 on March 13, 2008

Okay, here are my responses to 9 of the biggest challenges people are having with their online marketing. (Note I've truncated the original questions down to single sentences.)

1. **[Phil] How to overcome 'internet marketing paralysis'.**

Marketing Paralysis, (and I'll drop the 'Internet' because this applies to ANY type of marketing), is where there are **so** many things you could do... you end up doing *nothing*.

When that happens a business can stagnate and go nowhere. (And believe me when I say I'm talking from **too much** experience of this since I started in 1996.)

I think marketing paralysis stems from one main root — not knowing **which** activity will produce the **best** results.

But here's the thing — you'll **never** find out until you try them. The key is to start small and **test** every step of the way.

For example, don't fork out on a full page national advertising campaign until you know the offer is capable of generating sales. Try regional or small line ads first.

In terms of Internet Marketing, that means you need to know a front-end offer first **attracts** visitors to your web site — and that the web site is capable of **converting** at least a small (but hopefully a large) percentage of those visitors into paying customers or clients on the back end.

Google Adwords is an easy one. You control the budget, so you can start with a very small budget and small amount of traffic to a web site — then when you know it's profitable, increase the daily budget. But again, until you test Google Adwords you won't know if your adverts get traffic and your site converts sales... and for less than a tenner you start to find out in the next few hours.

The key is to start testing.

I remember the first direct mail letter I put out — the feeling I got when all the response came flooding in... and then **kicking myself** hard because I could have done it years ago!

Also, if you start testing adverts and they DO attract visitors onto your sites... but none of them make an enquiry (or purchase) — that's a great result! You're already halfway there. Now all you have to do is tweak the site and run the advert again.

The key in all of this... well, there are two... **put testing systems in place.**

(For example, code your print adverts and require that code to be entered on your web site — so you can see how much response is derived from said campaign.)

One of the best cure of marketing paralysis is to know that you can clearly see whether your marketing is producing sales.

My book explains how to split-test web pages, (and I've blogged about the different multi-variate testing software options).

One more tip: I think it was my friend Richard Lee who said or pointed me to a great maxim: 'Don't focus on the end result... focus on the first step'.

For anyone who is seriously affected by marketing paralysis I recommend you read **Action!: Nothing Happens Until Something Moves** (available at www.carolbentley.org/nh.html).

2. [Karin] How to effectively use the web when the majority of your business appears to be front-

end/one off purchases?

There are lots of things you can do **offline** — and you seem very proactive Karin so you're probably doing most if not all of them :-), but my friend, Paul Gorman, has powerful advice on all some of the best offline tactics for dealing with front-end loaded businesses.

Here are 3 ideas in terms of Internet Marketing:

• Occasional customer e-mails offering hints and tips on product usage and maintenance will keep relationships active over the long term, and at no cost, and if you add "pass this onto a friend" type requests in those communications — that's one way of getting extra referrals and new business (combine it with an incentive for more response to it).

• Form **reverse strategic alliances**.... make deals to promote **other companies** (flooring/home related) products and services to your 'one time/very infrequent' customers, in addition to your back-end range of products that you mention.

• Are you using video on your sites? A one-off purchase or higher ticket price items will very much benefit from online video, and that's a great thing to promote in offline advertising. (Especially when used in conjunction with a landing page to capture interested prospects.)

3. [Dave] Where to find the most reliable advice on how to build a blog, SEO, traffic, etc.

Unfortunately I'm not aware of one place that tells you **everything** you need to know.

In fact I think your question relates to the first question above — you don't **need** to know everything.

The best you can do is choose your advisors carefully — look for people succeeding in doing what you want to do. Don't take advice off anyone who isn't demonstrating success in what they preach.

Reminds me of the story about the financial advisor who goes to the Millionaire and says 'ok show me the current state of your finances'. The millionaire looks the advisor in the eye and says, "No, show me yours first..."

I cover a lot of stuff here which works well for me, and I also recommend Richard Lee, Robert Phillips, Terry Dean, Chris Crompton, John Reese, Jim Sansi. Those are some of the best Internet Marketing minds I know of (hope I didn't miss anyone out).

As for SEO... whatever you learn today may change tomorrow anyway. My advice is to get the basics in place first. So start a link building campaign, start submitting articles, get backlinks by leaving comments on blogs, and so on.

And optimise your site for keywords as well... check out Richard Lee and Fred Black for the latest results based evidence on what works there... those guys have achieved some **very** impressive results with Google for highly competitive phrases.

I could go on, but I'll have to stop there. The fact is all of this is a journey. It's all constantly changing. You'll never know everything... and **you don't need to**. Just **get started**.

4. [Richard] Where and how to attract prospects (front end) traffic to either a new site or one that's been online a while but is still relatively unknown (low traffic).

Again a very broad question, and one that is entirely dependent on your business. I'd recommend revisiting the sections in my book on the best places businesses can start their Internet based promotions.

If I understand your business correctly then we're talking about a **local** based service business?

If so, I'd start by creating a strong (front-end) irresistible offer and getting that promoted locally — as direct to your target audience as possible. Use **landing pages** in your promotions. Also check out Google Adwords and its ability to restrict campaigns to geographically constrained areas.

5. [Steve] The best ways of not only getting prospects to a site, but to actually start a relationship that are more likely to result in one or more future sales.

I mentioned traffic above, and elsewhere on my blog, and also in my book, so let's talk about the strongest ways of forming online relationships.

I've found that to be **blogging**.

Unlike e-mail marketing you can type more freely. It's less formal, and people accept communications a lot more frequently than 'standard' e-mail newsletters for example. (If you're subscribed to my blog then you get an e-mail from me almost every weekday, my unsubscribe rate is very low, and I feel I have a strong relationship with my readers... (thank **you**.)

The key is that your blog has to accept subscribers — it's essential if you want to grow readership. I cover all that in my blogging course (read about it at www.carolbentley.org/rubb.html

****

I'll post my answers to the remaining questions (6 - 9) tomorrow.
****

To be continued...
~ © Ed Rivis

---

*Answer Time: Overcoming 9 Big Challenges; part 2 (of 2)

Posted by Ed Rivis
at www.edrivis.com/?p=234 on March 14, 2008

Following on from yesterday, here are the last four answers to my Question Time...

6. [Andy] How to commission the development of a web site that WILL increase sales without being ripped off or fed a load of 'brand building' B.S..

Andy's question is why my book exists — to help the small business owner define what they want from their web marketing without leaving it in the hands of someone else. Use my book to put blinkers on your web developers so they only give you what you know your company needs — not what they think it needs.

First of all, understand that **YOU** know more about your business than *anyone* else.

So one of the biggest mistakes I see small business owners doing is **completely** handing over the development of their website to a third party — either an internal member of staff or external web design company or individual.

It's a **BIG** mistake.

Before you give anybody the task of developing your web site you need to decide WHO do you want the site to attract the most. Who is it talking to? (Perform an 80/20 analysis on your business first if you need to discover who your most profitable customers are.)

Yet many web designers will simply go away and create a site with...

> * A homepage (that usually says not much more than 'Welcome.')

> * An About us page (it's a bitter pill to swallow but in most cases, who cares?)

> * A few brief pages covering products and services.

> * And the all important 'Contact Us' page. (You may need to dust off the cobwebs to find the submit button.)

Gee... where do I send my cheque?

No, you've got to drive the web development process by defining **what you need** for the site to achieve your business objectives.

Decide what action you want your 'Most Wanted' visitors to do on your web site.

And there are usually two types of visitors. The ones who **already** do business with you. And the ones who don't know anything about you, or your company and it's products or services.

So when you plan out what you want your web site to say, bear in mind you probably need at least two separate areas — one to generate new customers / capture sales leads, and the other part of the site (or separate site) to sell and communicate with existing customers.

Finally, when you know **who** you most want to attract, have decided **what** messaging and mechanisms you need to capture new customers or clients, and what mechanisms you need to keep a strong relationship with existing customers or clients... THEN you can confidently outsource your web development... because **you will be able to tell them what your business <u>needs</u> to succeed online.**

7. [Alan] How to ensure your site is legally compliant.

The laws are becoming increasingly strict, and will continue to do so. For example it's not illegal to send unsolicited e-mails to other businesses in the UK... but I suspect it soon will be.

Also, in the UK, at the very least a corporate site should have the registered company address, VAT number and other salient information on every page. And we could talk about accessibility and a whole lot more, so the best I can do is point you at the best online sources of information.

Start with your countries government web site(s). They usually contain everything you need to cover yourself for distance selling regulations, and in the UK I can also recommend Outlaw (www.outlaw.com/)—

a tremendous resource for IT related legal information.

One thing I read on the latter site — you will have received e-mails with the message 'Do not read this if you are not the intended recipient'... that goes at the bottom of a lot of corporate e-mails. Apparently that's legally useless because it's at the BOTTOM of the e-mail — people have already read the e-mail before they get to that statement. How many companies do that!?

8. [Juliette] How to visually and logically segment your web marketing (and site) if it sells different product lines and services to different customers (e.g. locally and nationally).

Whatever promotions you perform at either the local or national level, make sure the data you capture contains enough information that you know who are local prospects. (When someone buys from you you get their details anyway — I'm talking more about capturing the details of enquirers so you know if they are local or not.)

Then — and for you it's critical — segment your e-mail marketing so local offers **only** ever go out to local people.

E-mail marketing is always best when it's specific — always tailor your communications to be highly relevant.

The key to effective e-mail marketing is on you capturing enough information about customers and prospects on the front-end of your business first. Put systems in place to do that as soon as you can.

**9. [Graham] Asked why have I got an Alexa panel
on the right side of this page and what does the
number mean?**

Alexa is a service designed to rate a web site based on
its popularity. The LOWER your Alexa score the closer
you are to being the number 1 web site.

One marketer reckons that Google looks to Alexa's
score to decide how important your web site is in your
industry/category, and that the score affects where
Google ranks your site in its results. (In other words
the better your Alexa score, the better your SEO.)

I haven't done the statistical analysis to validate that...
but even if it's the case today it may not be tomorrow.
However, it only took a couple of minutes to add that
box to my web site, so what's the harm?

The other benefit of adding it to my page is less obvious. One of the main ways Alexa ranks a site is when
people install the Alexa toolbar into their web
browser. Then after that any sites that person visits
will be 'pinged' back to Alexa as more frequently visited.

However, not everyone has the Alexa toolbar installed

— so how do you increase your Alexa score even when a visitor doesn't have the toolbar?

Simple.

Add the panel that I have in the sidebar — then each time anyone visits your site, Alexa knows about it (although it's totally anonymous — Alexa never finds out the identity of my web site visitors, unless they have installed the toolbar **and** told Alexa who they are).

Finally, it's also a handy gauge to how my site's doing — and a constant reminder that I can do a lot better! (In terms of traffic)

It also makes a few readers curious....

Thanks for all your questions and I hope you feel I did them justice.

Have a great weekend, ~ © Ed Rivis

5 Powerful Ways to Increase Blog Readership
Posted by Ed Rivis at
www.edrivis.com/?p=253 on March 31, 2008

When I first started blogging, there was a lot of virtual tumbleweed blowing across it. Some days my blog was only read by one person... me! That was quite disheartening, and made it hard to stay motivated (in fact for a while I simply gave up).

However, I thankfully discovered a number of powerful ways of getting people here, and today I want to share some of those with you.

First of all you must...

1. Accept subscribers.

Encouraging readers to **return** to your blog in future is one of the — if not *the* — most powerful ways of increasing blog readership. And the easiest tactic to encourage return visits is to allow your visitors to subscribe, so they get e-mail reminders each time you add fresh blog content.

I use a service called aweber , which I have set up to automatically check my blog every hour of the day (www.carolbentley.org/aweber.html). If aweber sees I've added a new blog post, they automatically send an e-mail to my subscribers to let them know about it.

Obviously when subscribers receive that e-mail, a lot of them click the link in it and come back to my blog.

This is great for them because they don't need to remember my blog web address and keep checking my blog on the off-chance I've updated it. And as a result of that, I get a increasingly higher readership.

One more tip about offering blog subscription — usually it helps to offer an extra incentive for subscribers. For example on my blog anyone who signs up gets the first three chapters of my book, plus other valuable resources to go with it.

A strong incentive can more than double the rate at which people subscribe.

2. E-mail your *existing* list.

The first thing you should do when you launch your new blog is tell everyone you currently have permission to e-mail, and ask them to visit and subscribe.

It's unlikely that all of the people on your e-mail list subscribe, so you also want to schedule occasional reminders to anyone who has not yet subscribed. Tell them what they're missing out on — be specific.

- What do you blog about? (The subject matter.)
- Point out it's totally free, even to subscribe.
- How will they benefit by subscribing?
- Mention the incentive(s) if you offer any.
- If an industry figurehead has endorsed your blog be sure to mention that!

3. Comment on other blogs & forums.

Commenting on other blogs is a powerful way of increasing readership of your own blog, because people who read your comments may end up clicking the link you give, and therefore end up on **your** blog.

The same applies for forums relevant to your industry.

If you spend time on there being helpful and answering people's questions, people may spot and click the link in your signature, (which is the text that appears underneath your name whenever you post a comment).

4. Look for guest posting & interview opportunities.

Some blogs openly welcome guest posts — where you write and submit an article that is then published on the third party blog.

Also one tactic I've used which has increased my blog traffic is to respond to other bloggers who offer to be interviewed.

You simply email them some questions, they email back the answers and you publish the interview on your blog.

However, most times the other blogger will then link to your interview blog post (because it makes them look good) and at the same time a percentage of **their** blog readership will follow that link to read the interview on **your** blog... and your traffic spikes yet again.

5. Strategic Alliances.

I've formed a number of relationships with other professionals who are in the marketing sphere but who I don't compete with.

Most of those professionals I've helped out in one way or another (like helping them get started blogging, or created landing pages and websites for them). In turn, they promote my blog to **their** list.

I've had a **lot** of traffic from referrals through strategic alliance referrals.

Who do you know who will promote your blog to their list — either for payment for each subscriber that produces, or simply in return for you helping them?

These are just a few tactics I and other professional bloggers use to increase our blog readership. Try them out for yourself and see what happens.

~ © Ed Rivis

BLOGGER'S BIOGRAPHIES

In alphabetical order:

Mark Brownlow:

Mark is an independent web publisher, writer and accredited journalist. With the *emphasis* on independent. He published his first email newsletter in 1998 and has been in and around the business of email marketing ever since. His 2001 book on creating e-newsletters that have influence and impact is available for free at www.carolbentley.org/bnewsletter.html

Tui Bijoux:

Tui divides her time between Italy, London and the Pacific Northwest. When not battling jet lag, she enjoys composing music, writing, photography and blogging at her website www.mentalmosaic.com

Terry Dean:

Terry is offering you his Free Report, **"10 Key Strategies to Earn More, Work Less, and Enjoy Life!"** Discover how you too can have a profitable business, spend more time with your family, and concentrate on elements of your business you truly enjoy. Check out his free report and blog today at: www.terrydean.org

Marc Kline:

Marc works with the Education Team of AWeber, a permission-only email marketing solution.

Along with the blog this article was originally published to, they also provide other free resources for new and experienced email senders, such as webinars and a holiday calendar you can use for your email scheduling: www.carolbentley.org/calendar.html

Visit AWeber www.carolbentley.org/aweber.html

Jill Konrath:

Jill, author of **Selling to Big Companies**, is an internationally recognised sales strategist. As a frequent speaker at national sales meetings, she helps salespeople crack into corporate accounts, speed up their sales cycle and win more contracts. Jill also publishes an industry-leading newsletter, hosts a widely read blog and has written hundreds of articles on sales success

Read more about Jill's insightful book, **Selling to Big Companies** at

www.carolbentley.org/konrath-book.html

Check out Jill's article library at

www.carolbentley.org/konrath-articles.html

Jill's free report *Can LinkedIn Increase Your Sales?* is at www.carolbentley.org/konrath-report.html

Ed Rivis:

Ed Rivis has been in the web industry for more than 10 years. He's learnt all the strategies and tactics in his book, **The Ultimate Web Marketing Strategy**, (find out more at www.carolbentley.org/ruwm.html) through extensive training, experience and - most importantly - testing. His straight forward approach brings you an easy to read, jargon busting and fully comprehensible book that delivers web marketing techniques you can start implementing immediately.

Ed also shares his expertise in regular posts on his blog at www.edrivis.com

Hill Robertson:

Hill Robertson is the ultimate geek when it comes to creating websites.

He got started building websites from scratch in the early days of the Internet just for the fun of it. His fanatical hobby evolved into several successful internet businesses.

He loves to share his success principles about the Internet, business and family on his blog at http://hillrobertson.com and what's more, he talks in plain English!

Martin Russell:

Martin is a medical doctor with a difference. After creating his own counselling practice in 2001, he decided to share his experience of building his business through referrals.

www.WordofMouthMagic.com is the incredibly successful result.

Martin's passion, in both his counselling and in business, is helping people get access to incredible tools that make their lives easier and their efforts more rewarding, both in business and their personal life.

Rich Schefren:

They call Rich Schefren the "Coach to the Internet Gurus".

His unique philosophy about how to build real businesses online gets big money results for his clients. And that's the reason he formed Strategic Profits in 2004. Read more from Rich at the Strategic Profits website:

www.carolbentley.org/ssp.html

Cindy Silbert:

Cindy Silbert is the ultimate guide for successful women who want to thrive in all areas of their life from home, work, love, body and soul. She is an Author, Coach, Speaker and Creator of Life Cultivation, a fusion of eastern and western practices that transforms your personal or business life through one-on-one coaching, books, workshops and online programs.

She founded Bring U to Life, Inc.. and http://cindysilbert.com/blog to inspire and guide women across the globe to full self-expression and lasting personal fulfilment.

I'd like to express my heartfelt thanks again to these contributing authors who agreed to let me share their valuable insights with you.

Carol A E Bentley

BOOKS WORTH READING...

Here is a list of books to help you gain massive business growth. Many of them are sitting on my own bookshelf and are well thumbed, highlighted and have notes scribbled in them. I constantly refer to them to refresh my own thought processes and gain additional golden nuggets.

Some of these books help you to write compelling, results generating sales letters, adverts, web pages, brochures and flyers. Others help you with your marketing, sales and business strategies.

I Want to Buy Your Product... Have You Sent Me a Letter Yet?'
Carol A E Bentley. ISBN: 978-0954920609

Tested Advertising Methods
John Caples. ISBN: 978-0139068911

The Power Process – an NLP Approach to Writing
Dixie Elise Hickman & Sid Jacobson.
ISBN: 978-1899836079

Million Dollar Mailings
Denison Hatch. ISBN: 978-1566251624

The Greatest Direct Mail Sales Letters
Richard S. Hodgson. ISBN: 978-0850132380

How To Write a Good Advertisement
Victor O. Schwab. ISBN: 978-0879803971

Ogilvy On Advertising
David Ogilvy. ISBN: 978-1853756153

Influence: The Psychology of Persuasion
Richard Cialdini. ISBN: 978-0061241895

Don't Work for Your Business, Make Your Business Work for You
Brian James. ISBN: 978-0954891602

Get Clients NOW!
C.J. Hayden. ISBN: 978-0814479926

How To Out-Sell Out-Market Out-Promote Out-Advertise Everyone Else You Compete Against...
Paul Gorman. ISBN: 978-0953266609

Selling To Big Companies
Jill Konrath. ISBN: 978-1419515620

The Ultimate Sales Machine
Chet Holmes. ISBN: 978-1591841609

Marketing Plans
Malcolm McDonald. ISBN: 978-0750656252

Marketing - A Complete Guide in Pictures
Malcolm McDonald and Peter Morris.
ISBN: 978-0750661980

The Irresistible Offer
Mark Joyner. ISBN: 978-0471738947

Rapid Results Referrals
Roy Sheppard. ISBN: 978-1901534047

Meet, Greet & Prosper
Roy Sheppard. ISBN: 978-1901534054

The Ultimate Web Marketing Strategy
Ed Rivis. ISBN: 978-0955831201

Lightning Source UK Ltd.
Milton Keynes UK
14 February 2011
167503UK00007B/55/P